MW01468977

Daily JAM

Daily JAM

DAILY ENLIGHTENMENT IN JUST A MINUTE

A GENTLE WEAVE OF STOIC AND YOGIC PHILOSOPHIES

SARAH GARDNER

Cover Design: Hania Khuri-Trapper, Khuri Design
Cover Photo: Patrick Quinn-Paquet, PQP Photo
Back Cover Photo: Iliana Nunn Photography
Page Design: Willa Worsfold, willaworks design

To stay connected, please join the Daily JAM Family at

www.dailyjam.net

Amy,

This daybook is dedicated to you.

Let's walk together.

I look forward to
sharing Just A Minute
with you every Day.

With gratitude,

Sarah

WITH GRATITUDE TO:

My incredible editor: Barbara Perlo.
I bow and simply say "Thank you."
This book would not have happened without you.

My family: Geoff, Will, Emma, and Mocha.
Thank you for being patient and so supportive.

My mum:
Thank you for being my first editor and number one fan.

My daddy:
Who has shown me that through the deepest sorrow,
love is still stronger.

My very talented yogi friends:
Hania Khuri-Trapper for designing the book cover and
Willa DeVoti Worsfold for page design.

My Daily JAM family:
You have been by my side every step of the way.
Thank you.

INTRODUCTION

W elcome to the Daily JAM. JAM is an acronym for "Just A Minute", as it will take you only one minute a day to read. My goal is to express how being human is actually very simple. It is not the story you have created in your mind. It is not about being perfect. It's about being the best version of yourself...today, at this moment. It's about the choices you get to make and the person you are becoming without a finish line.

I'm not an expert on life. I struggle, just like you, but I hope the Daily JAM will help us to navigate together toward more fulfilling and satisfying lives for ourselves and others. I share inspirational ideas, strategies, and quotes, from those more intelligent than I*. I weave Stoic philosophy and yogic philosophy into a writing form that is modern and digestible. Both are ancient philosophies that intertwine so well together and are still relevant today. They guide us to be better, to give more to ourselves and to one another, and to be present to what life is offering in every moment.

It is my hope to help you live every day with greater purpose, love, patience, and awe in the magic of being a human being. Please enjoy this daily journey that potentially, in just a minute of reading, could bring greater understanding and joy to every minute thereafter.

Namaste,
Sarah

*A short glossary is found in the back of the book.

Daily JAM

CONTENTS

JANUARY

DAILY JAM

JANUARY 1

SANKALPA

"May all your troubles last as long as your New Year's resolutions."
- Unknown

Happy New Year! This year, I encourage you to not set a New Year's resolution. Instead, I would love to introduce you to *sankalpa*. While resolutions are often set from a belief that you are not good enough and are driven by the ego, a sankalpa starts with the awareness that you are right where you are supposed to be.

In the yogic tradition, a sankalpa is a phrase that harmonizes the heart and mind. It's not about changing an aspect in your life. It is a vow and commitment to be your true self. It is a foundational phrase for your purpose in life. Sankalpa originated from Sanskrit, the classical language of South Asia.

Everything you need to fulfill your sankalpa is already inside of you. It is a heartfelt desire. Resolutions reinforce the mistaken belief that happiness comes from the outside. A sankalpa comes from a place of innate completeness and wholeness.

A sankalpa is true now. Your phrase is in the present tense as a reminder that whatever is required is already within you. It does not require a change of action. It is a statement of who you are and comes from deep within. Examples could be: "I am already whole and already healthy." Or, "Kindness is my true nature." Or, "I radiate love."

Quietly listen for your sankalpa. Don't struggle to come up with a phrase. Be gentle with it. Let it settle and then, when you are ready, go out into the world and let the phrase silently trickle out with every action you take.

1

JANUARY 2

GO LIGHTLY IN LIFE

"People think angels fly because they have wings.
Angels fly because they take themselves lightly."

- Anonymous

D on't you sometimes wish that life came with a "How To" manual? You try to do it all. You blame yourself for everything. You wish you could be better. You wish there were more hours in the day and that you could get more sleep. Can you stop this way of being? Take a deep breath, exhale and imagine you are sitting in a chair in your home watching YOURSELF and listening to your thoughts. How does that make you feel? Now imagine your child or your best friend listening and watching. Is that who you want to be? Awareness is being able to observe and challenge your own thoughts.

Live one day at a time, one breath at a time. Don't take everything so seriously. It truly is simple: Be the best you can be at this very moment. Let go of all the what-ifs and be open to the possibility that you are the best version of yourself today, no matter how messy it looks.

JANUARY 3

LEARN TO RESPOND

"Pain is inevitable; suffering is optional."

- Buddha

We have emotions. They are part of our chemical make-up. Think back to the last time you truly got scared by something. Maybe you almost got in a car accident, maybe you lost your child for a moment in a store. That is real fear. Hormones are sent through your body to react. But after that initial period in time, you have the choice of how you will respond. Do you notice the change in my wording? It went from react to respond.

In every situation in life, you have the opportunity to choose. Isn't that amazing? What does it take to flip fear to rational thinking? What does it take to flip anger to patience? What does it take to flip worry to surrender? It takes awareness. Pause, come back to this moment, be the observer of your thoughts and then respond in a thoughtful, compassionate way.

It will take practice, a lifetime of practice, but every time you pause you create space for more kindness and love in your life.

JANUARY 4

HEART CENTER

"Dig deep, the water-goodness-is down there.
And as long as you keep digging, it will keep bubbling up."
- Marcus Aurelius

I n yoga, we talk about finding your "true north" which is an internal compass that successfully guides you through life. It is your fixed point in a spinning world. In Stoic philosophy, it's your "logos". There is an energy that the world is organized in a rational and coherent way. Your logos is directing you down the right path. You may just refer to it as "finding my way" or being connected with your "heart center". Our minds are cluttered with thoughts but underneath those thoughts is just you - your true self. Simple and open.

When I was little, my dad and I loved to eat artichokes together. We would sit and enjoy leaf by leaf, the unwrapping of this mysterious vegetable. We knew that enjoying each moment along the way would lead us to the heart.

We are like artichokes—so many layers cover our hearts. Focus today on unwrapping your layers. There is a beautiful, pure heart in there that is ready to be discovered.

JANUARY 5

CHANGE YOUR THOUGHTS

"We don't see things as they are, we see things as we are."
- Anais Nin

W hat if you were able to let go of putting meaning into everything that comes your way. What if you decided right now to accept that life just is. What an incredible awakening when you realize you have control over your thoughts.

Marcus Aurelius, Roman Emperor from 161-180 and one of the first Stoic philosophers, wrote this line in his written work titled *Meditations*: "The mind is the ruler of the soul." American spiritual teacher Ram Dass said, "Our karma is our mind."

Become aware of the dialogue in your mind. Are those thoughts positive? Are they kind to your soul? Be in charge of yourself. When your past begins to tell you a story, learn to let it go and take the lesson you learned from it. When fear and worry begin to talk, focus on what is in your control and then let go of the rest. When anger takes over, focus on your breath and then lead from your heart.

You get to choose how you think and act every day. When you create new habits of thought you essentially rewire your brain. In science this is called neuroplasticity. You can change the course of your thoughts.

JANUARY 6

WHAT IS STOICISM?

*"It's a philosophy designed to make us more resilient, happier,
more virtuous and more wise—and as a result,
better people, better parents and better professionals."*

- Ryan Holiday

H ave you ever been on your way to an appointment and got stuck in traffic? I'm guessing yes. What is your go-to reaction when things do not go as you planned? Anger, frustration, the thought of why me? Stoicism is an ancient Greek school of philosophy founded in Athens by Zeno of Citium around 304 BC. Many hear the word stoic and think it means someone that doesn't show emotion. This is not Stoicism. Stoicism was created to guide all people to navigate life with rational, connected thought and a belief that our world is connected in a way bigger than ourselves. You learn to release your need to control. You engage in life as it comes. And you let your ego be devoted to something greater than yourself.

So back to the traffic…Stoicism takes the wheel and says, "Ok, there is nothing I can do about this but I can control how I respond. First, I'm going to breathe in and breathe out, then I'm going to call my appointment and let them know my situation, then I'm going to _____ (fill in the blank with what makes you happy: listen to music, call a friend, listen to a podcast, etc). Isn't that so much more fun than road rage?

JANUARY 7

WHAT IS YOGA?

"The poses bring a feeling of well-being that stays with you. They do so through a balance of effort and relaxation; and through endless forms of balanced meditation."

- Master Patanjali

I believe that yoga is a way of living. Similar to Stoicism, yoga is a way to approach life through a different lens. It extends far beyond the postures to an awareness of why you are here. The teachings of yoga are a practical, step-by-step methodology that brings understanding to your experience and also guides you to the next experience. Like a compass, yogic philosophy tells you where you are and how to navigate to the next chapter.

The first and most important book ever written about yoga is *The Yoga Sutra*. It was written by the Indian Master Patanjali about two thousand years ago. Many incredible ideas of how to lead your best life are shared in this book. In addition, yogic philosophy stems from the *Yamas and Niyamas*. They are guidelines to live a life of joy and purpose.

As I often end my yoga class with, "Let the yoga not be just what you do, but who you are."

JANUARY 8

BREAKDOWNS ARE GOOD

"What is to give light must endure burning."
-Victor Frankl

D id you know when you break a bone it grows back stronger? This is true for breakdowns in your life too. Life is about falling down and getting back up - but not getting back up with anger, frustration, and resentment. It's getting back up a better, stronger person. We have breakdowns to have breakthroughs.

When something does not go your way today, look at it as an opportunity to learn and grow. Look at it as happening for you, not to you.

Life just is; we put the meaning into it. A year after graduating from college I married my college boyfriend and three months after that he told me it wasn't what he wanted. I was young, I was heartbroken, and I knew I had to learn quickly how to begin again. The wounds were deep but for the first time in my life, I learned to love myself. I look back at this time in my life as a gift. Breakdowns make you stronger. The cracks in your life let the sunshine in.

JANUARY 9

TURN "HAVE TO'S" INTO "GET TO'S"

*"On those mornings when you struggle with getting up,
keep this thought in mind - I am awakening to the work of a human
being. Why then am I annoyed that I am going to do what I'm made
for, the very things for which I was put into this world?"*

- Marcus Aurelius

I believe in this passage from 2000 years ago, Marcus Aurelius is saying that when you look at every situation in your life as, "I get to…" instead of "I have to…" you are filled with purpose and gratitude. Marcus Aurelius was the Emperor of Rome. He could have stayed in bed, but he knew that his life mattered and he got to help make the world a better place.

Try today to change your "have to's" into "get to's". I get to exercise. I get to make phone calls today. I get to bring the kids to school. I get to do the laundry. I get to make a presentation. I get to make dinner. I get to put the kids to bed. When you change the word "have" to "get", you feel a sense of appreciation and gratitude instead of feeling that it is a chore or a burden. It also opens your heart to all the blessings in your life.

JANUARY 10

HOW DOES YOUR GARDEN GROW?

"We have billions upon billions of seeds in our minds,
planted there by hurting or taking care of those around us."

- Geshe Michael Roche

*T*he *Yoga Sutra* tells us that every minute of our lives we are choosing to plant "good seeds" or "bad seeds". These seeds store up and then will "sprout" throughout your life. If bad seeds have been planted in the past you can stop them from sprouting by viewing the world differently. How you view the world determines whether you suffer or find true happiness.

The seeds decide how our minds perceive things. We can change the seeds by cultivating our actions and our thoughts to those of goodness. Yoga Master Patanjali says, "The storehouse is planted by the things we do." Here he is referring to the storehouse as our own mind where the seeds stay until they sprout images and thoughts. Every action we take, every word we say, every thought we have plants seeds in our mind and determines how we see the world later on.

The important message in planting your garden of seeds is to know that everything that ever happens to you only happens to you because you have done the same thing to someone else. This is often referred to as "kharma" or in the Bible the "Golden Rule": Do unto others as you would have them do unto you. Epictetus, the black slave that studied and became a Stoic philosopher said, "Where is Good? In our reasoned choices. Where is Evil? In our reasoned choices."

What type of seeds will you plant today?

JANUARY 11

THE MOST IMPORTANT VIRTUE

"Use kindness; it makes the mind bright and clear as pure water."

- Master Patanjali

G rowing up my dad would always say, "be sweet." For my children, they will often hear me say, "choose kindness". Kindness is the most important virtue.

Kindness is about bringing happiness to others. Why is this so important? Because it takes you out of your own head when you think about others. Your life is directed by how you treat others. The greatest seed you can plant is the compassionate act of helping someone else.

Stoic philosopher Seneca wrote 2000 years ago in his essay, On the Happy Life, 24.2-3: "A benefit should be kept like a buried treasure, only to be dug up in necessity...Nature bids us to do well by all...Wherever there is a human being, we have an opportunity for kindness."

Let your life be a gift to others. When you interact with others today, even someone you pass on the street, send them kindness through your thoughts, use your words to fill them up, and let your actions enable others to keep kindness flowing.

JANUARY 12

BEING PRESENT TAKES PRACTICE

*"Nothing is more precious than being
in the present moment. Fully alive, fully aware."*
- Thích Nhất Hạnh

B eing present takes practice. It may be the most difficult thing
you've ever done. So how do we practice? The first step is awareness.
This happens by becoming the observer of your thoughts. You pause, observe
if your mind has taken you to a movie; a story created in your head. You
become the awareness of seeing both the past and the future on your mind's
movie screen. Then you come back to where you are at the present moment.
The present moment is as it is. Always. Can you let it be? Can you enjoy it?
Can you learn from it?

The human condition is lost in thought. Why are we so afraid of looking
at what is right in front of us here and now? If you don't feel comfortable in
the present moment no matter where you are or where you go, you will
always carry unease with you. But when you deeply accept this moment as it
is, no matter what, you are still, you are at peace.

Being present doesn't mean that you are not learning from the past or
planning for the future. When your mind focuses on a past event you
become the teacher: What did you learn? How can you become better from
it? When your mind dives into the future you become the fisherman and reel
it in to focus on that one catch.

The beautiful thing is that you are in control of your thoughts and the
present moment keeps showing up to give you a second chance.

JANUARY 13

CHARACTER

"Character is destiny."

- Heraclitus

I t really is simple: Do the right thing. Always. Your character is what is remembered when you are no longer here. It is what defines you and carries you through life. Marcus Aurelius said, "Waste no more time arguing about what a good man should be. Be one."

The four virtues of Stoicism that make up one's character are courage, temperance, justice, and wisdom. Courage is your fortitude and strength to endure. Temperance is your restraint and self-control. Justice is fairness and doing the right thing. Wisdom is your ability to be driven by reason when acting because of what you have learned navigating your life.

Think about your day and all the opportunities you have to make a choice. Choose to do the right thing the first time so you don't have to clean up the mess later. In the actor Matthew McConaughey's famous commencement speech to the 2015 University of Houston graduating class he called this "leaving crumbs." Remember planting the good seeds will build the foundation for your future. Yogi Master Patanjali said, "If you make it a way of life never to hurt others, then in your presence all conflict comes to an end."

JANUARY 14

NATURE

"We depend on nature not only for our physical survival.
We also need nature to show us the way home,
the way out of the prison of our own minds."

- Eckhart Tolle

Y ou must create the space to explore and ponder. No matter where you are, you can open your door or a window and find nature at your fingertips. Nature is a healer. It is a comfort available to all and helps you to regain your balance.

Holocaust survivor Anne Frank writes in her diary about the awe of looking out her small window and despite her cramped hide-a-way for two years she saw the beauty and comfort in nature: "As long as this exists, this sunshine and this cloudless sky, and as long as I can enjoy it, how can I be sad?"

In nature, there is rhythm and flow to everything. There is a calm and peacefulness to this flow. Nature rests in being - completely at one with what is and where it is. When you appreciate nature and spend time soaking it up, this beautiful flow and presence seeps into you. Watch the birds, look at the trees, listen to the wind…they are not trying to be something they are not. There is a peace and an energy that cannot be understood through thought.

Marcus Aurelius wrote in *Meditations* about the "charm and allure" of nature's process, the "stalks of ripe grain bending low, the frowning brow of the lion, the foam dripping from the boar's mouth."

Spend time outside today. Let nature quiet your mind, bring you comfort, and awaken the awe of what is right in front of you.

JANUARY 15

THE PEN

"There is nothing either good or bad, but thinking makes it so."

- William Shakespeare

I n the wonderful book *How Yoga Works* a story is told about how the teacher explains to her student about perception. She holds up a "pen" to her student and asks him what it is. The mind quickly answers with, "It's a pen." Then she opens the window to a grazing cow and shows him the "pen" and the cow proceeds to eat it. The important message is that anything in life is not itself *by* itself. Your eyes, your mind, the seeds you have planted… *you* make it appear as something. Someone else may see the same thing as completely different. If the pen was a pen by itself the cow would have seen it as a pen too. Things are not themselves—they are ourselves.

Your eyes do not think, your mind does. Open your eyes and your heart to see things differently so your mind can begin to create new patterns of viewing the world. The Greek Stoic philosopher Epictetus said, "Don't let the force of an impression when it first hit you knock you off your feet; just say to it: Hold on a moment. Let me see who you are and what you represent. Let me put you to the test."

Life just is—you put the meaning into it. You choose how you look at things and this gives you the power to change. Practice today looking at what you make things mean. Can you view it differently? Can you make it mean nothing?

January 16

Have a Routine

*"The truth is that a good routine is not only
a source of great comfort and stability, it's the platform
from which stimulations and fulfilling work is possible."*
- Ryan Holiday

I love my morning routine. It is my sanctuary, my peace, my comfort. You can create routines throughout your day. We all do better with structure and routines create that. American televangelist, Mike Murdock said, "The secret of your future is hidden in your daily routine."

When you have a routine, it helps to quiet your mind because it limits the number of choices you need to make. It creates structure inside the chaos. A routine provides a platform to practice presence. The greater number of details in your life that you can set to a routine, the less amount of clutter you will have in your mind.

When you have a routine that becomes a ritual it helps you to end and begin again. Your great work will come from having rituals and habits. Epictetus said, "Every habit and capability is confirmed and grows in its corresponding actions, walking by walking, and running by running… therefore, if you want to do something make a habit of it."

JANUARY 17

DIGITAL NOISE

"Ask yourself at every moment, 'Is this necessary?'"

- Marcus Aurelius

There's a lot going on in our world right now and no doubt it is important to become aware, acknowledge, and act on the contribution you can make to help any situation. But don't let digital noise become your taskmaster. Remember...you are in control of you. Is your phone, computer, or television controlling you?

When you are listening to the news or scrolling your social media ask yourself, "Is this information making me better? Can I use this information to help someone?"

We have become a country that can't be still. We don't let our minds rest because we are always checking something in fear of missing out. Often this information is toxic. The TV personality, Bill Maher, said, "The tycoons of social media have to stop pretending that they're friendly nerd gods building a better world and admit they're just tobacco farmers in T-shirts selling an addictive product to children. Because, let's face it, checking your 'likes' is the new smoking."

You have important work to do today. To become the best version of yourself limit your inputs. "If you wish to improve," Epictetus said, "be content to appear clueless or stupid in extraneous matters." And if the information does matter...do something about it.

JANUARY 18

LESS IS MORE

"Luxury is the wolf at the door and its fangs
are the vanities and conceits germinated by success.
When an artist learns this, he knows where the danger is."
- Tennessee Williams

It is the simple things that stir our soul. Find the joy in simplicity. When your life is filled with "stuff" there is not enough space to enjoy the present moment. Perhaps the new outfit or new car fills a void emotionally for a short time but what is left is an item that takes up space literally and figuratively in your mind. When you free yourself from the weight of all the extras in your life, you create a lightness of being.

Less is more applies to many aspects of your life: your words, your pursuits, and your belongings. Listen more than you speak, pursue serving others and appreciate what you have. It is not the accumulation of things that brings us fulfillment in our lives, but the accumulation of values and character. Marcus Aurelius said, "I was once a fortunate man but at some point fortune abandoned me. But true good fortune is what you make for yourself. Good fortune: good character, good intentions, and good actions."

JANUARY 19

APPROVE OF YOURSELF

"I'm constantly amazed by how easily we love ourselves above all
others, yet we put more stock in the opinions of others than in our
own estimation of self...How much credence we give to the opinions
our peers have of us and how little to our very own!"

- Marcus Aurelius

We spend an incredible amount of our life trying to win admiration from others. It is an innate trait to want to be accepted; to be welcomed into the pack. But the struggle occurs when instead of being a part of the community, we see ourselves as a separate entity. Our focus is on how to prove ourselves to others.

When you spend your life's energy trying to prove yourself, you are at the mercy of things beyond your control. You become helpless.

Why do you need to prove anything to anyone? Maybe what's happening is you're trying to prove something to yourself. Instead of trying to prove something, try *approving* of yourself. Change the judgment of yourself and others to acceptance. You are right where you are supposed to be today, at this moment.

JANUARY 20

SUPERPOWER ENERGY

"Wherever you stand, be the soul of that place."

- Rumi

J ust like with your thoughts and actions, you are responsible for the energy you bring into a room. Can't you feel the energy of someone that has the weight of the world on their shoulders versus the energy of someone that lights up a room with peaceful joy? It's palpable.

Be the kind of person that has authentic energy. An energy that bathes in contentment no matter what is happening. It's important to know that your energy comes *from* you, not *at* you. And the energy that comes from you then surrounds you by a few feet. Today acknowledge that energy. Just be when you walk into a room. What are you radiating out into the world?

There may be different beliefs in what happens after we die, but it is quite evident that who we were is no longer in our bodies. Our life force, our energy, is separate from the vehicle that moved us throughout our life. Think of your body as the sun and your energy as the heat it releases to the world. Let your superpower be your energy. The kind of energy that warms the hearts of others just by your presence.

JANUARY 21

ENJOY THE PROCESS

*"The process is order, it keeps our
perceptions in check and our actions in sync."*
- Ryan Holiday

Y ou do know what the finish line is, right? It's your last breath. We spend so much time trying to achieve this or finish that. We miss our life when we don't enjoy the ride. When you are attached to the outcome, the joy you experience is short-lived because you are already on to the next thing.

It's the work, the training, the process that fills you up. When your mind focuses on the outcome you are letting things outside of your control take over. Be here now. Step by step live and learn.

There is peace in the process. Think about learning a new language or a new instrument. You begin with one word or one note and then you add a second. If you began by setting a goal to be fluent or accomplished within a short amount of time, all the fun and joy would be taken away. Slow down, pace yourself, be grateful for where you are in the process and be mindful of the present moment because that is where the magic is. Let the journey be the reward.

JANUARY 22

NEVER STOP LEARNING

"It is impossible to learn that which one thinks one already knows."

- Epictetus

F all in love with learning. Become an explorer and discover all that you do not know. In 426 BC, Socrates was known as the wisest citizen of Athens, Greece, but he spent most of his life proclaiming what he did not know and was eager to ask questions and learn.

Let the world be your teacher. Let books be your teacher. Let the experiences in your life guide you to ask questions, to ponder, and to solve. It's important to surround yourself with people that are more intelligent and wiser than you. You can benefit from their knowledge. When you are learning something new, be open to feedback. It is the critical feedback that makes you better.

In yogic philosophy, the word *prajna* expresses how we gain wisdom through an open state of mind, open eyes, and open ears. Pema Chödrön writes in her book *Comfortable with Uncertainty,* "It is a state of basic intelligence that is open, questioning, and unbiased. Whether it comes in the form of curiosity, bewilderment, shock, or relaxation isn't really the issue. We train when we're caught off guard and when our life is up in the air." In other words, we learn when we let ourselves receive in every aspect of our life.

Be like Socrates and go around and look for the things you do not know. You will never stop learning because the more you learn, the more you are exposed to the things you do not know.

JANUARY 23

FLIP JUDGING TO REPORTING

"He was sent to prison. But the observation
'he has suffered evil,' is an addition coming from you."
- *Epictetus*

We often interject our thoughts and opinions because we think we are helping. In our mind, we add a dialogue to almost everything that we witness. Take a moment to pause before you speak. Listen to the dialogue in your mind and stop being the commentator.

Try flipping judging to reporting today. It's very different. When you report you simply state what happened without adding a judgment after it. For example, "I did this; therefore I'm wrong." When there is not a condition or a story after something that has happened to you, your life is filled with so much more clarity and ease.

Epictetus said it beautifully, "Don't seek for everything to happen as you wish it would, but rather wish that everything happens as it actually will— then your life will flow well." Stoicism calls this the "art of acquiescence" - to accept what has happened to you with gratitude. In yogic philosophy, this way of being is found in the study of the *Niyamas* - you watch what you do and what you think without adding judgment.

Today, practice not adding a semicolon after a thought or a statement. Be the reporter and leave it at that.

JANUARY 24

LEAVE EVERYTHING BETTER

"Always leave things better than you found them...especially people."

- Henry Cloud

Y ou know what it feels like when someone borrows a book and doesn't return it, or stays at your home and doesn't offer to help, or the one that always breaks my heart...when someone litters. We must practice taking better care of everything. We must have more respect for others and our world.

It can be the simplest act. Pick up a piece of trash when you are out for a walk, compliment a friend, leave a room neater than you found it. Create opportunities in your day to leave something or someone better.

I love this from the book *All I Ever Needed to Know I Learned in Kindergarten* by Robert Fulghum:
"All I really need to know about how to live and what to do and how to be, I learned in kindergarten. These are the things I learned: Share everything. Play fair. Don't hit people. Put things back where you found them. Clean up your own mess. Don't take things that aren't yours. Say you're sorry when you hurt somebody..."

Commit to being a person who makes life a better experience every day. Leave a touch of grace mentally, physically, and emotionally as you go about your day.

JANUARY 25

WORRYING ABOUT WHAT OTHERS THINK

"The tranquility that comes when you stop caring
what they say. Or think, or do. Only what you do."
- Marcus Aurelius

It really is wasted energy when your mind is exploding with thoughts of what other people might be thinking about you. Think about this: 99% of what bothers you is about you. 99% of what bothers others has nothing to do with you. So why are we spending so much of our precious time caring about 1%?

When you catch yourself wondering what someone else is thinking about you, pause and redirect that thought to sending them kindness and telling yourself, "I am the best version of me today." You cannot control what other people think but you can use your mind and body for good. When you let go of worry surrounded by ego you create space for what truly matters.

I do think as we age we care less and less about what others think and we find this so freeing. In a world of social media and an obsession with self, we have to focus even more on being the observer of our thoughts and silencing the ones that are not important.

You have too much good to do today. Let your heart guide you and let your mind focus on the work you have to do to help make this world a better place.

JANUARY 26

MEMENTO MORI

"Let us prepare our minds as if we'd come to the very end of life.
Let us postpone nothing. Let us balance life's books each day. ...
The one who puts the finishing touches on their life each day
is never short of time."

- Seneca

Memento Mori is an ancient practice of reflection on mortality. In both Stoicism and yogic philosophy, this practice creates awareness of living life fully. Most of us avoid thinking about death. What happens if we use the end as a beginning every day? When you look at your life as a gift that can be taken away at any point you open the door to living with clarity and gratitude.

Marcus Aurelius wrote in *Meditations*, "You could leave life right now. Let that determine what you do and say and think." Live your life now. Don't wait for the perfect time or perfect situation. Memento Mori reminds us to do what we can now.

Viewing your life this way is not about dying, it's about living because they are the same. To truly live you must think about your mortality. Let go of death bringing you anxiety or fear and let it be a gentle reminder to wake up and live your life with purpose.

JANUARY 27

WHAT IS THE EGO?

"It is by surrendering the limitations of its own banks that a river becomes the mighty ocean; do not be afraid to throw away the trinkets of your ego to gain the diamond of grace."

- Swami Veda

When the mind says, "I," that is the ego. Our mind does this to help organize and differentiate how we are engaging with every event in our lives. The ego is essential to our existence. The trouble comes when we believe the "I" is more important than anything else.

Remember, life just is: We put the meaning into it. Think about being at the grocery store and you hear a child having a tantrum. The ego makes it personal by saying, "I hear that child screaming." Then based on your past experiences you put a value judgment on the event. You might become sympathetic because you can relate to how the caregiver is feeling or you might be annoyed because you were hoping for some peace and quiet. The ego makes it about you and then adds a story to it.

Let your ego come from your soul, not your mind. Focus on others and that will soften the "I".

JANUARY 28

PRACTICE THANKSGIVING

*"If the only prayer you say
in your entire life is 'Thank You' that would suffice."*
- Meister Eckhart

It is impossible to feel gratitude and anger at the same time. It is impossible to wish for something else when you are grateful for what you have. It is impossible to be selfish when you are grateful. The key to happiness is living a life of gratitude.

There are so many opportunities to practice thanksgiving. Try this one today: Pause and be thankful for events throughout your day as they conclude. This can be done verbally or silently. As you complete your exercise, thank your body for allowing you to move. After you take a shower, thank the water and the source that brought it to you. After you finish a meal, thank the food and those that helped bring it to you. After a meeting, thank everyone that participated. After spending time outside, thank the sun and the birds. After dinner with your family, thank them for sharing that time together.

Learn the art of giving thanks in all situations. Every encounter you have today conclude with "thank you".

JANUARY 29

DIFFERENCE BETWEEN STILLNESS AND SILENCE

"To hold the mind still is an enormous discipline,
one which must be faced with the greatest commitment of your life."
- *Garry Shandling*

Silence can be found in a church. Stillness can be found in the middle of Grand Central Station. Stillness is a feeling. Silence is a lack of sound. You know that feeling when you are so absorbed in something that you lose track of time…that is stillness. You could be working on a project, listening to every word your loved one speaks, practicing your golf swing, or playing an instrument in the middle of a busy train station. Stillness can be found in anything that brings you focused joy.

Stillness is what you feel when your mind and your heart only focus on one thing. You are happiest in the moments of stillness. Stillness inspires new ideas and it is where greatness comes from. You must create space in your life to let stillness flow.

Practice stillness today. Nature is a beautiful way to explore stillness. Let it guide you, let it cleanse you. Watch how nature allows stillness to constantly flow. Then become aware of stillness in the busyness of your day. Mark the moments when your mind is not drifting and you are loving what you are doing. That is stillness.

JANUARY 30

ALWAYS SEEKING

"Happiness is like a butterfly which, when pursued, is always beyond
our grasp, but which, if you will sit down quietly,
may alight upon you."

- Nathaniel Hawthorne

O scar Wilde, the Irish playwright and poet, said there are two kinds of unhappiness in the world. One is *not getting* what you want; the other *is getting* what you want. So much of our time and energy is spent wishing we had something different. In yogic philosophy, one of the *Niyama's* is *Santosha* which explores contentment. There is a paradox to Santosha: The more we seek contentment or need it to look a certain way, the more it eludes us. Freedom is found when you let go of seeking and realize that each moment is exactly how it is supposed to be.

Seneca said, "No person has the power to have everything they want, but it is in their power not to want what they don't have, and to cheerfully put to good use what they do have." There can be an enormous shift in your quality of life when you open your eyes and your heart to all that you do have. Gratitude is the key to letting go of the endless pursuit of seeking.

A whole new world opens up when you look at all that you have instead of what you don't.

JANUARY 31

CHOICE

"Life is a matter of choices, and every choice you make makes you."
- John C. Maxwell

Y ou are the sum of your parts. In other words, you are a collection of the choices you have made in your life. Every event in your life has been an opportunity for choice. You are the cumulative effect of all of your choices; your waistline, your wallet, your relationships, your character. What is so beautiful and powerful is that you have complete control over your choices.

As we are learning through Stoicism, you can't control everything that happens to you, but you can control how you respond. I believe choice happens before the response and it is completely up to you. What is interesting about choice is it's the little, insignificant choices over time that add up in a positive or negative way. Let's take exercise for example. If you were to walk an extra 2000 steps a day after 27 months you would have walked 900 miles and lost 30 pounds. But you have to choose every day, even when you don't see a change, to be disciplined and committed.

Making the right choice often doesn't bring immediate gratification but it does plant the right seeds to strengthen your life. You are who you choose to be.

FEBRUARY

FEBRUARY 1

YOU MUST FAIL

"The key to success is massive failure."
- *Thomas Watson, President IBM*

W hat you need to succeed is failure. We must make mistakes over and over again to triumph. Those that succeed in life the most seek out failure. They are not afraid and failing becomes part of the process.

There are countless examples in history of those that failed before they succeeded. Thomas Edison made 1,000 unsuccessful attempts at inventing the light bulb. Michael Jordan said, "I've missed more than 9,000 shots in my career. I've lost 300 games. Twenty-six times, I've been trusted to take the game winning shot and missed. I've failed over and over and over again in my life. And that is why I succeed." This one is kind of fun: Your go-to product to get out the squeaks and what not, WD-40, is named because it was the 40th attempt to create the useful lubricant.

We must fail to succeed. When you become comfortable with beginning again you change your emotional habit pattern of giving up. You become a master of your emotions and you become a master of success.

FEBRUARY 2

LEARN TO SAY NO

"It's only by saying 'no' that you can concentrate
on the things that are really important."
- *Steve Jobs*

I t is hard for us to say "no" because we don't want to hurt someone's feelings or because we think we can do it all. Every time you say "yes" to something you are creating less space in your life for what is truly important. "No" is a short and powerful word that needs to be said more often.

It may take practice to learn how to say "no" but when you flip it to what the no is allowing you to focus on it will become less difficult. When you say "no" it shows people your time is valuable. One trick to try is to use the word "don't" instead of "can't". When you say, "I can't" it may come across as an excuse while "I don't" implies you have set certain rules and boundaries for yourself. An example could be: "Thanks so much for thinking of me for your evening workshop but I don't do any appointments after 6 pm so that I can be with my family."

When asked to do something, if it is not a clear yes, it's a no. As C.S. Lewis said, "Is my 'yes' coming from a dark corner or from the light in my heart?" Watch your life become more meaningful each time you say "no".

FEBRUARY 3

DON'T ONE UP

*"Most people do not listen with the intent to understand;
they listen with the intent to reply."*
- Stephen R. Covey

We often do this without even knowing. How often have you been in a conversation and someone is telling you about their experience and your response is adding something personal that is more significant. For example, my friend says, "I am so excited we are going on our first family vacation to Aruba next year!" My response, "Oh fun! I've been there three times and next year we are going to Hawaii." How do you think that makes my friend feel?

It's important to listen, to let others feel heard and validated. When you "one-up" someone their joy or heartache is diminished. The conversation has become about you and not them. When you feel compelled to add your own experience it's your ego talking. Be thoughtful and stop yourself. Find the joy in their experience. Feel the heartache or concern for the other human being when they are sharing a struggle. Learn to hold space for others without the urge to add your own story.

FEBRUARY 4

EQUANIMITY

"Learn to keep your feelings in balance,
whether something feels good or whether it hurts;
whether something's enjoyable or distasteful..."
- Master Patanjali

T he definition of equanimity is mental calmness, composure, and evenness of temper, especially in a difficult situation. I think this is the perfect word for Stoicism and yogic philosophy. Marcus Aurelius wrote in *Meditations*, "To be like the rock that the waves keep crashing over. It stands unmoved and the raging of the sea falls still around it."

In the *Yoga Sutra*, the Four Infinite Thoughts are infinite kindness, infinite compassion, infinite joy, and infinite equanimity. Here equanimity refers to helping everyone the same achieve happiness and this begins by avoiding extremes of feelings. Equanimity is learning to not be thrown off balance by how you feel.

Calmness is strength. Equanimity is not about not caring. Quite the opposite: It's about caring so much that you don't let your emotions lead the way. You lead from your heart and not your head.

FEBRUARY 5

LIFE'S WHISPER

"Difficulties come when you don't pay attention to life's whisper.
Life always whispers to you first, but if you ignore the whisper,
sooner or later you'll get a scream."

- Oprah Winfrey

L isten for the whispers in your life. It feels like a gentle nudge to
wake you up to your life. Maybe it's a nudge to put your phone
down when you are driving. Maybe it's a call from your doctor's office to
schedule your annual physical or that inner voice that says, "something is
off". The whisper is trying to wake you up from sleep walking through your
life but you must listen.

Everything is signaling you to be a better version of yourself in some way.
The universe is trying to take care of you by the whispers. Life whispers to
you all the time and if you don't hear it, it gets louder and louder.

Listen to your inner voice. The voice that comes from your heart, not
your head. It's whispering to you and will help guide your life.

FEBRUARY 6

GIVE WITHOUT RETURN

"Even after all this time, the sun never says to the earth,
'You owe me.' Look what happens with a love like that.
It lights the whole sky."

- Hafiz

We often think in relationships that the give and take should be 50-50. It actually should be 100% you and you should not expect anything back. When you engage in a relationship this way you are not only taking responsibility for your actions but you are showing unconditional love.

You can give without return in all aspects of your life. You give because you genuinely care. Look for what needs to be done and not the credit to be gained from doing it.

Marcus Aurelius wrote this passage over 2,000 years ago: "Some people, when they do someone a favor, are always looking for a chance to call it in. And some aren't, but they're still aware of it—still regard it as debt. But others don't even do that. They're like a vine that produces grapes without looking for anything in return. A horse at the end of the race…A dog when the hunt is over…A bee when its honey stored…And a human being after helping others. They don't make a fuss about it. They just go on to something else, as the vine looks forward to bearing fruit again in season." We should be like that.

FEBRUARY 7

LOVE IS A VERB

"Love without action is meaningless
and action without love is irrelevant."
- *Deepak Chopra*

L ove is action. Love requires movement of your mind, your heart, and your body. Love for yourself, love for others and love for beliefs can only be strengthened by your effort.

Love is challenging and rich and multi-layered. When you love something so profoundly your every step is action. When John Lewis led a peaceful Civil Rights march across the Edmund Pettus Bridge on March 7, 1965, in Selma, Alabama he said, "You beat me, you arrest me, you take me to jail, you almost killed me but despite that I'm still going to love you." He believed you never gave up on anyone, and he also believed in his cause so strongly that he was prepared to die for it.

Love is not a feeling. It is a way of being. There is an African proverb that says, "When you pray, move your feet." That is love in action. Love with your actions today.

FEBRUARY 8

FOCUS ON ONE THING

*"Every second of every day, our senses bring in
way too much data than we can possibly process in our brains."*
- Peter Diamandis

I'm fascinated with how our minds work and frankly how often they don't work to help us to enjoy our lives and stay present. How often are we multi-tasking? How often are we "listening" but our mind is thinking about something else? Have you ever finished a meal and can't even remember what it tasted like?

Our brains can only focus on one thing at a time. Here is the challenge—you have five basic senses that send information to the brain: touch, sight, hearing, smell, and taste. Practice not double sensing. Meaning: When you are driving use your eyes to drive; not to look down at your phone and back at the road. When you are listening to your child tell you a story; use your ears to only hear them. When you are eating a meal today, put all distractions away and truly enjoy every bite.

FEBRUARY 9

FIVE SECOND RULE

"The 5 Second Rule: The moment you have an instinct to act on a
goal you must 5-4-3-2-1 and physically move or
your brain will stop you."

- Mel Robbins

I recently ran into a friend who is actually a well-known author and public speaker, Mel Robbins. I had been wanting to read her book but just hadn't "gotten around to it". After seeing her I said, "That's it, I'm ordering her book as soon as I get home!"

It turns out that what I did was exactly what her book is about. We often let life get in the way or we let our emotions get in the way. Mel's "Five Second Rule" is to count backward from five and then act. This practice interrupts our habitual pattern of always letting our feelings run the show.

Mel first came up with the strategy to stop hitting the snooze button every morning. She committed to herself that when the alarm went off she would say, "5-4-3-2-1, go!" She got out of bed before her mind could tell her something different.

Often our decisions are made by our feelings and they are usually not aligned with what is best. Use the "5 Second Rule" today. If you are in a meeting and are thinking of sharing an idea—5-4-3-2-1 speak up and share. If you have been wanting to have that difficult conversation with a loved one —5-4-3-2-1, have it.

Replace the chatter in your mind with courage. 5-4-3-2-1 GO!

FEBRUARY 10

ENJOY A HOBBY

"This is the main question,
with what activity one's leisure is filled."

- Aristotle

R emember what you enjoyed playing as a child? So many of our best memories are at play. The things you loved as a child represent your inner child. Bring something back as a hobby.

A hobby is a physical action that replenishes and strengthens your soul. Your hobby should fill you up with joy and focus. It challenges you and relaxes you at the same time. Your body is busy and your heart is open. Your hobby should not have an external justification. It can help you get better at something but that is not the point.

Your hobby can be anything that helps you rest your mind and actively bring joy to your life. Examples could be: cooking, assembling a puzzle, collecting stamps, gardening, playing a recreational sport or exercise-whatever speaks to your inner child.

Having a hobby is important to your life. We all need balance and a time to let go of striving to get ahead. A hobby teaches you that you are enough. You don't need validation from something outside. Make time in your life to have a hobby.

FEBRUARY 11

AWARENESS

*"Awareness allows us
to get outside of our minds and observe it in action."*
- Dan Brule

T he first step in being present is becoming aware that you are *not* present. Think about how often you are lost in thought. The majority of our thoughts are repetitive and are stories from the past or guesses on the future. To become present in your life, awareness must come first because you cannot change what you are not aware of.

When you recognize that you are lost in thought, you realize that who you are is not the voice in your head but the one who is aware of it. When you no longer believe everything you think, you step out of thought and see clearly that the thinker is not who you are.

We have the power to stand back and look at things. This is essential and the first step to becoming more present. Awareness is being able to question your own thoughts. You are in charge of your thoughts. Awareness of your thoughts opens the door to presence.

FEBRUARY 12

BECOME THE OBSERVER

*"The highest form of intelligence
is the ability to observe yourself without judging yourself."*
- Deepak Chopra

Did you know that we have approximately 60,000 thoughts a day? Studies have shown that 80% of those thoughts are negative and 95% are the same thought you had yesterday. After becoming aware that we are not present because we are lost in thought, the next step is to become the observer of those thoughts. Your mind is a conversation and the observer of this dialogue is your soul. When you recognize your wandering mind, you realize that who you are is not the voice — but the one who is aware of it.

Practice listening to the chatter in your mind. You will notice that the 60,000 thoughts are filled with judgment, speculation, complaints, comparison and so on. An awakening begins to happen when you see how you have made up your realities.

What is truly important in our lives is beyond the thinking mind. The more you practice observing your thoughts, the more you will awaken your true self and become more present.

FEBRUARY 13

THE SPACE BETWEEN

"It has been said that it's the space between the bars that holds the tiger. And it's the silence between the notes that makes the music."
- Wayne W. Dyer

We are learning that to become more present we first need awareness, then we learn to become the observer of our thoughts and then we learn how to spend time in the space between our thoughts. The present moment isn't what is happening now...it is the space in which it happens. The present moment is the silent space between the thoughts.

So how do we create space between those daily 60,000 repetitive thoughts? Practice breathing in a way that you notice the pause. Take a deep inhale, notice the pause, slowly exhale, notice the pause, and repeat two more times. Feel this experience in your body and let it begin to retrain your mind to look for the gap between your thoughts.

Everything emerges from the space between thoughts. You must have this pause, this space, this gap for all creativity in your life to happen. You can activate the space between your thoughts at any time. Your true self is there.

FEBRUARY 14

CHOOSE WHAT YOU THINK

"What you're supposed to do when you don't like a thing is change it.
If you can't change it, change the way you think about it."

- Maya Angelou

W hat is so amazing and powerful on this journey of learning to become more present is that we get to choose our thoughts! You now know that you are not the repetitive, negative voice in your head but the observer of those thoughts. So if you are the observer, can't you then be the director of that voice?

Our minds think. That is what they do, but we have become victims of identifying our lives with the negative voice in our heads. Begin today to choose how you think. I have said before: Life just is...we put the meaning into it. Situations aren't bad or good, our thinking labels them as such.

Since we have the power to stand back and look at things, why not choose to look at them in the present moment with positivity. Ask yourself, "Is there anything wrong with this moment?" Choose what direction your thoughts will go. Practice directing your thoughts to work for you and not against you.

FEBRUARY 15

ACCEPT THIS MOMENT

*"Accept — then act. Whatever the present moment contains,
accept it as if you had chosen it...
this will miraculously transform your whole life."*
- Eckhart Tolle

Become aware of your thoughts and realize that your true self is not the voice in your head. You are deeper than thought. You are the one that is observing those thoughts. Once you observe your thoughts and stop identifying with them, being present begins to knock at your door and you look for the space between your thoughts.

To fully be present you must accept each moment as it is and not the story your mind has created around it. The one constant factor in your life is this moment, and it is painful when you stand in opposition to what is. Try to not argue with each moment in your day. When you surrender and accept that each moment is exactly as it is supposed to be, your life will unfold with ease and presence.

You cannot find the present moment in your mind. Be. Here. Now. Let go of the past and the future. Find the space between your thoughts and accept this beautiful moment as it is.

FEBRUARY 16

ALWAYS A WHITE BELT

"In my walks, every man I meet is my superior in some way,
and in that I can learn from him."
- Ralph Waldo Emerson

There is an adage in the sport of Jiu-Jitsu that says, "Always a white belt." A white belt is a beginner. One who is learning with enthusiasm, with humility, without ego. This is how we should live our lives.

Everybody has something they can teach you. Be open-minded and have a willingness and ability to learn from anyone. Pay attention and look for what you may not know. To do this you need to let go of your ego and be like a sponge soaking up knowledge regardless of its source.

An exercise you could try is to write down all the things you admire about people you respect and what it would take to acquire those skills. Learn from them, seek advise and then apply what you have learned. It is important to practice what you learn because, as Epictetus said, "If you didn't learn these things in order to demonstrate them in practice, what did you learn them for?"

Unless you are a master at something, you should continue to learn as if you were a white belt.

FEBRUARY 17

SERVICE IS YOUR PATH

"To see people who will notice a need in the world
and do something about it... Those are my heroes."
- *Fred Rogers*

The common thread in yogic philosophy, Stoic philosophy, and many spiritual practices is the understanding that our purpose is to help others. I have found that the greatest joy in life is felt in being of service.

Stoic philosopher Marcus Aurelius said 2000 years ago, "Humans were made to help others. And when we do help others — or help them to do something — we're doing what we were designed for. We perform our function."

The rhythm of life is found in serving others. Look around at nature and how effortlessly it serves. The sun's rays, the raindrops, the trees, the ocean are all one beautiful, continuous gift of giving.

We are here to shine our light. The best way to be of service is to be yourself. Let your service come from your heart. I remember the pivotal point in my life when I realized that it wasn't about me. It was about helping others. I have never been happier or more fulfilled. Find a way to help someone today and then pay attention to how it makes you feel.

FEBRUARY 18

THE ART OF ACQUIESCENCE

*"The Fates guide the person who accepts them
and hinder the person who resists them."*

- Cleanthes

The Stoics used the term "art of acquiescence" to refer to an attitude of acceptance and moving on from things that are outside of your control. Imagine if a surfer fought the conditions of the water. To succeed, a surfer must be calm and let the wave carry him with faith.

The "art of acquiescence" in Stoicism is found in yogic philosophy through the word "surrender". This is not a passive surrender but a way of taking life on by yielding to events in your life rather than opposing them. This shift happens on the inside. You can still take action on the outside but with an understanding and acceptance of what is happening now. Practice letting go of resistance and let life flow.

The "art of acquiescence" can only be found in the present moment. It takes great character to accept things as they are instead of wasting time on how they should be. Let go of your need to control and joyfully engage in life as it is.

FEBRUARY 19

PRACTICE NON-EXCESS

"The point in life is to know what's enough."

- Gensei

G reet each day with a sense of abundance rather than indulgence. When exploring yoga's ethical practice in the yamas and niyamas, the fourth observation is one of non-excess referred to as *Brahmacarya*. It invites us to live our lives with a sense of wonder and contentment rather than burdened with excess.

Practicing non-excess is not about non-enjoyment. It's about living in moderation which allows you to experience your life with clarity and gratitude. Following this philosophy challenges our perception of what it really means to have everything we need.

If you pay attention to your life there is a moment in time where you reach the perfect limit of whatever you are engaged in. Listen to what your body needs and not what your mind is telling you. Look at yourself and ask where you may have excess. Is it too much social media? Too much food? Too much discipline? Too much ambition? When you embody moderation you find balance in your life.

Excess is draining. Too much of anything is not a good thing. When you become aware of the "enough", you cultivate a sense of satisfaction and ease.

FEBRUARY 20

EMPATHY

"Could a greater miracle take place for us than to look through
each other's eyes for an instant?"

- Henry David Thoreau

E mpathy is a way of being connected with another human being by feeling their heart center. It is accepting the journey of another person and relating to what they are going through. I often say to my kids, "Imagine how you would feel if…" Having empathy is the ability to deeply understand and feel the experience of another person.

Empathy is different from sympathy. Empathy involves understanding or trying to understand how one feels while sympathy is sharing your feelings about someone else's situation. With empathy, you feel from the inside and often there are no words; with sympathy, you verbally speak to the outside. Empathy is a lot harder than sympathy.

Empathy helps us feel connected with others. We are connected with their feelings and what they think. Empathy involves taking someone's situation and putting yourself in it to truly feel what they are going through.

To deepen your empathic connection, become a better listener. When you engage with someone, pause and have stillness as you see into their heart. What you will see is that you are meeting yourself.

FEBRUARY 21

THE WISDOM OF OBSCURITY

"It is wisdom to be silent."

- *Wayne Dyer*

In the 36th verse of Lao-Tzu's *Tao Te Ching* he talks about following a path where you release your need to be more *anything* in the eyes of others. He calls this "the wisdom of obscurity."

It really is true in life that the harder you try to impress or succeed based on ego, the harder your path will be. The more you pat yourself on the back, the less you are acknowledged by those around you. Marcus Aurelius wrote in *Meditations*, "Is an emerald suddenly flawed if no one admires it?"

Lao-Tzu uses the metaphor of fish leaving the deep water to see the "big world" but when they do they are caught by nets. The lesson is that you will outlast those that try to be recognized. Practice not drawing attention to yourself. Stay your course, and you will flourish.

It has been said that those who know do not speak. The message here is a paradox. The quieter you become the louder you are heard. Try having "the wisdom of obscurity" today. Let your wisdom come from your inner being.

FEBRUARY 22

PERCEPTION

"It's all in how you perceive it. You're in control.
You can dispense with misperception at will, like rounding the point.
Serenity, total calm, safe anchorage."

- Marcus Aurelius

The Stoics practiced an exercise called Turning the Obstacle Upside Down. It is a beautiful yet challenging way to live your life. You have control over how you perceive *everything*. You have the power to take a "bad" situation and look for the "good".

I lost my dad, my best friend, to Lewy body dementia. Undeniably, it was the hardest experience of my life. I let myself feel the sadness daily, but I also choose to be grateful and focus on all of my wonderful memories. It fills me up to know I had the opportunity to say everything I could possibly say before he passed. I am thankful that the disease took him when he still knew who I was.

We are what we feel and perceive. When you change your perception, you change your world. You are the one that is holding yourself back from throwing away your misperceptions. No matter what happens in your day, your perception of those events is under your control.

FEBRUARY 23

ASK FOR HELP

"Don't be ashamed to need help. Like a soldier storming a wall, you have a mission to accomplish. And if you've been wounded and you need a comrade to pull you up? So what?"

- Marcus Aurelius

Why is it that we think that asking for help is being weak? Maybe it began in the classroom when we were afraid to raise our hands and ask a question? Let's teach our children that asking for help makes you strong; it makes you better.

To live a productive life with less struggle it is necessary to ask for help. When you ask for help it shows you care about what you are doing. It shows you are willing to learn.

When you ask for help you receive support and this exchange of energy is essential. We all need help. If you are afraid to ask for help remember that human beings are basically wired to want to give help. We feel good when we help others so your asking becomes a win-win.

Barack Obama said, "Don't be afraid to ask questions. Don't be afraid to ask for help when you need it. I do that every day. Asking for help isn't a sign of weakness, it's a sign of strength. It shows you have the courage to admit when you don't know something, and to learn something new."

FEBRUARY 24

HAVE A COMPLAINT FREE LIFE

"When you complain, you make yourself a victim. Leave the situation,
change the situation, or accept it. All else is madness."
- Eckhart Tolle

There seems to be a lot to complain about right now. Is it helping?
When you complain you tell yourself and the world that you
believe a situation should be different but then, most often, you don't do
anything about it. Complaining helps you to feel like you are involved but
you're not. Instead of helping you are actually making matters worse.

It's important to remember that what we get or don't get in our lives is
dictated by the law of karma or the law of "cause and effect". So when we
complain, we receive more of what makes us unhappy. Essentially, you are
asking the universe for more of the same.

The first step in having a complaint free life is to never complain about
something that is out of your control. Doesn't it seem ridiculous to complain
about the weather? The second step is when something is in your control,
change the complaint to a positive. For example, I'm turning the car around
because I left my briefcase at home; For example, instead of complaining that
I have to turn the car around because I forgot my briefcase, I can say to
myself, "Oh well. Now I get to give my daughter at home an extra hug
today."

You can either handle what is placed before you or you cannot.
Either way, don't complain and as Marcus Aurelius said, "Don't be
overheard complaining...Not even to yourself."

FEBRUARY 25

MIND FEAR

"We are more often frightened than hurt;
and we suffer more from imagination than from reality."
- Seneca

We spend a great majority of our time fearing the unknown. It appears in our life as worry, anxiety, nervousness, and more. Fear of what might happen is psychological fear. It comes from thoughts based on stories in our heads about the future. Since we are so identified with our minds, we are in a constant state of fear.

There is an exercise that began in the Stoic tradition called: *premeditatio malorum*. This practice helps you to look at your fear, whether it is asking for a raise, starting a new project, asking someone out on a date, etcetera, and to think about the worst case scenarios of what would happen if you took action.

Best-selling author and podcaster, Tim Ferris practices Stoicism and created a written approach to this called "Fear Setting". With the use of three pages, you write out 10-20 examples of all the worst things that could happen if you took action on what you are fearful of. I remember my daughter's CrossFit coach doing this with her the night before a competition. She wrote down every possible thing that could go wrong. On the second page, your Prevent Page, you write down what you could do to prevent these things from happening and then on page three you write down how you would repair each worst-case scenario.

Don't let fear stop you today from being your best.

FEBRUARY 26

HAPPINESS IS FOUND IN GRATITUDE

"The journey of your life will change when you emphasize gratitude for all that you are, all that you accomplish, and all that you receive."
- Wayne Dyer

We search and search for happiness. Happiness is found in each opportunity in your life through gratitude. By becoming aware that every experience is a *given* moment, gratefulness spontaneously arises. It is given to you and when you make a conscious effort to be grateful, happiness appears.

Be grateful for this moment and relinquish the pursuit of more. Train yourself to value the things that cannot be taken away. When your heart is filled with gratitude there is no need for excess. If you need to be excessive know that you can never be grateful enough.

The practice of gratitude is not difficult. You need to stop and become aware so you do not miss the opportunity. Then you need to look by using your senses and take in the beauty of the moment. Enjoy what is given to you and then take the opportunity to do something with the gift that has been given to you.

FEBRUARY 27

START A JOURNAL

"I hope I will be able to confide everything to you,
as I have never been able to confide in anyone, and
I hope you'll be a great source of comfort and support."

- Anne Frank

Anne Frank wrote the above in her first journal entry on June 12, 1942. Journaling is a restorative and creative way for you to get to know yourself. It creates an opportunity for stillness. Your journal is your journey.

Journaling lets you write and examine. It allows you to become the observer. You get out what is in your head by putting it on paper. Journaling is a way of letting go and will help you get through difficult times. It can also be a place where you write down what your soul wants.

There is no correct way to write or time of day to journal, but it's important to give yourself the gift of this practice. I choose to journal as part of my morning ritual. Recently, I have been journaling as if the day was complete. I write in the past tense about what I did, how I felt, and always what I am grateful for.

Begin today and let your journal become your companion.

FEBRUARY 28

WORRY

"Worry a little bit every day and in a lifetime you will
lose a couple of years. If something is wrong, fix it if you can
but train yourself not to worry."

- Mary Hemingway

Worry stops you from joy. When you worry, you use your imagination to create an outcome you do not want. You worry because it makes you feel like you are doing something. Most of the things you worry about are not important. Worry does not help anything. It is your ego shouting at you, and it tricks your brain into thinking you are doing something to help the situation.

Constant worrying takes a toll on your emotional and physical health. The good news is that chronic worrying is a mental habit that can be broken. You can train your brain to stay calm. As we are learning through Stoicism, the training is guided by what you can control and what you cannot.

Think of your worries as solvable or not solvable. If your worry is solvable start brainstorming solutions that are in your control and then take action. If your worry is not solvable then accept the uncertainty. Embrace the opportunity to learn to adapt, to overcome challenges, and to increase your resiliency.

Worry is not healthy, productive, or loving. When you worry you are not trusting yourself, others, or the universe. Choose joy over worry.

FEBRUARY 29

SEEK A MENTOR

"The relationship between a Guru and a sisya [disciple] is a very special one, transcending that between parent and child, husband and wife, or friends. A Guru...inspires confidence, devotion, discipline, deep understanding, and illumination through love."
- B.K.S. Iyengar

Throughout history, the importance of having someone to guide you, to question you and to challenge you has been one of the keys to living a fulfilled life. This guide has been referred to in different philosophies as a mentor, a tutor, a master, or a guru.

Finding your own mentor takes time and respect. In yogic philosophy, we learn how our teachings have been passed down to us from one mentor to the next. Yoga is taught best when the teacher is a *vessel*. From the book *How Yoga Works*: "We hold something inside us which is bigger and more beautiful than us as individuals. Yoga has been passed down—poured from vessel to vessel, poured from teacher to student, and then to their students—for hundreds and hundreds of centuries."

Mentors can often see what you cannot. Your mentor guides you to become more self-aware and encourages you to reach your full potential. You will know you have met your mentor when you find someone that lights up your soul.

MARCH

MARCH 1

FORGIVENESS

"The weak can never forgive.
Forgiveness is the attribute of the strong."
- *Mahatma Gandhi*

Forgiveness is letting go of something that you are holding against yourself or someone else. Forgiveness is part of our journey. To become, to grow, to be, you must go down the path of forgiveness. When you practice forgiveness, you heal. Instead of being stuck in the past, you allow yourself to move forward.

There needs to be a level of safety for forgiveness to happen. When you are ready to forgive let it come gently and authentically. Never rush or force forgiveness. Become aware if you are holding on to negative feelings. Are they serving you? You are not ready to forgive if you hold onto anger, because the anger is your protection from healing your heart. To forgive you must let go of your ego because your ego thrives on being the victim.

Forgiveness begins with you. Forgiving yourself opens the door to love. A method of practicing forgiveness is found in Patanjali's *Yoga Sutra* 2:33: "When obstructive thoughts arise, practice the opposite thought." Maybe that is flipping the negative and destructive voice in your head to a dialogue your best friend would have with you. Or, if you are angry at someone for a wrongdoing, send them kind wishes. Remember, what you offer others will return to you.

MARCH 2

WISDOM

"Wisdom is often nearer when we stoop than when we soar."
- William Wordsworth

W isdom is not about having all the answers. It is about being
inquisitive, curious, thoughtful, and aware. After many wrong
turns, wisdom allows us to find the best way to navigate life. You cannot
gain wisdom if you have not experienced failure. Wisdom grows through
experience and witnessing or participating in situations that do not succeed.

Buddhists refer to wisdom as *prajna* which is a state of wisdom higher
than knowledge. It goes beyond the knowledge in one's brain and the
storehouse of our thoughts on to a higher wisdom of understanding the
true nature of reality. You can rely on wisdom but not on your mind.
Clearly stated in the 33rd verse in the *Tao Te Ching*: "One who understands
others has knowledge, one who understands himself has wisdom."

Wisdom is having an open mind while you search for truth. It involves
asking questions, studying, and reflecting. Wisdom is built on managing
expectations, considering all possibilities, and being prepared when life puts
an obstacle in your way. As Antisthenes said, "To the wise, nothing is
alien or remote."

Be intellectually humble and let your wisdom come from your heart.

MARCH 3

THE WIND OF EMOTION

"Never apologize for showing feeling.
When you do so, you apologize for truth."

- Benjamin Disraeli

Think of your emotions like the wind. Sometimes they are still, sometimes gentle and sometimes fierce. It is part of our nature to have emotions. Allow yourself to feel your emotions. Let them run through you. Pay attention and observe them without judgment. Try identifying and labeling your current emotion: "This is what sadness feels like." Acknowledge the emotion, embrace it, and then let it go if it is not serving you.

Just like you are not the negative thoughts in your mind, you are also not your negative emotions. They are part of your experience, but they don't define or control you. Don't let your emotions change who you are - your true self.

Many of our emotions are self-inflicted. We are emotional because we think the world should be different than it is. Be aware of your wandering mind creating emotions that have no justification.

Let the wind of your emotions pass through you. Feel it, learn from it, and then move on.

MARCH 4

Take Action

"Waste no more time arguing about what a good man should be.
Be one."

- Marcus Aurelius

We spend a great deal of time wishing and hoping things could be different. One of the primary disciplines of Stoicism is action, or more accurately the *right* action. These actions define your character. Instead of just thinking about change, we must become enrolled, engaged, and productive. Marcus Aurelius said, "To talk about something is one thing, to do it is another."

It is important for you to know what your values and principles are before you can take meaningful action. Turn your desire for change into an undertaking and consciously choose action over and over again.

Civil Rights leader, John Lewis, believed we all should find a way to get in the way in a peaceful, loving, non-violent way. In addition, Ibram X. Kendi explains in his book, *How to be an Anti-Racist*, that one is an anti-racist if they take action. If you do not do anything, you are contributing to the injustice.

Don't just interpret the world around you, take small steps toward what you know is right. You can be a gentle force for change. Let your words become your work.

MARCH 5

DON'T HATE THE HATER

"You must continue to help others—you must devote your life to it.
It's important to realize the person you may be helping the most
is the person who was committing the violence. Your act of kindness
here is towards the person doing the violence. That's why it is so
crucial that you avoid hating him as you try to restrain him."
- from How Yoga Works

How can we have a better world if we hate the hater? Our job is to plant good seeds. Negative energy cannot be lifted if we do not meet it with love. In Martin Luther King's words, "Hate cannot drive out hate, only love can do that."

Haters hate because it fills up their egos. They are not capable of being happy for another person's success. If you are around someone like this, it is important for you to know it is about them, not you. Try responding with the opposite of what they are saying.

Being around a hater can help you become a better person. Become aware of the emotions that come up, ask yourself if the opinion is inside your control, and respond humbly. Observe how it makes you feel to not add fuel to the fire.

MARCH 6

INNER PEACE IS POWER

"Self control is strength.
Right thought is mastery.
Calmness is power."

- Buddha

Inner peace is found in the joy of Being no matter what the circumstance. You have this incredible inner peace that gives you power. While others may be arguing, complaining or falling apart around you, you stay strong and steady. You know whatever you are experiencing is happening for you, not to you.

Learn to soften everything in your life. The harder you resist the natural flow of life, the more difficult the journey will be. When you live from a place of least resistance, you witness the magic of essential goodness.

When you have inner peace there is an end to suffering. This does not mean that you will not have obstacles in your life...you will, but the power of your inner peace will guide you through. You know, that like the lotus flower, you must be in the mud to grow.

A turbulent mind cannot be at peace. Learn to say "yes" to whatever is happening to you in the present moment. Accepting what is, brings peace instead of struggle.

MARCH 7

YOU ARE NOT A LABEL

"The more labels you have for yourself, the dumber they make you."
- Paul Graham

Our identity is wrapped up in what we think others think of us. As a result, we chase what others think we should, and then label it. We live someone else's dream. Because of labels, our identity is cast into a box of what we should or should not be.

Who do *you* want to be? Can you let go of labels and just be you? We lose our true self when our identity becomes so layered. We become restricted by our labels because they close us off to possibility.

Again, it comes back to our ego. Your ego thrives on labels which allow you to mask your true self. Practice not letting your thoughts create your identity. Your thoughts become obsessed with the labels you have created for yourself and how to live up to them. When you pursue what others have carved out for you, the road ahead will often be barren. You will have lost your power and someone else will be sitting in the driver's seat.

Wayne Dyer eloquently says in *Change your Thoughts, Change Your Life* that when you follow someone else's path, "You'll become a slave to outside messages of praise — someone else's opinion will be directing your life."

You are enough. Labels are superfluous.

MARCH 8

VIEW GREATNESS DIFFERENTLY

"We are only as strong as we are united, as weak as we are divided."
- J.K. Rowling

When we think of the word "greatness" we often think of power, success, wealth, and fame. We think of those that stand out. Imagine a world where there was no ladder of success, no one person or group more powerful than another.

Wayne Dyer encourages us in *Change Your Thoughts, Change Your Life* to discover a new definition of greatness. "Offer yourself a definition that doesn't use any standards of appearance or traditional external measures of success. Notice those who give much, boast little, nurture others, and decline recognition or credit, and put them in your greatness file. Encourage yourself to practice these same kinds of behaviors."

Greatness is when you see yourself in everyone. To do this you must have stillness in your life. Seneca said that "nothing is great unless it's also at peace." A great person never claims their greatness.

Practice letting go of dominating any relationship in your life. See the good, see the greatness in all beings.

MARCH 9

PERSEVERANCE

*"Success comes to the lowly and to the poorly talented,
but the special characteristic of a great person
is to triumph over the disasters and panics of human life."*
- Seneca

What do you learn when things come easily? Maybe that you were lucky? Maybe it is an opportunity for your ego to grow? When there is no effort or struggle, we are often left feeling unsatisfied or empty. It is through perseverance that we feel our best. We chose not to give up when others may have.

When you push yourself past the hard work into more hard work, that is perseverance. Throughout history, you will hear about inventions, causes, and personal goals that came to fruition after an endless amount of effort. There is no doubt the same is true for you.

You can train your soul to be strong and resilient. You can turn hardship into an opportunity for growth. Dedicate yourself to something important to you and take the right actions over and over again to reach your goals. At the end of the day when we know we persevered through difficulties using our own true grit and fortitude, we rest peacefully.

MARCH 10

TAKE THE COMPLIMENT

"Accept both compliments and criticism.
It takes both sun and rain for a flower to grow."
- Marek Kośniowski

I'm not sure why we feel the need to say anything but "thank you" when we receive a compliment. We often add commentary to something nice someone has said to us. For example, "You did so great with your presentation today!" We reply with, "Oh gosh, really? I didn't feel good about it at all." Why can't we just say "thank you"?

When we receive praise or recognition, it can feel awkward. It feels uncomfortable to have the attention so we rebut with a self-deprecating statement. Instead, in that moment, pause and be filled with gratitude. Positive energy is then relayed back to the sender. Offering sincere thankfulness acknowledges a person's recognition and appreciation. When we undermine a compliment, it makes your conversational partner feel pressured into saying more nice things about you.

It is your ego talking when you say anything to contradict a compliment. Become comfortable receiving and then reflect on the praise and believe it to be true. Let the kind words fill you up. Today when someone offers you a compliment say, "Thank you. I really appreciate it."

MARCH 11

LET LIFE FLOW

"It is by surrendering the limitations of its own banks that a river
becomes the mighty ocean; do not be afraid to throw away
the trinkets of your ego to gain the diamond of grace."

- Swami Veda

I t is an incredible awakening when you allow life to just flow. When
you shift your thinking to, "I don't *mind* what happens" you will
experience tremendous freedom. The keyword in that phrase is "mind". Try
to not let your mind become a barrier in your life.

We have become possessed by our thoughts. We let them guide us against
the current. Let go of what is outside of your control. Whatever is could not
be otherwise. Marcus Aurelius wrote in his journal, "That every event is
the right one. Look closely and you'll see. Not just the right one overall, but
right. As if someone had weighed it out with scales."

You let life flow by deciding to let go of worry, stress, and fear. Trust that
you are right where you are supposed to be on your journey through life. To
stay in the flow all you have to do is take one step forward.

MARCH 12

GOOD

*"Our greatest glory is not in never falling,
but in rising every time we fall."*

- Confucius

How do you deal with failure? Turmoil is part of life and we must expect it and welcome it. It may seem hard to say "good" when life does not go according to your plan, but I promise you, it will make you a better person. Something good comes from everything.

Flip how you look at setbacks in your life. Find the opportunity for growth, reevaluate the situation, and begin again. Use each situation in your life as a teaching tool.

Some of my favorite writers have used the word "good" so powerfully and beautifully. Ram Dass wrote, "You may experience despair that you'll ever know that. Good! Because through the despair and through that surrender you get closer to it." In Marcus Aurelius's words, "Something happens to you. Good. It was meant for you by Nature, woven into the pattern from the beginning."

When something doesn't go your way today, say "good" and be ready for a change in perspective.

MARCH 13

HURRYING DOESN'T WORK

*"Your entire life journey ultimately consists of
the step you are taking at this moment. There is always
only this one step, and you give it your fullest attention."*
- Eckhart Tolle

The most important moment is now. How often are we rushing through something to get to the next thing? The only way to get through something is to stay present. When you try to hurry up the process you will often have to begin again. Whatever you are rushing to next will be there. Hurrying only makes life more difficult.

Why not enjoy the process? As Mary Poppins said, "In every job that must be done, there's an element of fun. You find the fun, and SNAP, the job's a game." Be like Mary Poppins and find the fun in the task. Turn the ordinary into the extraordinary. The only way to do that is by putting your attention exclusively on the present.

Marcus Aurelius wrote in *Meditations*, "If you do the job in a principled way, with diligence, energy and patience, if you keep yourself free of distractions, and keep the spirit inside you undamaged, as if you might have to give it back at any moment - If you embrace this without fear or expectation—can find fulfillment in what you're doing now, as Nature intended, and in superhuman truthfulness (every word, every utterance)—then your life will be happy."

MARCH 14

YOUR ONE LIFE

"We have two lives, and the second begins
when we realize we only have one."

- Confucius

Your life begins when you realize your true self, your sacred self is who you really are. You are a spiritual being having a human existence. Your true essence is loving-kindness. You were placed on this earth for a purpose. Your job is to unwrap all the layers that have formed over your soul and be a light while you walk this path here on earth.

Live your one life with the awareness that you will return to how you began. Spiritual teacher and author Eckhart Tolle wrote, "The collective disease of humanity is that people are so engrossed in what happens, so hypnotized by the world of fluctuating forms, so absorbed in the content of their lives, they have forgotten the essence, that which is beyond content, beyond form, beyond thought. They are so consumed by time that they have forgotten eternity, which is their origin, their home, their destiny. Eternity is the living reality of who you are."

Ask yourself constantly if you are moving back to your original spirit or away from it. Daily examples abound: letting a car go in traffic, saying you're sorry, enjoying an uninterrupted meal all bring you back. Anger, worry, resentment all bring you away from your sacred self.

Use your mind intentionally to see in which direction your action will take you. Walk life's path without fear because you will simply return to how you began.

MARCH 15

IDES OF MARCH

"Cowards die many times before their deaths; the valiant never taste
of death but once. Of all the wonders that I yet have heard it seems
to me most strange that men should fear, seeing that death,
a necessary end will come when it will come."
- William Shakespeare

I find it quite interesting that we have a date on the calendar that makes us think of fear, doom, and death. Ides actually refers to the first full moon of every month which usually fell between the 13th and 15th day of the ancient Roman calendar. The Ides of March corresponded to March 15 in ancient Rome. During this time, before 44 B.C., this date actually marked not just the full moon but a new year and was reason to celebrate.

This changed in 44 B.C when Julius Caesar was assassinated or perhaps in 1600 when William Shakespeare coined the phrase, "Beware the ides of March" in his play *Julius Caesar*. For as long as we can remember, March 15th has had a connotation of being dark and gloomy.

It's interesting to wonder if this ominous day came from life imitating art or art imitating life. Let's choose to make this day exactly what it is…today. No burden of the past, no omen for the future, just joy in the moment.

MARCH 16

SERVE A PURPOSE

"Although not consciously trying to guard the rice field from
intruders, the scarecrow is not after all standing to no purpose."
- Bukkoku Kokushi

Maybe we should say one aims to serve a purpose rather than have a purpose. When you look at nature, do we say that the ocean has a purpose or do we look at it as serving a purpose?

Having purpose seems to imply singularity while serving unifies and projects to the greater good. Serving is gentle and helpful. Having is greedy and ego-based. When you serve a purpose, you share with others. When your purpose comes from a place of serving, you are present with virtue and add value to the world.

Serving a purpose is why we are here. Like the scarecrow in the quote above, it doesn't have to move mountains but it does need to touch the hearts of others in a helpful way. Pablo Picasso said, "The meaning of life is to find your gift. The purpose of life is to give it away." And in the words of Ralph Waldo Emerson, "The purpose of life is not to be happy. It is to be useful, to be honorable, to be compassionate, to have it make some difference that you have lived and lived well."

MARCH 17

LESS BUT BETTER

"Many things are good, many are important,
but only a few are essential."

- Todd Christofferson

W e have so many options, so many opinions, so many choices. Do you ever pause and ask, "What is most important now? What is truly essential?"

Author and public speaker Greg McKeown wrote *Essentialism: The Disciplined Pursuit of Less.* The book explores how we can achieve so much more in our lives by doing what is only essential. It's about doing what is most important with the time and resources you have now. McKeown talks about eliminating what is not essential in your life so you can focus your attention on how to make your "highest contribution."

An Essentialist thinks almost everything is nonessential while a non-essentialist thinks almost everything is essential. It is a mindset, a way of life that discerns as McKeown puts it, "the vital few from the trivial many." An Essentialist starts small and looks for simple wins in areas of importance. Never forget that making progress is meaningful work.

Essentialism is about living a life of simplicity with high contribution.

MARCH 18

CONSPICUOUS CONSUMPTION

*"Life's necessities are cheap and easily accessible
and the man who adapts himself to his slender means
and makes himself wealthy on a little sum, is the truly rich man."*

- Seneca

C onspicuous consumption is defined as "the expenditure on the consumption of luxuries on a lavish scale in an attempt to enhance one's prestige." The ego plays a huge role in conspicuous consumption driving us to stand out, to look wealthy, to feel successful and superior.

Conspicuous consumption can be found in those who can't afford what they strive to portray to the world. It can also be found in those who are wealthy on the outside but are poverty-stricken within.

Material items do not ultimately bring you happiness. They may fill a temporary void, but soon you are emotionally back to where you started. Repeated acquisition will land you on a never ending treadmill.

Live a life that gives you meaning rather than wealth. Give, instead of collect. Serve, instead of accumulating. Be rich in your heart. William Shakespeare said in his play *Henry VI*, Part 3:

"My crown is in my heart, not on my head;
Not deck'd with diamonds and Indian stones,
Nor to be seen. My crown is call'd content;
A crown it is that seldom kings enjoy."

MARCH 19

THE INNER CITADEL

"I am the master of my fate. I am the captain of my soul."
- *William Ernst Henley*

In Stoicism, the Inner Citadel is a fortress that protects your soul. We can all build an Inner Citadel. It is built by not letting judgment invade our soul. Marcus Aurelius repeatedly said in his journal, *Meditations*, that "stuff cannot touch the soul."

It is our mind that lets our soul be invaded by outside forces as well as inside forces. Become a warrior of your soul. You can strengthen your Inner Citadel by anticipating and welcoming failure, by feeling your emotions and then letting them go, and by looking at adversity as an opportunity for growth.

An incredible example of living from your Inner Citadel was displayed by Thomas Edison when he witnessed a fire destroy his research facilities. Edison turned to his son and said, "Go get your mother and call her friends. They'll never see a fire like this one again." Seeing his son's panic and confusion he continued, "It's all right, we just got rid of a lot of rubbish."

MARCH 20

PRACTICE GRATITUDE FOR BOTH

"The journey of your life will change when you emphasize gratitude
for all that you are, all that you accomplish, and all that you receive."

- Wayne Dyer

W e tend to practice gratitude for what is going right in our lives
which is wonderful, but it is also important to practice gratitude
for what goes wrong. Ralph Waldo Emerson said, "Cultivate the habit of
being grateful for every good thing that comes to you, and to give thanks
continuously. And because all things have contributed to your advancement,
you should include all things in your gratitude."

When you live your life from a place of gratitude you view the world
through a clear lens. *Eucharistos* is the word Stoic philosopher Epictetus used
for gratitude. It translates into "seeing" what is actually occurring in each
moment, and recognizing that each moment is freely given to you as an
opportunity. Choosing to be grateful for all that happens changes your life.
When adversity strikes, gratitude helps you to bounce back faster.

Notice how gratitude makes you feel. When you stand back, become the
observer and witness that being grateful for the "good" and the "bad" makes
you who you are today.

MARCH 21

BE VULNERABLE

"Vulnerability is not winning or losing. It's having the courage
to show up when you can't control the outcome."
- Brené Brown

M any of us fear vulnerability. We are afraid if we expose our true self we will be judged or we will fail. Often, we feel vulnerable because of something that happened in our past. We don't want to put ourselves in that situation again so to protect ourselves we don't live to our full potential.

Think of vulnerability as a good thing because it means you are challenging yourself; you are creating possibilities and opportunities. You have grit because you are exposing yourself to fear on purpose. You are a warrior.

Practice vulnerability. Put yourself in a situation that you may typically walk away from. Embrace the fear so that you can own it. Once you have identified the fear, you can change your narrative around it.

Vulnerability is about intention. You have the power to take that step forward. It is about taking risks and having courage. Let it be your badge of honor.

MARCH 22

LAUGHTER

"Laughter is the sound of the soul dancing."
- Jarod Kintz

I s laughter part of your day? Laughter is a universal language that heals all. It occurs spontaneously and can catch us by surprise. It gives us an opportunity to pause, to be presents and to find joy in the moment.

Laughter helps us connect, bond, and build relationships. It is a way to show our love by helping people to smile, relax, and feel better. Laughter helps us to stay positive and it eases tension. When you laugh at yourself it changes how you physically feel.

Laughter makes us healthier. It lowers our blood pressure, reduces stress hormones, and makes us more resistant to infection. Did you know that laughter is the fastest and easiest way to regulate your breathing and flush out your lungs? When you laugh, your heart rate, respiratory rate, and oxygen consumption increases. Sometimes you may laugh so hard that your abdominal muscles feel like they got a workout!

Let's bring more laughter into our lives. Just look to children for an example. They laugh on average 200 times a day. Laughter is contagious. Let's spread that.

MARCH 23

PERFECTION IS AN ILLUSION

"We don't abandon our pursuits
because we despair of ever perfecting them."
- Epictetus

N othing in life is perfect. Being human means not being perfect. We have created this unattainable goal of perfection that is an illusion. We think that we have to strive for perfection because of the images we are inundated with via marketing and social media on all of our screens. The truth is, perfection does not exist.

You are beautiful with your imperfections. They are your guide to learning and growing. How boring it would be to be perfect. Choose to see imperfections as perfect. Your human existence is a journey of imperfections but within you, at all times, is your perfect sacred self. Rumi said, "You <u>are</u> the truth from foot to brow. Now, what else would you like to know?"

Chasing perfection is a waste of your precious energy. Your aim should be progress. Don't abandon your dreams, your pursuits, your life, because you think you can't be perfect. Live with meaning and intention and that is as perfect as it gets.

MARCH 24

VISITORS

"The mind is by nature radiant. It's shining.
It is because of visiting forces that we suffer."
- Buddha

Imagine sitting at home and there's a knock at your door. You get up and discover a guest on your doorstep. Your guest is fear. At that moment you have a choice. You could fling open the door and say, "Welcome home," or you could slam the door shut and pretend the guest was no longer there. A third option might be to invite your visitor in for a meal without letting it have the run of the house.

We all have uninvited visitors that come into our lives. They may have names like greed, hatred, jealousy, fear, and doubt but they are not who we are. They are born out of conditions, but like a house built on a strong foundation, these visiting forces do not need to tear you down.

When a visiting force arrives, acknowledge it by its name. "Hey jealousy, there you are." If you don't become the witness of these emotions they will find a way to take up residence. The practice becomes what you do when you open the door. Can you remember who lives there? What can you learn from this visitor? How long do you want your visitor to stay knowing they have arrived to bring you suffering?

These uninvited visitors are not why we suffer. We suffer only when we attach an emotion to our identity. When a visiting force comes to your home today, try greeting it with compassion and maybe sit with it for a few moments. Then send it on its way.

MARCH 25

WHAT MAKES A GREAT LEADER?

"No one should feel the heaviness
of your directions or be hurt by your instructions."
- Wayne Dyer

W ho we are is how we lead. Humility is one of the most important characteristics of a leader. Nelson Mandela said, "If you show people you are not a threat, they will listen to you." A great leader leads from below not from above. He or she serves as the foundation, the roots, the support system. They embody a sense of stillness that brings peace and comfort to those around them.

True leadership is found in those who guide rather than direct. To be a great leader you have to relinquish control. Encourage those around you to make their own decisions by setting a good example. Lead with collaboration and empathy.

The job of a leader is to serve. To be *for* the people and not *above* the people. When we look at our history, we can easily see that goodness prevails under this kind of leadership. Incredible examples include Jesus Christ, Buddha, Muhammad, Gandhi, Mother Teresa, amongst many others. Leadership from above has caused war, terrorism, famine, the holocaust, and more.

Today I pray for great leaders. Not just in our government, but in our work, our communities, and in our families.

MARCH 26

NOTHING LASTS FOREVER

"Nature is merciful and does not try her children, man or beast,
beyond their compass. It is only where the cruelty of man
intervenes that hellish torments appear. For the rest—
live dangerously; take things as they come;
dread naught, all will be well."

- Winston Churchill

Winston Churchill wrote the above quote in 1931 after he was nearly killed by a car when he was crossing a street in New York City. What was most important to Churchill immediately after he was struck was that the driver of the car was not held responsible for the accident. When the driver visited him in the hospital, Churchill tried to offer him some money because he knew that he was out of work. Winston Churchill is showing us that undesirable events will happen but how you respond to them conveys your true nature.

There are many challenging times in our lives. Remember that so much of what happens is outside of our control. Your fear will not make the situation go away but your positive energy will help lighten the load. We will endure, and, like Epicurus says, "Nothing is unending."

Train yourself to not be surprised. Be ready, be calm. Let go of fear because it can penetrate your soul.

MARCH 27

WE SHOULDN'T INTERFERE

*"The most important thing to do in your life
is to not interfere with somebody else's life."*

- Frank Zappa

T he 37th verse of the classical text, *Tao Te Ching*, opens with, "The Tao does nothing, but leaves nothing undone." I believe this means that when we let life flow without interfering, the natural rhythm of life unfolds exactly how it was intended.

Think about all the ways we interfere with our world - from our environment, to our government, to our family, and so much more. When we interfere, we let fear enter. We stop our lives and the lives of others from flourishing.

Watch how life unfolds when you let life just be. Learn to meddle less and be still more. Your life is not someone else's story to tell. Your life is beautifully, quietly told through your soul. When you interfere with your true self, you cause friction and put up barriers.

In addition to not interfering with the natural rhythm of your own life, practice not interfering in the lives of others. Your children can be a great place to start. As long as they are safe, let them find their way. When you tell your children or anyone in your life how to do something, you interfere and cause resistance. Pause and let others discover what they are capable of.

MARCH 28

WE ARE PIECES OF THE WHOLE

"A man's life brings nothing
unless he lives in accordance with the whole universe."
- *Lao-Tzu*

E verything in life is a part of the whole and it begins with humility. Imagine humility as the roots in the ground and every aspect of our world growing from that foundation. Wouldn't that be amazing?

When you realize you are a piece of the whole, your contribution becomes critical and your lack of contribution becomes detrimental. Everything including nature, spirit, and human existence are parts of the whole.

Conflict arises when we see ourselves as better than or separate from this wholeness. When we harm the whole, we harm ourselves, and when we harm ourselves, we harm the whole.

We usually think of our body as a whole. We don't put value on one organ over another, and we don't question their roles. Imagine how our body would work (or not work) if the brain said to the heart, "I'm more important than you."

The body works harmoniously to allow wholeness. This is how we should exist. Working together with an understanding that we are all equal, that we are all parts of the whole.

Marcus Aurelius wrote, "Nor can I be angry with my kinsman, nor hate him, for we are made for cooperation, like feet, like hands, like eyelids, like the rows of the upper and lower teeth. To act against one another then is contrary to nature."

MARCH 29

WILLINGNESS IS THE KEY

"When you are willing to feel it, you can heal it."

- Unknown

We have all experienced sadness, pain, and disappointment. Your breakdowns occur so that you can experience breakthroughs. The key to getting to the other side of your hardship is to let it flow through you. Feel the emotion, witness how it makes you feel, and then let it slowly drift out of you. The length of time it takes you is not a judgment. It is not a race. The key is to be willing to feel the pain in order to heal your heart.

When you suppress your pain, you may think that you are being strong, but it wraps another layer of armor around your true self. To find joy again, you must reconcile with your pain. Be willing to heal. Opening up your wounds will not feel good but it is how you mend.

Don't be afraid. Be willing to take action to heal. Marcus Aurelius said, "Get active in your own rescue." There is such freedom and joy on the other side. Forgive yourself and others, feel the pain on a cellular level, and begin again on the other side of your hardships.

MARCH 30

ACT TO BECOME

"First tell yourself what you want to be;
and then do what you need to do."

- Epictetus

E very moment is an opportunity to become a better version of you, but it must be done through action. You can't think your way to becoming something, you have to act. The goal in life then becomes the pursuit of that achievement.

If you want to learn a new skill, or start a company, or create a product, or write a book, you must put value on becoming. Ask yourself, "What do I need to do to create what it is that I want to do?" Be relentless in your pursuit and find joy in the process. The only thing you should fear is standing still. To become, you must take steps forward and when you lose your step, you must dust yourself off, reevaluate, and then take your next step forward with more wisdom and confidence.

Marcus Aurelius said, "Devote yourself completely to achieving the goodness that is uniquely yours. It would be wrong for anything to stand between you and attaining goodness—as a rational being and a citizen."

MARCH 31

VIRTUE

"Our virtues and our failings are inseparable, like force and matter.
When they separate, man is no more."

- Nikola Tesla

V irtue is defined as the quality of being morally good but, I think the term signifies excellence in what is most important to you. Having virtue allows us to live with peace because we know we have control over the way we act and respond. Virtue helps you to live in harmony with yourself, with others, and with external events.

Another word for virtue could be fulfillment - to act in a way in which every action helps bring your inner spirit into harmony with your life. Virtue is strengthened by wisdom and then applied through your actions.

The Stoics believed what we were aiming for in life is virtue. The four virtues in Stoicism are wisdom, courage, temperance, and justice. In yogic philosophy, the four virtues are friendliness toward the happy, compassion toward the unhappy, delight in the virtuous, and indifference towards the wicked.

Other great virtues include patience, honesty, gratitude, consistency, humility, and humor. What virtues are most important to you?

APRIL

APRIL 1

VALUE REST

*"When you lose touch with inner stillness,
you lose touch with yourself. When you lose touch with yourself,
you lose yourself in the world."*

- Eckhart Tolle

T he rest that I am referring to here is not sleeping; it is about allowing a pause in your life whether it be for two minutes or two weeks. This pause is crucial to your happiness and growth. When you give yourself the gift of rest you create an opening for gratitude and time to reflect on what is most important to you.

Place value on rest. Allow your body, mind, and spirit to rest so you can begin again with renewed energy and purpose. It's important to rest enough to replenish. Listen to your body so you know when to rest or better yet, make it part of your daily routine. Take time every day, even for two minutes, to sit, be still, and let your mind and body rest.

It is good to periodically step away from the world and find connection with yourself. Microsoft founder, Bill Gates, takes what he calls a "think week" twice a year. Alone, in a cabin in the woods for seven days, he reads, reflects, writes, learns, and plans. He rests from his daily responsibilities and busy life to learn more about himself and how he can offer his best self to this world.

Learn to unwind whenever possible. Take time to reflect and recharge. Let rest be important to you. Let it be essential in your life.

APRIL 2

YOUR INNER PURPOSE

"Your inner purpose is to awaken. It is as simple as that.
You share that purpose with every other person on the planet—
because it is the purpose of humanity."

- Eckhart Tolle

E veryone has the same inner purpose. Your inner purpose is to be here now. To be present, to be conscious, to be awake. Your outer purpose is unique to you and changes often. It is what you do with your life to offer a contribution to this world. Think of your inner purpose as *being* and your outer purpose as *doing*. The being is primary and the doing is secondary.

Let's look at an example. If you are reading a story to your child at bedtime, the reading is the doing but it is not what is most important. It is your awareness of being fully present that is most important. If you are able to see and witness this shift, you realize that your life's journey is not about the destination, it is about the step you are taking right now. This step, now, is your primary purpose. The destination is your secondary purpose.

It always comes back to being present. When you are present, your inner purpose shines. Since there is never anything but this moment, your inner purpose always comes first. Your success in life comes from aligning your inner purpose with your outer purpose. Looking at our example above, if your outer purpose is to be an incredible parent but your mind is always lost in thought, then you are not fully present. Your inner purpose is not put first and as a result, your outer purpose is not realized. When you focus on being completely present as your primary purpose, your life will change.

APRIL 3

CHANGE IS ESSENTIAL

"Progress is impossible without change,
and those who cannot change their minds cannot change anything."
- George Bernard Shaw

E verything is changing. From the seasons, to our bodies, to our thoughts and beliefs, to our environment. Marcus Aurelius wrote, "The universe is change. Life is opinion."

Embrace change instead of fearing it. Since every moment your life is changing, make a shift to welcome it and look for the opportunity for growth. Change allows you to try something new. It can give you a different perspective. When you fight change, you go against the natural flow of life.

Change happens within you and around you. You are an evolutionary being produced through change. Think of yourself as a wonderful book. Each change is a turning page. You close one chapter and open another and each chapter brings new beginnings and excitement to your life.

Change also expands your mind and challenges you. You learn about your limitations and about what you are capable of. Change is necessary for the realization of anything and everything.

Step outside of your comfort zone today and welcome change.

APRIL 4

HIGHER POWER

"The sun makes me believe there is a higher power."
- Unknown

Look around you. Feel your heart beat. Listen to the sound of the morning birds. It's magical, it's spiritual, it is there for you in every moment of every day. When you become aware of this magic, you know there is something out there bigger than you. When the sun rises and sets every day, when a baby is born, when rain arrives just as things are wilting, when a friend calls just as your spirit is fading...you know there is a greater power.

Believe in something greater than yourself. Call it whatever your soul desires: God, grace, universe, life. Know that it deeply cares about you. It wants you to surrender to life and be present to your purpose. There is such a sense of relief when you realize you are not the center of the universe. You and your actions play a key role in the natural rhythms and melodies of life, but ultimately there is a higher power that conducts our universal orchestra. You are an essential string on an instrument that can contribute to making beautiful music.

Let this higher power be your teacher. Everything that occurs in your life is a lesson. Know that you are not alone. Believe in something that is guiding you, that is watching over you, and is loving you.

APRIL 5

BE LIKE A PALM TREE

"When criticism comes, listen. When powerful forces push you
in any direction, bow rather than fight, lean rather than break,
and allow yourself to be free from a rigid set of rules—in so doing,
you'll be preserved and unbroken."

- Wayne Dyer

D id you know that palm trees can withstand 200 mile per hour hurricane force winds? They truly are aerodynamic marvels. You would think they had limbs of steel, but palm trees are actually related to grasses and don't have the woody structure like most trees. They are composed of flexible tissue which allows them to bend all the way to the ground.

We can learn from the palm tree. We can choose to be flexible, to bend, to sway, so we do not break. We can weather the storm and not be uprooted. When you allow flexibility to become a part of your character, you open to all possibilities.

Being flexible allows you to give and receive with grace. In place of your ego is a kind and open human being. Be flexible in your conversations. Listen to someone's point of view, process it, lean into the possibility of a different perspective.

Be like a palm tree—bend so you do not break.

APRIL 6

CHOP WOOD, CARRY WATER

"Before enlightenment; chop wood and carry water.
After enlightenment; chop wood and carry water."
- Zen Proverb

C hopping wood and carrying water is your life. It is up to you how you want to take it on. In Zen philosophy, the belief is the way a person does one thing is the way they do everything. If you look at your life as chopping wood and carrying water and do it mindfully then you will see that everything has purpose.

Ram Dass said, "Everything is part of waking up." Everything is sacred. True awakening happens when you find the joy in the mundane. It is not what you are doing but how you are being. You know that everything comes from within. This awakening allows for your labors not to be a burden.

Like chopping wood and carrying water, there is always more to do. But remember it's not about the destination, it's about the journey. If you wish to be doing something different, then the task has control over you. If you do the work without wishing for something else, you will have peace.

Keep this proverb in mind as you go about your daily projects.

Ask yourself: Is the wood chopping you and the water carrying you? Or, are you chopping the wood and carrying the water?

APRIL 7

THE FOUR NOBLE TRUTHS

"Suffering is universal. The origin of suffering is attachment.
The cessation of suffering is attainable.
Path to the cessation of suffering is detachment."

- Buddha

We all suffer. There are four truths that Buddhism teaches which guide us through suffering. The Four Noble Truths are: the truth of suffering, the truth of the cause of suffering, the truth of the end of suffering, and the truth of the path that leads to the end of suffering.

The first noble truth is that life always holds an element of unfulfillment. It is called suffering. Anything and everything in the physical world carries the potential for suffering because of impermanence. The passage of time brings suffering. Since everything is changing, we are always accommodating. Suffering is part of the experience of our existence.

The second noble truth is that the cause of suffering is desire. It is the craving for something, the holding onto something. We are often wishing things could be different and this causes suffering. The opposite of craving is the awareness that life just is. You accept the present moment as it is. The way to reduce suffering is to become less reactive to difficult things.

The third noble truth is that suffering does not cease; it is our craving not to suffer that ceases. When you try to avoid suffering it only makes you suffer more. The key is to give up attachment.

The fourth noble truth is that the eightfold path leads to the end of suffering. This eightfold path is intertwined and an ongoing practice that directs us into skillful ways of living. Once you accept that life is suffering, you can transcend it and you will no longer suffer.

APRIL 8

SEEING CLEARLY

> "Once you know there's no place to hide
> then you wonder who you are hiding from?"
>
> *- Ram Dass*

There's a *Sikh* story about a holy man who gave two men each a chicken and said, "Go kill them where no one can see." One man went behind the fence and killed the chicken. The other man walked around for two days and came back with the live chicken. The holy man said: "You didn't kill the chicken?" The man said: "Well, everywhere I go, the chicken sees."

Since we are all one, there is no such thing as no one. In this story not only can the chicken "see" but the man can "see" as well. When you strip away your armor and realize that your greatest offering to this world is your soul and your love, you will wake up to seeing clearly.

Learn to embrace oneness by seeing yourself in everyone you interact with. See one instead of two. Beautifully said in this poem by Hafiz:

"The illumined one
Who keeps
Seducing the formless into form
Had the charm to win my heart.
Only a Perfect one
Who is always
Laughing at the word two
Can make you know of love!"

APRIL 9

KEY TO A GOOD LIFE

"Nothing delights the mind as much as loving and loyal friendship."

- Seneca

The key to a good life is to have good relationships. Eight decades of research at Harvard Medical School reveal that social connections are good for your health and happiness. This Harvard study has followed a large group of individuals since the 1930's. At a young age, like many of us, the study participants thought happiness was found through wealth, working hard, and achieving "the American dream." What the study found is what brought them the greatest joy and the greatest health benefits were the meaningful relationships in their life.

Dr. Waldinger, director of the Harvard Study of Adult Development, said that "social connections are good for your health. Those that are connected with others are happier, healthier, and live longer than people who are less well connected." The Harvard study found that those who were the most satisfied in their relationships at age 50 were the healthiest at age 80.

Humans want a quick fix that will make them happy. Relationships take work but the reward is a full life. The study also found that those who were happiest in retirement were the people that actively looked to "replace work mates with new play mates."

Find your tribe. It's the quality of your relationships that matter not quantity. Learn and grow together. Be there for each other.

APRIL 10

COMMON GOOD

"There is no higher religion than human service.
To work for the common good is the greatest creed."
- *Woodrow Wilson*

T he common good refers to providing an opportunity for each individual to reach his/her full potential. Much of Stoicism stems from the belief that each of us is part of the human race. We each play a role in contributing to the common good of our species. Think of an athletic team; the common good of the team is to win. Individual athletes must all work together. The coach is thinking about the whole team, not just the individual.

Common good is about doing the right thing because it will affect the collective world around us. Since we are made for community, we are mutually interdependent. My good includes your good. We make choices that align with what is best for all. The common good continually calls us to see, reflect and act on what will help us all thrive.

In nature, you will observe how everything inherently works together. When you work towards the common good, you go with the flow instead of against it. To work towards common good there needs to be optimism. We need to think of others as well as ourselves. We are one human family so we must continually seek a universal common good.

APRIL 11

WHAT IS REASON?

*"What defined a Stoic above all else was the choice of a life
in which every thought, every desire, and every action
would be guided by no other law than that of universal Reason."*
- Pierre Hadot

R eason is the defining characteristic of one's self. Reason is your GPS in life. It guides you in navigating your way. To stay on course, there needs to be a balance. If you sway too far to the side of logic then there is no room for creativity and if you sway too far to the side of "everything happens for a reason," then you may not take action to improve yourself and this world.

During the 17th and 18th centuries, a philosophical movement dominated Europe called the Age of Enlightenment or the Age of Reason. Thinkers of the Enlightenment desired a new understanding of the human condition. At the forefront was reason. Their belief was that reason was non-negotiable and logic guided you to understand the world.

In Stoicism, reason was often referred to as logos. The idea is that nature is governed by reason. Logos is a way to understand how the world works. You make peace with the fact that life is always changing and we are united by change, by logos. Heraclitus described the world in terms of a river: "No man ever steps in the same river twice, for it's not the same river and he's not the same man."

APRIL 12

YOUR SOUL

"If there is light in the soul, there will be beauty in the person.
If there is beauty in the person, there will be harmony in the house.
If there is harmony in the house, there will be order in the nation.
If there is order in the nation, there will be peace in the world."
- Chinese Proverb

I t starts with you and hopefully it starts with your soul. The energy you bring into a room, the way you listen, the way you respond, the words you use - your way of being affects those around you. As the proverb says above, the first step in having peace in the world is to let your soul shine.

Your soul is your truth, your true self. You must create space and find stillness to hear your soul speak. Your soul speaks to you and then through you by quiet action. When you shift away from your ego towards growth and self-love, it is a call from your soul. You may notice you have a new desire to make a difference in the world. Your values may change and you might rearrange your priorities. You may be unclear what your soul is trying to tell you, but you know change will be part of the plan.

I believe your soul leaves your body when you die but until then, it never leaves you. In the Indian text, *Bhagavad Gita* it says, "The soul is never touched; it is immutable, all-pervading, calm, unshakable; its existence is eternal."

APRIL 13

THE PARADOX OF SUFFERING

*"In some ways suffering ceases to be suffering
at the moment it finds a meaning,
such as the meaning of a sacrifice."*

- Victor Frankl

S uffering is a paradox: The more we focus on our suffering, the more suffering we face. The more we try to get rid of our suffering, the more intense our suffering becomes. The key is to accept suffering as part of life and then you will no longer suffer.

Life is not complete without suffering. Accept suffering as your task. Look for the opportunities. Try changing the word suffering to learning. Look at life's situations as opportunities to learn and find meaning in the suffering. Once you find the meaning in the suffering, the suffering ends.

We can only grow through suffering. Benjamin Franklin said, "Those things that hurt, instruct." Look at what your sufferings have done for you. Have they made you play the victim role or have they made your life worthy?

Bring presence and meaning to your suffering. Then your suffering will be transcended and you will no longer suffer.

APRIL 14

BE A TEACHER AND A STUDENT

"If the teacher is not respected and the student not cared for, confusion will arise, however clever one is. This is the great secret."

- Lao-Tzu

In the passage above the meaning stems from the belief that our purpose is to help others. You are driven by a guiding light to be of service to all. This path allows you to be the giver and the receiver, the teacher and the student. The key is to be compassionate to even those who have wronged you or the world. Literally, it is your job to raise your vibration to help lift others up.

Wayne Dyer similarly offers, "The great secret is this: waste no opportunity, abandon no one, respect the teachers, and care for the student." Think of the "student" as the one who has not found inner peace. Maybe it's your friend who is always complaining, your sister who wished her life was different, or your child who uses anger to communicate. You teach them by how you live your life. You are centered, finding the good in every situation and are ready for whatever comes your way.

When you find *yourself* judging or criticizing, become the student. Observe and redirect your inner voice to find the positive. The world is your classroom. Find opportunities to be both the teacher and the student. Help others as if it were your job.

APRIL 15

TAPAS

"Can you show courage and stay in the fire
until you find the blessing?"

- Catharine Larsen

C an you put yourself in uncomfortable situations on purpose to strengthen your resilience to difficult challenges? This type of training is referred to in yoga's ethical practice as *Tapas* and in Stoicism as *voluntary discomfort*.

Tapas is the determined effort to become someone of character and strength. Tapas literally means "heat." It is the practice of putting oneself into situations that light you up like there is a flame underneath you.

Examples of Tapas in India involve people sitting for three hours for 45 days in very cold conditions. During this time, they will also have cold water drip on their heads. A similar practice is done with heat in the summer time. The Stoics would fast regularly and emperors would dress in rags, living with as little as possible.

"Tapas eventually changes our nature," Deborah Adele writes in *The Yamas & Niyamas*, "turning us into a cauldron that can withstand any of life's challenges." When you practice self-discipline regularly, you become a higher version of yourself.

You can create your own Tapas. You could take a cold shower, sleep on the floor for a night, fast for a day, or stand in the rain without a jacket or umbrella. These actions result in gratitude. You realize what you were taking for granted and prepare you for hardships that may lie ahead.

APRIL 16

HABITS

"Capability is confirmed and grows in its corresponding actions,
walking by walking, and running by running...therefore,
if you want to do something, make a habit of it."
- *Epictetus*

Developing good habits can add so much freedom and meaning to your life. The key is to take small steps with huge attention. You need to know the why behind the habit you are creating. Ask yourself, "Why do I want to _____?" Get as specific as possible here. For example, perhaps you want to start meditating. The why could be I want to start meditating so I can learn to become aware when my mind wanders. Then after you determine the why, ask yourself, "Who do I need to become to make meditation a habit?"

James Clear identifies in his book *Atomic Habits,* that there are four main components to developing habits. First is a cue or a trigger to act, then a craving for a change in state, followed by a response or action, and ultimately there is a reward. Using the meditation example, the cue could be a special timer that you set, the craving is your desire to become more present in your life, the action is sitting down for a set amount of time and practicing meditation, and finally the reward would be a more peaceful day and increased mental awareness.

To make the process more successful and enjoyable, add immediate gratification to your habit building. For example, after you meditate reward yourself with your morning coffee or read a chapter from your favorite book.

APRIL 17

MINDSET

"If parents want to give their children a gift, the best thing they can do is to teach their children to love challenges, be intrigued by mistakes, enjoy effort, seek new strategies, and keep on learning."
- Carol Dweck

How does it make you feel if I were to say to you, "You are so smart?" How does it make you feel if I said, "You work so hard?" This is the key difference in developing what Carol Dweck has coined a "fixed mindset" versus a "growth mindset." A child who is told that the outcome is what is most important and not the process, will believe that his/her abilities are pre-determined. When the learning process is highlighted, the child understands that his/her abilities are always evolving.

It's important for parents, teachers, and coaches to lead by example with a growth mindset. Children learn by observing how we respond. Show them that success comes from effort and learning from one's mistakes.

A student who obsesses over grades instead of enjoying the learning process has a fixed mindset. Unfortunately, when failure on any level occurs, it becomes part of his/her identity and the only way to handle it is to avoid failure altogether. Working hard, building character, and being the underdog are all traits of those with a growth mindset. Even when they reach their goal, those with a growth mindset know there is still more to experience.

We all have elements of both mindsets. Mindsets can be learned and can be changed. Notice when you are being open with a growth mindset or closed with a fixed mindset.

APRIL 18

EFFORTLESS EFFORT

"I fear not the man who has practiced ten thousand kicks once,
but I fear the man who has practiced one kick ten thousand times."
- *Bruce Lee*

To feel alive, you must live with effort. Instead of thinking about what you want to do, you must move with intention and effort. When the Wright Brothers were trying to create the first airplane, there were many others that were trying to do the same thing. With only a thousand dollars to work with, the brothers put all their focus on testing and re-testing their creation. They had 1,900 test flights in a month. Meanwhile, their corporate rivals with millions of dollars, had a comparable amount of test flights in a year! As a result of their efforts, the Wright brothers were able to learn more quickly and get the result they knew was possible.

If you keep making the effort, time will be on your side. Everything worthwhile takes effort. Whatever you are inspired to do will take effort and action and ultimately greatness will be achieved when intense practice makes the task appear effortless. Think about watching the greatest athletes. It's magical. It's a form of stillness. It is grace in action because their effort defines not just what they do, but who they are. There is no struggle. The beauty of their effort just comes to them naturally as a result of the hard work.

You can achieve this too.

APRIL 19

LIVING VIRTUOUSLY

"Know the strength of man, but keep a woman's care!
Be a valley under heaven; if you do, the constant virtue
will not fade away. One will become like a child again."

- Lao-Tzu

L iving virtuously is being at peace with what is. You are guided by an understanding that your life matters. To make an impact, to be the change - practice radical humility. To feel this, look up at the sky tonight.

Living virtuously involves going with the natural flow of life. You put your ego aside and accept the world as it is but embrace it with compassion and an understanding of how we are all one. Guided this way, you will live a life of abundant virtue.

Living virtuously is not about obeying laws or being a good citizen; it's about living who you truly are embodying love, kindness, and peace. You are consciously connected to yourself and understand that you are a piece of the whole.

Living virtuously is not about meeting someone else's standards or checking a box to see if you have achieved success in being virtuous. Virtue fills you up and never leaves you. It is the natural way of being. Keep coming back to your true virtuous self.

APRIL 20

RE-CREATE YOUR LIFE

"It's your road and yours alone.
Others may walk it with you, but no one can walk it for you."

- Rumi

We often have to re-design our lives. Sometimes over and over again. Some of the reconstruction is the natural progression of life. Then there are unplanned events that lead to re-creating your life. Many years ago, I realized that after my very young and short first marriage ended, the only way to heal was to begin again. I moved to Boston and went to graduate school to follow my passion. I created a new life and happily remarried. I began a new chapter.

Be willing to start over. Epictetus said, "How long are you going to wait before you demand the best of yourself?" To re-create your life, you need to take action. Dig deep, find courage, and face the unknown.

Think of those that have overcome addiction, survived illness, lost their job, or bravely stepped outside of their comfort zone. What have they done to carry on? They reinvented themselves. They learned from their past but then moved on to start fresh.

Each day is your opportunity to re-create your life. In the yoga practice, one of the final poses is the fetal pose. It signifies how we all began and how we can always begin again. Stoic philosopher Seneca expressed it like this, "Begin at once to live, and count each separate day as a separate life."

APRIL 21

10,000 THINGS

"That the self advances and confirms
ten thousand things is called delusion;
that the ten thousand things advance and confirm the self
is called enlightenment."

- Dogen

P icture your life as a spinning ball that is composed of events, material possessions, and countless thoughts. This spinning ball of life is your 10,000 things. This concept was first introduced by Lao-Tzu, a Chinese philosopher 2,500 year ago. The world of 10,000 things is the outer world of form. It is a representation of the categorized, classified, and scientifically named objects of earth. The 10,000 things help us to communicate and identify what we talk and think about.

The 10,000 things signifies all manifested reality. It is a Chinese way of saying "myriad of things" or "innumerable things." I like to think of the 10,000 things as man-made constructs. What is of nature, mystery, awe, higher being was not and can never be built by a human being.

Live outside of the 10,000 things as often as you can. Step back, observe, and let life flow. Your wandering mind lives in the center of the 10,000 things. Practice how it feels to step outside of that perpetual, repetitive spinning ball. Then, when you step back into the 10,000 things, know that you are both form and formless. You are both a human being and a spiritual being. You are both the 10,000 things and no thing.

APRIL 22

MAKE SLEEP A PRIORITY

"Each night, when I go to sleep, I die.
And the next morning, when I wake up, I am reborn."
- Mahatma Gandhi

Sleep is built into your biology for a reason. Sleep is necessary for you to make your highest contribution. It resets your brain and your body. Gone are the days when more work and less sleep meant that you were "successful." Sleep is not a luxury; it is a necessity.

Sleep allows your brain to unpack. Many of the trivial memories from the day are forgotten in order to free up space for the next day. If you don't sleep well, your memory can be impacted. During sleep, new brain connections occur and your body regenerates. As you sleep, hormones are released at certain times. Every time you wake up, the cycle begins anew.

We often find ourselves tired during the day because we hit the snooze button that morning. What happens when you fall back asleep is your body enters a new sleep cycle. Each cycle is 90-110 minutes. If you wake up before the cycle is over your brain will stay foggy for four hours. This is called sleep inertia.

Sleep is a meditative practice. Make it a priority. Go to bed and wake up at the same time every day. Leave your phone in another room. Make the room dark, quiet, and cool and never hit the snooze button.

APRIL 23

CARE, DON'T CARE

"Never believe that a few caring people can't change the world.
For, indeed, that's all who ever have."

- Margaret Mead

C are reveals itself when thought becomes action. For some, care is their profession. For others, it's their responsibility as a family member. Some people are born with a nurturing way of being. We care for others because it's primal. It's what we were born into. We care for others, and we care about them.

What do you truly care about? I bet it lights you up. It makes you feel strong, courageous, loved. Caring for ourselves and others is what will heal our world. I often end a conversation saying, "Take care." I'm thinking: be well, be careful, be good to yourself and others.

There are times though when you should not care. Pay attention to when you care what others think of you. If someone is judging you, then they don't care about who you really are. In both Stoicism and yogic philosophy, one of the core beliefs is that you should act independently of other people's opinions. Marcus Aurelius wrote in *Meditations*, "Don't waste the rest of your life worrying about others — unless it is for some mutual benefit. The time you spend wondering what so-and-so is doing, saying, thinking or plotting is the time that's lost for some other task."

APRIL 24

FREE WILL

"I have noticed even people who claim everything is predestined,
and that we can do nothing to change it,
look before they cross the road."
- *Stephen Hawking*

Free will is your ability to choose. Your character and your fate are shaped by your choices. Free will allows you to make your own choices and the corresponding actions are up to you. There are many arguments about whether free will exists. Those that don't believe in free will suggest that our lives are run by fate. That everything is predetermined. I would contend that our free will determines our fate.

You are the source of your action. If you choose to go through a red light, the consequence is not because of fate. It is because of your free will. As we live our lives, our moral compass directs us to make positive choices. Our free will becomes a rational desire. You choose to do the right thing because you know it is best for the common good and making the wrong choice can have dire consequences.

Think of free will as anything you could have done otherwise. Remember that your free will determines your fate. Weather could be an example of fate. It is out of your control, but how you respond is in your control. It is your free will if you choose to go outside in a thunderstorm and then the fate of nature is no longer in your hands.

APRIL 25

FLIP IT

"You can't see the picture while you're in the frame."

- Les Brown

W hen you change how you look at a situation, the situation changes. I like to call it "flip it." When you find yourself unhappy, flip whatever is bringing you down. You can turn it into a game. Change the meaning in your head to something that makes you feel good. Angry that it's cold outside? Great, I get to wear my new jacket. Ugh, I don't want to workout…I am so lucky that my body is able to exercise. It's endless. You create your thoughts.

It's a choice. A positive response will build you up; a negative response will tear you down. When you see differently, you think differently. Instead of focusing on what is going wrong, flip it and ask: What is going right for me right now? The joy of being present will unveil that in this moment, all is well. Give up the interpretation, "There is something wrong here."

You cannot change what you are not aware of. Learn to become aware of how you respond. When you want change, flip it. Stop thinking someone else should change and instead, lead with the change you desire. For example, if you want your spouse to appreciate you more then you need to become the kind of person that appreciates your spouse.

Look at your life for all that it is instead of what you think it is not. You will see, you have all that you need.

APRIL 26

DOES YOUR BRAIN GET TIRED?

"You gain strength, courage and confidence
by every experience in which you really stop to look fear in the face.
You are able to say to yourself, 'I have lived through this horror.
I can take the next thing that comes along.'"

- Eleanor Roosevelt

Your brain is a muscle and like any other muscle in the body, it can be overused and become tired. The brain is designed to look for problems as a survival mechanism. The brain is always thinking and is never satisfied. However, when the brain is not given an opportunity to rest and have peaceful thoughts, it begins to slow down which results in an inability to focus.

We spend a lot of our energy thinking, processing, planning, and worrying. As a result of the unknown, our brains are actively re-sourcing and constantly looking for new ways to do things. At some point, your brain will tire and you will feel exhausted.

You are not alone if you feel weary. Our brains are working so hard to understand what is happening in our world. Everything is constantly pivoting. Be kind to yourself. Take mini breaks throughout your day, get enough rest, and allow time for your brain to be quiet.

APRIL 27

MEDITATION

"Commune with your own heart, and in your chamber, and be still."
- Book of Common Prayer (1662), England

Meditation is a stillness and an invitation to awaken. It is being with the quiet that is always there. Meditation is a beautiful place to get to know yourself. To sit, become still, and observe. It's not about stopping your thoughts but rather offering an opportunity to witness them. What are your thoughts saying? Can you rise above them and let them float by?

Meditation is an inquiry. What are you thinking? How are you feeling? How are you breathing? Be curious and aware. Can you enjoy the space between the thoughts? Can you soften your mind and open your heart?

Mediation is surrender. Beyond the thoughts is the ecstasy of surrender. Breathing in to what is. Breathing out to what you think it should be. Fill up, let go.

Meditation is self-love. You become at peace with yourself through meditation. It is an extraordinary gift to give yourself. Well-known meditation teacher and writer, Jon Kabat-Zinn said, "It is indeed a radical act of love to just sit down and be quiet for a time by yourself."

APRIL 28

SILENT KNOWING

"Those who know do not talk. Those who talk do not know."

- Lao-Tzu

T his is one of life's greatest paradoxes. If you know that all of life's answers will naturally flow, you have no need to voice how you think things should be. We think that we must communicate by expressing and showing our knowledge but this is merely our ego "speaking". Underneath the ego, is your highest state which is silent knowing.

When we are attached to something, we feel compelled to discuss its importance. True knowledge comes from the awakening of non-attachment. When you realize you are not attached to anything in life, you will discover that you are attached to everything. As soon as you let go of attachments to things, ideas, winning, profiting, etc., you will see that all you need is already inside of you. That vital energy you carry, connects you with everything you encounter. You are attached to everything around you through love.

When you become the kind of person that is peacefully knowledgeable and confidently quiet, you lose interest in being "right" and defending a point of view because it is now irrelevant. You carry an energy of silent knowing, not of what is right or wrong, just of what is.

APRIL 29

LIVING INTENTIONALLY

*"Those who love peace must learn
to organize as effectively as those who love war."*
- Martin Luther King, Jr.

You can control many aspects of your life through the power of intention. Your intention is not about wishing. It is about doing. Let your intention come from the kind of person you want to be for yourself and others. It's not what kind of job you want or how much money you would like to make. If those are things that you desire, script your intention on what characteristics you will need and what actions you will need to get the result you are hoping for. Your intention is the energy that you bring to a deed or to your words.

Your intentions reveal your values. Set your intentions from within. What is the why beneath the why. For example, you want a bigger home. The why beneath the why could be because you want to impress your neighbors or because you have adopted four children.

First see the vision, then the steps it will take to achieve it, and then take the first step. When you set an intention, plan with the end in mind. In Robert Greene's book, *The 48 Laws of Power,* Law 29 is: Plan All The Way To The End. "By planning to the end, you will not be overwhelmed by circumstances and you will know when to stop. Gently guide fortune and help determine the future by thinking far ahead." Make time every day to set intentions and create opportunities to work on the ones you have set. The journey of the intention is what is most important.

APRIL 30

WHAT IS SPIRIT?

"The possibility of stepping into a higher plane is quite real
for everyone. It requires no force or effort or sacrifice.
It involves little more than changing our ideas
about what is normal."

- Deepak Chopra

Y ou are spirit. It is not something found outside of yourself. Your spirit is your essence. It is your innate presence. There is an inner silence and mystery to it. Spirit is the part of you that is seeking meaning and purpose. The part of you that is drawn to hope and believes in goodness.

Your spirit needs stillness to awaken. The beginning of spirituality is to separate what you are from what you are not. We listen to the voice in our head and think that it is us. That inner dialogue is not you. Your true self, your spirit, is the one who is observing those thoughts. This is where consciousness resides. This is the most important thing to realize: you are not all of those thoughts, and you know this to be true because you are observing them.

Spirituality is an instinct. Inside every one of us is the instinct to know life is meaningful and we are connected to everything. There is a yearning for something more than our mind and our body.

Create opportunities to watch and marvel. When you see the world through your eyes as a spiritual being it changes how you act and how you view the world.

MAY

MAY 1

SLIDING DOOR MOMENTS

"I want to look for and lean into those moments of trust."
- Cara Meredith

Trust is built in very small moments. In what has been coined "sliding door" moments, Doctor John Gottman discovered the pivotal moment in people's lives that changes their trajectory often occurs without awareness. He named this occurrence the "sliding door" moment after the 1998 Gwyneth Paltrow film, *Sliding Doors,* in which a woman lives two alternative lives after missing a train.

We have a few big sliding door moments in our lives and countless smaller ones that happen every day. In every interaction, there is a possibility of turning toward or away from connection. There is an opportunity for a choice. Will you open the door emotionally to someone or to an opportunity, or will you choose to let the door close?

These moments often surface in interactions between two people. There is an imaginary sliding door that you can choose to go through and become engaged with the feelings and thoughts of another or you can simply allow the door to close and stay locked up in yourself. Choosing to respond to someone you care deeply about fills the need for validation that we all desire.

Be aware of the sliding door moments in your life. They are often the little moments in relationships. They are a bid for connection. In a giving action, the door opens relationally. Become aware of moments today where you can make a difference because you chose to turn toward the connection.

MAY 2

MANTRAS

"You identify with this new thought you have added, until you and
that thought become one and all other thoughts are
passing just like clouds in the sky."
- *Ram Dass*

A *mantra* is a single thought that you consciously make dominant in your mind. It can be a single word or a short phrase. It can be meaningful or simply a word to focus on to clear and calm the mind.

When you choose to recite a mantra in your head, your mind relaxes and the constant chatter becomes softer. Ram Dass stated, "No other thought can capture your attention which remains fixed upon the single thought."

The purpose of a mantra is to break free from the habitual reactivity of thoughts and thinking. Most of us, without even realizing it, have a mantra running through our heads. Maybe it's "I'm not good enough" or "I'm always right." When we let this kind of mantra occupy our thoughts, our perception of ourselves is an illusion.

Choose a mantra that fills you and others up. A mantra often shared in a yoga class is: "May I be happy, may I be at peace, and may I be free from suffering." Then you extend the mantra to friends, family, and strangers. "May you be happy, may you be at peace, and may you be free from suffering." You can also choose a mantra that you separate with the inhale and the exhale. For example: inhale love, exhale kindness.

MAY 3

LOOK FOR THE OPPORTUNITY

"While it's true that someone can impede our actions,
they can't impede our intentions and our attitudes, which have the
power of being conditional and adaptable. For the mind adapts and
converts to its action into a means of achieving it. That which is an
impediment to action is turned to advance action.
The obstacle on the path becomes the way."

- Marcus Aurelius

T he greatest lessons learned in life are usually taught through an
obstacle. There is such freedom when you choose to view the
obstacle as a teacher instead of a problem. There is a lesson in everything.
Let what impedes you, empower you.

Obstacles are part of life. When you turn a trial into a triumph the
reward is unmatched. You have gained wisdom and confidence. The
challenge elevates you. There are so many beautiful examples of people who
have overcome a serious illness or faced tragedy and turned their hardship
into love and hope for others.

You can be transformed by your obstacles. Use the obstacle as fuel. Tell
yourself you can learn from the challenging situation. Seneca said, "A good
person dyes events with his own color...and turns whatever happens to his
own benefit."

Our mind is often our greatest obstacle. Become aware when you have
placed an imaginary boulder in your own way. Change your perception of it.
You are strong. You are resilient. You are wise. Pick it up and toss it to the
side. You make your own path in this life.

MAY 4

YOU ARE YOUR WORDS

"Happiness is when what you think,
what you say, and what you do are in harmony."
- Gandhi

What you say, you create. Listen to yourself and others today. Your words have incredible power. When you say, "I am so tired," you will stay tired. When you say, "I am unhappy," unhappiness is the energy you carry into the world.

There is a great sermon by Pastor Joel Osteen where he talks about the power of "I Am". He says what follows the "I am" comes looking for you. You are inviting whatever comes after the "I am" into your life. You are sending it an invitation.

You get to choose your words. If you know that you create what you say, why not choose words that uplift you? I have found saying, "I am grateful" has changed me on the inside. I am more at peace and aware of the beauty of my life.

When you criticize yourself, you bring negative energy into your heart. Words are powerful. Wake up in the morning and say, "I am beautiful. I am healthy. I am compassionate. I am awesome!" What you say, you will become.

Let go of what someone may have said about you in the past. You control who you want to be. Begin today to use your words to empower yourself because you are awesome!

MAY 5

TIME IS AN ILLUSION

"Time is the horizontal dimension of life, the surface layer of reality.
Then there is the vertical dimension of depth, accessible to you
only through the portal of the present moment."

- Eckhart Tolle

Y ou never truly experience time itself. There is only this moment. We think of time as a succession of moments, but the truth is, time is only happening right now. Your past was, and your future will only be in the now, the present moment.

Our mind is constantly thinking about what happened or what could happen so that our perception of time is not real. Our ego lives in the mind-made world inside of our head. Our ego loves time and defines it by all the stories we create.

You may see evidence of time - your children growing up, milk going bad in the refrigerator, a butterfly that used to be a caterpillar - but you never see it happening as an experience of time. You only experience what happens in the present moment. Practicing being present brings you into alignment with your true self. You will find all that you are looking for by making the present moment your primary focus. This doesn't mean that you don't have goals and dreams, but you can't achieve them if you miss this moment. You are always right here. The clock may go around but it's always right now.

MAY 6

In Control of Only Two Things

"This is why we say that nothing happens to the wise person
contrary to their expectations."

- Seneca

We are in control of only two things: 1) how we prepare for what might happen and 2) how we respond to what just happened. Today we will focus on preparation.

You prepare for what might come your way by strengthening your character today. You practice being resilient with this moment no matter what transpires. You're tired and your child is asking you a million questions; take a deep breath and let your patient, loving side surface.

Preparing for what might happen does not mean that you create disaster scenarios in your head. It's about learning to let life flow naturally. Seneca writes, "Don't seek for everything to happen as you wish it would, but rather wish that everything happens as it actually will—then your life will flow well."

When you surrender to the little occurrences in your life, your inner strength will be ready when the big, "life-changing" events happen. You prepare for what might happen by loving yourself. You meet the trying times in your life with compassion and understanding.

If you prepare for what might happen by blaming, worrying, and letting your ego be the driver of your life, you will live your life unconsciously. You will miss the moments to learn and grow.

Preparation lies in thought, word, and deed. Choose your thoughts to be positive and actionable. Speak only if it is uplifting and helpful and always take action that strengthens your character.

MAY 7

RESPONSE

*"Life is ten percent what happened to you
and ninety percent how you respond to it."*

- Charles Swindoll

W e are in control of only two things: 1) how we prepare for what might happen and 2) how we respond to what just happened. Yesterday, we focused on preparation and today we consider the importance of the response.

How you respond to what has just happened reveals so much about you. Everything you do matters. Without even knowing it, your response sends energy to everyone around you. If you stay calm when a crisis happens, those around you will tap into that. If you yell at someone, everyone within earshot feels deflated.

Practice responding without reacting. If someone cuts you off in traffic, just smile. If your spouse makes a rude comment, don't say a word. It's not what others are doing, it is what *you* are doing and how you respond that is important.

How you respond to a situation is in your control and the best way to let your true self shine is to respond after a pause. Victor Frankl said, "Between stimulus and response there is space. In that space is our power to choose our response. In our response lies our growth and our freedom."

Learn to mindfully respond instead of mindlessly reacting. Practice the pause and perhaps the response will be simple, peaceful silence.

MAY 8

SET YOURSELF FREE

"To truly practice forgiveness
we must first forgive ourselves for not being perfect."
- *Thích Nhất Hạnh*

F orgiveness is essential to live your best life. Often when we are wronged by someone else, the act of forgiving that person sets *you* free. When you forgive yourself and others, you let go of resentment and open the door to freedom.

Forgiveness is about letting go and moving on. Learn to let go of your expectations of others. If forgiveness is hard for you, start with yourself. Keep forgiving yourself over and over again. Feel the forgiveness in your heart.

When you stop playing the victim, you find the space to forgive. Our ego chooses punishment as the price for forgiveness. Your heart forgives. Our world is lost without forgiveness. There's a true story about two prisoners of war who met years later and one said to the other, "Have you forgiven your captors?" And the other replied, "No, I never will." "Then they still have you in prison, don't they?" said the first prisoner.

Set yourself free. Forgiveness is such a beautiful way to clear the path to find your true self.

MAY 9

RELAXATION

"The mind must be given relaxation—it will rise improved and
sharper after a good break. Just as rich fields must not be forced—
for they will quickly lose their fertility never given a break—so
constant work on the anvil will fracture the force of the mind.
Constant work gives rise to a certain kind of dullness and
feebleness in the rational soul."

- Seneca

After vigorous action relaxation is necessary. An obvious example
is exercise. To become stronger, your muscles need time to repair.
If you don't build in rest days, you will stop getting stronger. Any competitive
athlete will tell you that recovery is as important as the workout.

How about you? Do you give yourself the necessary gift of relaxation?
Relaxing doesn't mean that you are not engaged with life. Maybe you enjoy
going for a walk or doing a puzzle. It is time spent when your thinking mind
can rest.

Relaxation is even more important the more active your body and mind
are. Einstein was famous for solving problems while he played the violin. He
had been playing since he was a child so the task was second nature to him.
After working intensely on a problem he would give himself a break to relax
and play the violin. As he played, his subconscious mind started working out
what his conscious mind had been working on.

You may notice that creative ideas flow more easily when you are at rest.
You have softened your armor to allow space for your mind to relax. You can
be more when you give yourself time to do less.

MAY 10

IT'S ADDICTIVE

"Seeking validation, voids you."
- Khateeja Munazza

W hy is it that we seek social validation so much? It's because what happens in our brain is similar to what happens to us chemically when we kiss the person we love or take a bite of delicious food; we want more. When we are validated the brain releases dopamine transmitters which make us feel good. We get a rush of good energy that we experience as pleasure.

Internal validation is important to personal growth but external validation can be harmful. Our brain can quickly become addicted to the rush of pleasure that we receive from our devices. We become dependent on this feeling. As with other addictions, we will need more and more to be satisfied.

It's not that all external validation is bad. As children, we needed it to learn what was right and wrong. As adults, we need it to know how to work well with others and to learn and grow. The problem is when what others say to us shapes how we perceive the world.

We all want to be validated and know that we matter. When you look at Maslow's hierarchy of needs, esteem and love/belonging are essential to human motivation. As with everything in life though, there is a balance. Soak up the dopamine that is released through human connection. Notice when you feel that rush from technology and remember that it is like a drug—it will not bring you true joy.

MAY 11

ENERGY

"Your energy introduces you before you say a word."
- Unknown

The energy you carry is palpable. Often it can be felt as soon as you walk into a room. The energy you send out, you often receive back. We feel the energy of others. No doubt you have experienced a calming, soothing feeling from some people whereas others have caused you to feel anxious and on edge. You are responsible for the energy you emit.

What is so powerful is when your energy aligns with a goal, the possibilities for growth and discovery are endless. When you are deeply passionate about something, your energy radiates connection and commitment. When you are not fulfilled, your energy is depleted. You are unstoppable when your purpose shines through. Mark Twain said, "The two most important days in your life are the day you are born and the day you find out why."

To bring your energy to a higher vibration start with how you talk to yourself. Your inner voice creates the energy you release to the world. Be in charge of your thoughts. Change the tone and content, and this will change your energy. Your brain listens to what your inner voice says. When you rescript, you feel the goodness that was always inside of you and create space for positive energy to flow.

MAY 12

WHAT IS YOUR PASSION?

"I have no special talents. I am only passionately curious."
- *Albert Einstein*

Is there something in your life that you can't imagine not doing? When you are truly passionate about something, it fills you up and gives you a deep sense of joy. This energy is released when you are actively experiencing something that has become your passion.

Your passion is a way to express yourself. Perhaps it is revealed through a creative source like painting or singing. Or perhaps you adore helping others, volunteering, spending time with your grandchildren, etc. Your passion could be playing a sport, cooking, or my favorite - learning. Find a passion that makes you feel alive, that invigorates you. Choose your passion freely and joyfully.

Maybe your passion is your job. But be cautious of taking your passion and making it your job. American non-fiction author Cal Newport said, "The more we focused on loving what we do, the less we ended up loving it." When your workplace becomes where you love to go to focus on your passion, you may find the work aspect drives away some of your passion.

MAY 13

FIND YOUR TRIBE

"The key is to keep company only with people who uplift you,
whose presence calls forth your best."

- Epictetus

Motivational speaker Jim Rohn famously said, "We are the average of the five people we spend the most time with." I'm not a huge fan of the word "average", and I'm also not a fan of math, so I would change this study to say that we are shaped by the company we keep.

The way we think, the way we feel about ourselves, and the choices we make are directly related to the people we spend the most time with. Your most important tool to sharpening your life is surrounding yourself with good people.

According to research by social psychologist Dr. David McClelland of Harvard, the people you habitually associate with determine as much as 95 percent of your success or failure in life.

If you want a glimpse of your future, look at who your friends are now. If you find that you are being held back, forge a new path that leads to a new tribe that awakens, challenges, and applauds your life. Find people that inspire you. Find a tribe that elevates you, not one that holds you back. Choose your future by choosing who you spend time with.

MAY 14

DEEPER KNOWING

"There is more wisdom in your body than your deepest philosophy."
- Friedrich Nietzsche

There is an enormous difference between knowledge and deep knowing. Just because you study and are filled with knowledge, doesn't mean you are taking appropriate action in your life. Lebanese-American author Nassim Taleb said, "…it is much better to do things you cannot explain than explain things you cannot do."

We let our heads get in the way of truly enjoying life. There's a deeper knowing inside of you. It is in your heart. Your heart knows what is right. Your heart sees clearly. Your heart has a deeper knowing than your mind. Deep knowing is beyond thinking. It's a quiet song inside of you that moves you to action.

Your heart communicates with you. It doesn't lie to you. Listen to the messages it is sending you. The voice of your heart is heard when you go inward and connect with the non-intellectual and non-analytic part of your being. When you hear your heart's voice you awaken to a deeper knowledge that guides and directs you. This knowledge lets you know yourself better and this, in turn, changes everything.

MAY 15

LIVE LIKE YOU WERE DYING

"This is the mark of perfection of character - to spend each day
as if it were your last, without frenzy, laziness, or any pretending."
- Marcus Aurelius

D eath unites us all. It is the one truth that we all will know. The way to human freedom is to not fear death. Why do we fear it so much? Is it because we feel we haven't lived enough? Is it because it is such a mystery? Or is it because we live like we are destined to live forever?

It is wise to think about death because it awakens us to live. This time you are given on earth as a spiritual being having a human experience is your responsibility. Don't look for the meaning in your life, look for the use of your life. And then use your days for that purpose.

When you pass, it is your identity that dies: your roles, your meanings, your many layers of armor. Living like you were dying is often associated with going skydiving or the like, but try shifting it to mean living without being attached to any label or to any of the many meanings you have associated yourself with. When you live this way, there is no fear of death.

MAY 16

KNOW THYSELF

"Death lies heavy upon one who,
known exceedingly well by all, dies unknown to himself."

- Seneca

The most important thing you can do in life is to know yourself. To know yourself you must go inward. The you on the outside changes from moment to moment but the you on the inside is who you need to get to know.

It takes hard, vulnerable work. As you explore inward, you may like what you find or you may not. Don't run from yourself. Begin to get comfortable in your own skin. Learn to be still and just breathe.

Look past your habitual self-image and into your essential being. Look and accept both the light and the dark within you. How you feel about yourself matters most.

In the yoga practice, self-reflection is called *svadhyaya*. It's not about analyzing thoughts and feelings. It's about self discovery. Studying yourself to know thyself.

One of my favorite quotes is from Nisargadatta Maharaj:

"Wisdom is knowing I am nothing.

Love is knowing I am everything.

And between the two my life moves."

MAY 17

STOCKDALE PARADOX

"You must never confuse faith that you will prevail in the end—which you can never afford to lose—with the discipline to confront the most brutal facts of your current reality, whatever they might be."
- Admiral James Stockdale

The Stockdale Paradox, which was first introduced by Jim Collins in his book *Good to Great*, illustrates how those that live their lives by optimistically wishing and hoping things will get better often fail, while those who have faith without knowing the outcome will survive and be better because of their struggle.

Admiral James Stockdale was the highest-ranking United States military officer in the "Hanoi Hilton" prisoner-of-war camp for eight years during the Vietnam War. Stockdale had no idea when his horrendous imprisonment would end, but he knew that he would turn it into the defining event of his life.

When Admiral Stockdale was asked who did not make it out he answered, "Oh, it's easy. I can tell you who didn't make it out. It was the optimists. They were the ones who always said, 'We're going to be out by Christmas.' Christmas would come and it would go. And there would be another Christmas. And they died of a broken heart."

Life brings us Stockdale moments. Have an unwavering belief that times will turn but don't put a date on it. Tell yourself that you will be stronger because of challenging times and our world will become a more compassionate and grateful place.

MAY 18

CIRCUMSTANCE

"Circumstances don't make the man,
they only reveal him to himself."

- Epictetus

Imagine you are a boat sailing in the ocean. The choices you make steer the boat. During times of adversity, it is your determination that is your tailwind. Fear is the headwind. Your inner compass guides you through and won't allow a storm of circumstance to take you off course.

In what direction will you let the circumstances of the day take you? The object is to not steer away but rather to avoid judgment as you navigate your course. Circumstances in and of themselves are neutral. We attribute meaning to all we encounter on our journeys when in fact, our discoveries along the way are neither good nor bad until we label them so.

Accept your circumstances with grace. Let life unfold as an opportunity. You will suffer if you believe that a situation should be a certain way. When you accept circumstances with equanimity and don't long for permanence, you move closer toward self-realization. In yoga, self-realization is called *Samadhi* and it is the ultimate end goal. It is seeing life the way that it is.

MAY 19

SOCIAL PROOF

"The five most dangerous words in business are:
Everybody else is doing it."

- Warren Buffett

I think we have all asked our children at least once, "If everyone were jumping off a bridge would you?" We are very driven by what others are doing around us. This idea has been coined social proof. It is a psychological principle that is the most potent way of influencing human behavior.

You see it every day. When human beings are uncertain about what they should do or unsure about what something means, they look to others to see how they should react or feel in new situations.

The greater the number of people doing something, the more others are likely to join in. Social proof persuades people to behave in certain ways. Often this behavior can have terrible consequences. In the 1960's, forty percent of the American adult population smoked cigarettes. Smoking became extremely popular and a social norm. This is a devastating example of social proof. Just because so many people are doing something, doesn't mean it is the right thing to do. Listen to your instincts. Follow your heart and blaze your own trail.

MAY 20

WHAT ARE YOU FEEDING YOUR MIND?

*"At any moment in time,
our reality is based on whatever we focus on."*
- Tony Robbins

D id you know that on average we spend seven hours a day watching TV? What you focus on becomes your reality. The quality of information that you consume matters. What we take in affects how we think, how we feel, and how we act.

Information is worthless without a purpose. You should have a reason to use the information. There is a part of our brain called the reticular activating system (RAS) that determines what information is significant enough for you to pay attention to. Your brain has to be told that something is important to you or it will not register it in your consciousness.

A classic example of your RAS is when you are thinking of buying a certain type of car and then you see it everywhere. The car has always been there but now that you have put significance on it, you become far more aware of it.

Put your brain to work for you. Let it know what your goals are and what information is important to you and watch them magically appear. Tell your brain what matters most. Before you read a book or watch the news, ask yourself what you want to get out of it. Have a purpose for your information gathering. Prioritize what is most important to you and watch it appear.

MAY 21

ACCOUNTABILITY

"You cannot escape the responsibility of tomorrow
by evading it today."

- Abraham Lincoln

Accountability is the bridge to unity and trust. When we don't hold ourselves and others accountable we move further and further away from peace. We all suffer when there is no accountability. How can you ever get to the other side of the bridge if you don't pay the toll of accountability?

There are plenty of examples in our own families, communities, and government where people get hurt, but instead of being held accountable we look for a quick fix like shame or pretending it didn't happen. We need to practice accountability. It's hard and uncomfortable, but it is our responsibility.

We think if we shame someone that we are holding them accountable but that is not true. There needs to be action and a behavior change. We hold others accountable because we care about them or we care about those whom their actions are affecting.

It starts with you. Become aware if you have made a mistake or harmed someone in some way. Admit your mistake and take responsibility for it. You will learn. You will feel liberated and you will develop more meaningful relationships.

MAY 22

OPPOSITES

"Learn the power of yin & yang and be able to translate this knowledge into your daily life. Everything has an opposite."
- The Tao

For everything that exists, there must also be its opposite. When you realize there are both sides to everything you will find peace. Watch how your life changes when you view opposites as compatible.

Think about everything in life: You would not know happiness if you had not felt pain. Without silence, there would be no sound. You can only succeed by failing. When you see indifference, know love is present. When you see darkness, know there is light.

Conflict arises when you think something should only have one side. Our world needs to see that the only way to solve conflict is through compassion. The only way to end hatred is through love. We must solve with the opposite.

Our rational mind does not think paradoxically. Transcend your rational mind to the truth that everything holds more than one interpretation. Be patient. There is a natural flow to everything. The ebb and the flow, the yin and the yang, the morning and the night. Life is continual destruction and healing.

MAY 23

THE OBSTACLE

"The mind is a superb instrument if used rightly. Used wrongly, however, it becomes very destructive. To put it more accurately, it is not so much that you use your mind wrongly — you usually don't use it at all. It uses you. This is the disease. You believe that you are your mind. This is the delusion. The instrument has taken you over."

- Eckhart Tolle

The obstacle is our thoughts. It is our own thoughts that stop us from becoming great. The problem begins when we think we are our thoughts and as a result, we must focus our attention on them. Your thoughts become in charge of your life.

Every situation is neutral. Your thoughts then attribute meaning to what you observe. Become aware when you label a situation. Just take note. Listen to that voice in your head and note the meaning you just created.

You are the awareness of your thoughts. Strip away all the stories, all the labels, and think of yourself as awareness dressed up as a human being. When you identify with your mind, meaning you think you are the story in your head, you live in a state of fear and illusion. Choose to not let your mind run your life.

MAY 24

GET COMPLETE

*"It is incredible how many hurts can be healed
by the two words, "I'm sorry."*
- Matshona Dhliwayo

I s there something in your life that always causes a dull knock on the door to your heart? Maybe it's a relationship in your life that has ended on the outside but not on the inside. Or did you say something hurtful to someone and never apologize? I remember years ago I said something I regretted to a friend and we drifted apart. I ran into her in a store years later, and I apologized.

Seek resolution for mistakes you have made and for others' mistakes that may have caused you harm. This could mean picking up the phone or it could be writing a letter that perhaps you never mail. It is a way to silence the knocking on your heart so you can be free.

Let yourself heal by getting complete with your life. Getting complete can also be a way to express yourself if you have been holding back. Maybe you call your dad and acknowledge that you have a difficult relationship but you love him unconditionally. Maybe your mom passed away when you were young and you never got to say goodbye. Write her a letter, express yourself, and feel your heart expand.

What are you holding on to that needs your help to become complete so you can move on?

MAY 25

RESIST THE TEMPTATION

"The beautiful and good person neither fights with anyone
nor, as much as they are able, permits others to fight...
this is the meaning of getting an education—learning what is
your own affair and what is not. If a person carries themselves so,
where is there any room for fighting?"

- Epictetus

R esist the temptation for conflict. When conflict is met by conflict
then the response is often resentment and revenge. Force always
causes a counterforce. The only way to solve conflict is to introduce peace.
Martin Luther King, Jr. said, "Love is the only force capable of transforming
an enemy into a friend."

When you feel conflict arise in a conversation you are having, pause, and
ask yourself if arguing is going to solve the issue or just appease your ego.
Be more interested in what others have to say and resist the temptation
to always be heard.

Let your interactions be of cooperation, not competition. You are
weakened when you are in conflict, but you are strengthened when you
cooperate. Make it a core value that you eliminate verbal and/or physical
force in all situations. This applies to what you watch and listen to.
Wayne Dyer explains this well, "Once you know that force is being applied
anywhere in the name of subjugating others, you'll realize that the constant
repetition of that news makes you a participant in the violence."

MAY 26

BEGIN AGAIN

*"Your principles can't be distinguished unless you snuff out the
thoughts that feed them, for it's continually in your power
to reignite new ones...It's possible to start living again!
See things anew as you once did—that is how to restart life!"*
- Marcus Aurelius

L ife is expecting something from you. Find your why.
Begin again and again until you do. Make it a daily practice to
do a course correction. Henry Ford said, "Begin again more intelligently."

Every day you are given an opportunity to begin again. A chance to
change, to learn, to grow. Every time you begin again you have
gained wisdom.

Improving yourself, self-study, inner work may seem selfish but it is the
most selfless work you can do because when you become better, we become
better. The more inner work you do, the less validation you will need from
the outside world.

Begin again to find all that you need is within you. Use your ego to work
for you. Have mindful self-focus. Ask yourself: "What did I do right today?"
and "What can I do better?"

You have the ability to change at any moment. Every day begin again
and unwrap a new layer in your self-cultivation.

MAY 27

CHAKRAS

"The body is the vehicle, consciousness the driver.
Yoga is the path, and the chakras are the map."

- Anodea Judith

You are energy. Your body consists of a beautiful, colorful system of energy fields called *chakras*. Each one of the seven main chakras is a spinning wheel that is connected to your nerves and major organs. They affect your emotional and physical well-being.

Starting at the base of the spine, in the tailbone area is the root chakra. It is identified with our physical identity, stability, and security. The next chakra is the sacral chakra and it is located just below the belly button, just above the pubic bone. The sacral chakra is connected with our self-worth around pleasure, sexuality, and creativity. The third chakra is the solar plexus chakra which is located in the upper abdomen. It is the chakra of personal power. It's related to our self-esteem and self-confidence. The fourth chakra is the heart chakra which is located in the center of the chest. It represents our ability to love and connect with others. The fifth chakra is the throat chakra and is connected to our ability to communicate verbally. When it is in alignment we speak and listen with compassion and confidence. The sixth chakra is the third eye chakra located between the eyes on the center of our forehead. It connects with our intuition and imagination. The seventh chakra is the crown chakra. It is located at the very top of our head. The crown chakra is linked to every other chakra and every organ in your body. It represents our connection to our purpose and spirituality.

MAY 28

WISHING WELL

"It's in keeping with Nature to show our friends affection
and to celebrate their advancement, as it were our very own.
For if we don't do this, virtue, which is strengthened
only by exercising our perceptions, will no longer endure in us."

- Seneca

A re you in a work situation or a school or athletic setting where you feel you are constantly being measured against others? Being motivated by others can play an important role in your life, but when it becomes a competition with those closest to you, often the outcome is less than positive.

Instead of feeling like you are up against others, shift to feeling you are working with them. Send your competition well wishes. Hope for them to do their best. Be compassionate when they fail. Practice empathy and selflessness.

Try this also with those you do not know. Become a well-wisher. Send those you encounter happiness and success through your thoughts. Notice how it makes you feel. As Benjamin Franklin said, "When you are good to others, you are best to yourself."

MAY 29

PANORAMIC VISION

"On this stony island of despair,
grant us the vision to paint a horizon; deep, lovely, and fair."
- Angie Weiland-Crosby

D id you know that you can take your body out of fight or flight mode just by the way you focus your eyes? Neuroscientist Andrew Huberman discovered that the way we focus our eyes affects the amount of stress we have in our lives.

We have two main ways that we look at things. When we are using our phone or reading a book, we are using our focal vision. This narrow, high vigilance vision has become our primary way of using our eyes. The other type of vision is panoramic vision. This is when you look straight ahead and allow the peripheral vision to open up. Your focal vision causes you to be on high alert while your panoramic vision has a calming effect.

Your eyes are two portals to your brain and a part of your central nervous system. Therefore, how you focus your eyes can either turn on stress or turn off the stress response. Since we spend so much time in close quarters and in front of screens, it is important to give yourself several panoramic views throughout your day. Stand outside if you can and gaze outward. Keep your head still and dial out your eyes. Notice how it calms you.

MAY 30

AMOR FATI

"My formula for greatness in a human being is amor fati:
that one wants nothing to be different, not forward, not backward,
not in all eternity. Not merely bear what is necessary,
still less conceal it...but love it."

- Friedrich Nietzsche

Amor fati is a Stoic and yogic mindset in which you make the best out of every situation. Amor fati, translated from Latin, is a love of one's fate. This means that you do not just accept what happens in your life but you love what happens because you know that it is happening for you.

No matter how hard you have worked or planned, ultimately the outcome is in the hands of something bigger than you. On the eve of the invasion of Normandy, General Dwight D. Eisenhower wrote to his wife, "Everything we could think of has been done, the troops are fit, everybody is doing his best. The answer is in the lap of the gods."

What happens to you is there to light your way. See the beauty in all that happens in your life. Be grateful for all events because they are teaching you something. You have the power to choose acceptance and even love for everything that happens to you.

When you live in the past or the future you are in opposition to amor fati. When you are present to each moment in your life and know that everything that happens was designed for you, then there is no reason to fear...there is only love.

MAY 31

Opponent and enemy

"There is no greater misfortune than feeling "I have an enemy";
for when "I" and "enemy" exist together, there is no room left
for my treasure. Thus, when two opponents meet,
the one without an enemy will surely triumph."

- Tao Te Ching

There is a difference between having an opponent and having an enemy. You lose your power when you have an enemy. You give it away by not taking responsibility. When you have an opponent, you focus on working together to resolve the conflict. With an enemy, your energy is spent on fearing and hating.

Just because someone disagrees with you, or vice versa doesn't mean they need to become your enemy. Make the decision to not have enemies. If you are faced with an opponent in your life, and you will be, let them become your ally, not your foe. Remember that the person "without an enemy will surely triumph."

When there is conflict, allow compassion to enter. There is no peace when you have an enemy. Look for yourself in your opponent. When you make someone your enemy there can be no union.

Anne Frank wrote in her diary when she was being hunted by the Nazis: "…in spite of everything I still believe that people are really good at heart… I can feel the sufferings of millions and yet, if I look up into the heavens, I think that it will all come right."

JUNE

JUNE 1

WHAT IS GRACE?

"I do not at all understand the mystery of grace - only that
it meets us where we are but does not leave us where it found us."
- Anne Lamott

G race doesn't give you an explanation. It quietly, gently transforms a moment into something better. Grace may be felt, it may be seen, and it may be given. Grace is the whisper in your ear that everything will be ok. Grace is an energy that pulls you away from doing something that might hurt you or others. Grace turns your mistakes into purpose.

You experience grace when you are open. When you surrender and fall into the center of now, you will find grace. Grace is saying yes to this moment and then yes to the next. Fill your life with more gratitude and you will witness more grace.

Grace can also be found in suffering. When we accept that suffering is part of life, our hardships can be met with grace. I remember standing in front of friends and family sharing my Dad's eulogy and being completely filled with grace. At what was the most difficult time in my life, I was overcome with his presence, an awe for the love we shared, and gratitude that I was able to honor him. As sad as I was, there was so much joy and conviction in my words because I knew that grace was holding one hand and my dad holding the other.

JUNE 2

THE SECRET OF NOTHING

"To attain knowledge, add things every day.
To attain wisdom, remove things every day."

- Lao-Tzu

One of the greatest secrets is the gift that is found in nothing. When you are able to see the joy in nothing, you unlock the doors to happiness, wisdom, and truth. You see that nothing is *something*. Actually, in nothing is everything.

When you are present to this moment and let go of the past and the future, you find everything in no-thing. Emptiness is a part of us. Everything in the universe originated from nothing.

Emptiness is creative. If you were to trace back all of your thoughts and all of your ideas, you would see that they all originated from nothing. You will have more clarity, more wisdom, and more happiness if you are completely awake to the presence of nothing.

There is power in emptiness. Think of shaping a piece of clay into a bowl—it is the space within that is useful. Or a room—it is only useful because of the space. In the emptiness you find usefulness. More eloquently said by Lao-Tzu, "The usefulness of what is depends on what it is not."

JUNE 3

CLEAR MIND

"But is Brain all that important? Is it really Brain that takes us
where we need to go? Or is it all too often Brain that sends us off in
the wrong direction, following the echo of the wind in the treetops,
which we think is real, rather than listening to the voice
within us that tells us which way to turn?"

- Benjamin Hoff

There is tremendous power in a clear mind. When you have a clear mind, you can see what is in front of you. A cluttered mind is lost in thought. It is often trying to figure things out and desiring for a situation to be different. Think of a bird singing; the clear mind listens to the bird singing while the mind that is full of knowledge wonders what *kind* of bird is singing.

Have a clear mind like a child. Always aware of what is around you and in awe of discovery and joy in the given moment. Your cluttered mind thinks too much and loses touch with its own senses. It can't hear or see the beauty that is placed right in front of it.

A cluttered mind is focused on gaining more, being someone different, or feeling a different way while a clear mind sees and feels what is right in front of it—not trying to change the moment.

Live your life with a clear mind. Listen for its wisdom. Linger in its simplicity. It is within each of us. This joyful, child-like mind will guide you to the peace within.

JUNE 4

CALM INNER LANDSCAPE

"You have the innate ability to choose calmness
in the face of situations that drive others to madness."
- Wayne Dyer

Have a sense of serenity no matter the circumstance. You are the master of your response. Stay poised and grounded regardless of what is happening around you. When you live your life this way, you let go of blame. You are responsible for your inner landscape. The outer landscape of our world does not need to cause you agitation and unrest. For every negative, there can be a positive. You choose how to let the outer world affect your inner world.

Become aware and responsible for how you are feeling. Become a master of your emotions. This doesn't mean that you don't feel and don't act to help a situation, it just means that you remain calm and centered in all that you do. Take control of your life or others will control it for you.

To find your calm inner landscape, begin by taking a few deep breaths and let go of judgments. Remember that your circumstance will not change if you meet it with anger…it will only make it worse. To remain calm shows strength. Marcus Aurelius wrote in *Meditations*, "The nearer a man comes to a calm mind, the closer he is to strength."

To have a calm inner landscape practice overcoming adversity, having self-control, and being conscious of your impulses. Be the calm in the storm. Be the steady in the unsteady. Be the stillness in the unrest.

JUNE 5

CONSCIOUS VERSUS SUBCONSCIOUS MIND

"Use the power of your conscious and subconscious mind to create
a vibrational match for the abundance you desire and deserve."
- *Jack Canfield*

D id you know that your subconscious mind is 30,000 times more powerful than your conscious mind? In his book, *The Power of Your Subconscious*, Dr. Joseph Murphy says your subconscious mind stores everything that happens in your life whether you are aware of it or not. The conscious mind averages only forty bits of information per second while the subconscious mind processes at four million bits per second!

Your conscious mind contains all of your thoughts, memories, and feelings that you are aware of at any given moment. Think of your conscious mind as your short-term memory and your subconscious as your long-term memory. There is communication between your subconscious and your conscious mind. I am sure you can remember a time when an idea just popped into your head. That was your subconscious handing it to your conscious mind.

Your subconscious mind can be a detriment or an ally. When you feel fear or anxiety it is your subconscious mind at work because it has everything stored from the past. But, by setting intentions, staying positive, and creating good habits, you can put your subconscious to work for you.

JUNE 6

YIELDING

"Yielding means inner acceptance of what is. You are open to life."
- Eckhart Tolle

Y ielding in life is a way to slow down, reflect, be grateful, trust, and have courage. You can choose between resisting and yielding. Resisting brings strain while yielding brings softening.

When you are driving, a yield sign means to pay attention to those around you and slowly proceed into the flow of traffic. If you are calm and aware, it is a natural progression. If you are nervous and fearful, you may come to a complete stop.

In life, we do need to yield for others, but most importantly we need to yield in our own life. Yielding is allowing your life to flow and surrendering to what is not in your control. Yield to the awareness that life peacefully flows when we don't push the pedal to the metal.

It's important to yield to your ego. Don't allow it to force itself out into the world. Soften it and go forth with humility and grace. Yielding means to pause before you take action, listen before you speak, and reflect before you move forward.

Place a yield sign inside your mind. Let it guide you gently, purposefully, and in harmony.

JUNE 7

SYMPATHEIA

"That which isn't good for the hive, isn't good for the bee."
- Marcus Aurelius

There is a Stoic concept called *sympatheia* (our word sympathy comes from this Greek word). Sympatheia is the belief that everything in the universe is part of a larger whole.

We are all woven together and therefore we are each a thread that plays an important role in the tapestry of life. We need everything around us. We need each other, the air, the water, the plants and animals in order to breathe and to be. Awareness of this will bring out the best in all of us. We experience a shift when we look out for each other.

Your actions should carry the good of the whole. Marcus Aurelius writes, "Meditate often on the interconnectedness and mutual interdependence of all things in the universe." Everything is connected and is dependent on this bond.

This living bond always chooses love over harm. There is a mutual benefit of goodness that prevails. We were made for each other. Why would we make others feel anything but equal?

Sympatheia is the unity of our souls. You are never alone. Remember the beautiful tapestry you are a part of. The greater good needs you.

JUNE 8

THE EYORE EFFECT

"I was so Upset. I forgot to be Happy."

- Eeyore

I think we all have a special place in our heart for Winnie the Pooh but for Eeyore, we often just shake our heads in dismay. Why does Eeyore always choose to look at the world as if his cup is half empty? He is constantly proving that what you say you create: "Oh well, I lost my tail. I guess this is going to be another lousy day." And then, of course, he has another lousy day.

The Eeyore Effect is actually created by your brain. When you feel overwhelmed and negative, your brain becomes less effective at down-regulating negative emotions and it loses its natural ability to extinguish those emotions. Your emotions will just continue on a downward spiral unless you reverse the flow.

Eeyores are afraid and let their fear take over. They create negativity by complaining. There can be no growth and no room for improvement when you live your life like Eeyore. You must believe in the good and stop creating worst case scenarios in your mind.

Become aware when you are acting like Eeyore and choose to turn the downward spiral upright again. Tell yourself, "Today is a great day." Say it again out loud, "Today is a great day."

JUNE 9

COMPARE YOURSELF TO YESTERDAY

"There is nothing noble in being superior to your fellow man;
true nobility is being superior to your former self."
- Ernest Hemingway

P ay attention today to how often you compare yourself to someone else or to an ideal. Unhappiness comes from always trying to measure up to something outside of yourself.

Shift your attention to measuring yourself against where you were before. This way of looking at your goals and accomplishments brings happiness and confidence. Appreciate the growth within you, not how your growth compares to someone else's.

Set goals and compare them with yesterday's accomplishments. What is most important is measuring against your former self. Greg McKeown stated, "If you focus on what you lack, you lose what you have. If you focus on what you have, you will gain what you lack."

You will achieve so much more if you keep focused on your own path. The key is to remember how far you have come. Be grateful for the steps you have taken and this will unlock a more hopeful future. You are your own measure of self-improvement.

JUNE 10

LIVE SIMPLY

"When life is simple, pretenses fall away; our essential natures
shine through. By not wanting, there is calm, and the world will
straighten itself. When there is silence, one finds
the anchor of the universe within oneself."
- Lao-Tzu

Give yourself permission to just be. Think of being more, not having more. We spend our lives trying to accumulate more: more knowledge, more success, more stuff. What would your life look like if you stopped adding and focused on subtracting? You can be more with less.

Marcus Aurelius wrote in *Meditations*, "If you seek tranquility, do less. Or (more accurately) do what's essential. Do less, better. Because most of what we do or say is not essential. If you can eliminate it, you'll have more tranquility."

See how you feel when you subtract things from your life. Maybe it's your clothes closet, excessive food intake, or non-essential appointments in your calendar. You will feel lighter and more productive with less. You will find joy in knowing that your happiness is not dependent on how much you accumulate.

You will not be fulfilled by seeking more. Have what you need and be grateful for it. When you want more, remember this passage from Kabir: "The fish in the water that is thirsty needs serious professional counseling."

June 11

The What-If's

*"You only live in the present, this fleeting moment.
The rest of your life is already gone or not yet revealed."*
- Marcus Aurelius

We don't know what the future holds. What is important to know is that whatever happens, we will be ok. Lamenting and worrying about the "what-if's" only causes more fear and uncertainty.

When you are worried about the future, remember that you are in control of this moment. Give yourself a break. You don't have to solve all of life's issues today. Focus on the task at hand. Calm the turbulence in your head by being completely present and becoming aware of your breath.

Consciously choose this moment and then the next. When you let go of your past and your future, you will find everything that you want.

Why do we say to ourselves that we should be unhappy now because of what happened in the past or could happen in the future? Seneca wrote in his *Letters From A Stoic*, "Wild animals run from dangers they actually see, and once they have escaped them worry no more. We however are tormented alike by what is past and what is not come. A number of our blessings do us harm, for memory brings back the agony of fear while foresight brings it on prematurely. No one confines his unhappiness to the present."

JUNE 12

LOVE YOURSELF

"You can search throughout the entire universe for someone who is
more deserving of your love and affection than you are yourself,
and that person is not to be found anywhere. You, yourself, as much
as anybody in the entire universe, deserve your love and affection."

- Buddha

You must find love in yourself and then the whole world will love
you back. We are only able to love others to the extent that we love
ourselves. Self-love is about patience, acceptance, commitment, and wisdom.

Learn to be your own friend. To be a compassionate person, you must
include yourself. Marcus Aurelius wrote, "By having self-respect for your own
mind and prizing it, you will please yourself and be in better harmony with
your fellow human beings."

Self-love directs you to be open to the possibilities in your life. When you
respect and care for yourself, there is clarity and direction. When you love
yourself, you are able to do what is right. You are responsible for your actions
and when they come from a place of loving yourself, the outcome can only
be filled with goodness.

Pay attention to how you treat others—this is a direct reflection
of how you feel about yourself. Love yourself and the whole world
will love you back.

JUNE 13

ALL NEGATIVITY IS RESISTANCE

"Positive anything is better than negative nothing."
- *Elbert Hubbard*

Whenever you experience negativity in your life, you are more than likely resisting something. Why do we have negative thoughts? Why do we speak words that cause a negative reaction? It is because our ego, which is not our true self, is strengthened by bathing in negativity.

Negativity will not solve anything. Instead of attracting goodness or making a situation better, negativity just causes more negativity. We often get attached to something negative in our lives because it gives us an identity. We are afraid to let go of playing the victim or holding onto our pain because we think it will be difficult. In *The Power of Now*, Eckhart Tolle writes, "Once you have identified with some form of negativity, you do not want to let go, and on a deeply unconscious level, you do not want a positive change."

We are the only life form that experiences negativity. Watch how nature never resists and always reveals its true self. When you feel a negative emotion come to your mind, try to separate yourself from it. Remember that you did not create negativity—your mind did. You have the power to let the emotion flow through you without attaching meaning to it.

Let go of the resistance and step into the present moment. It is in the now that we find that everything is just as it should be.

JUNE 14

ON BEING A PARENT

"Your children are not your children."
- Kahlil Gibran

I've been a parent for over twenty years, and I am still learning. Definitely still making mistakes which then make me a better mother. One of the hardest lessons has been that it is not my job to make my children happy. This challenges me to my soul. I always want to make things right. I never want to see my children in pain, but I know that they have to find their own way. It's important to let them fail. It's important to delight in their wins. It's important to let them become.

I find the below passage from Kahlil Gibran's *The Prophet* so important:
"Your children are not your children.
They are the sons and daughters of Life's longing for itself.
They come through you but not from you,
And though they are with you yet they belong not to you.

You may give them your love but not your thoughts,
For they have their own thoughts.
You may house their bodies but not their souls,
For their souls dwell in the house of tomorrow,
which you cannot visit, not even in your dreams.
You may strive to be like them, but seek not to make them like you."

JUNE 15

MALE AND FEMALE ENERGY

"What is the most beautiful in virile men is something feminine; what is most beautiful in feminine women is something masculine."
- Susan Sontag

We have both male and female energy within us. It's important to understand that this energy does not have to do with gender. It is through balancing these two energies that we become complete.

Feminine energy is like a magnet. It attracts what it wishes to experience and the energy outflows from the heart. Feminine energy is powerful and gentle at the same time. It isn't afraid of emotion and uses intuition as a compass. Feminine energy believes anything is possible. It thrives on creativity and expression. It is in sync with the natural rhythm of our world. Feminine energy flows in a circular motion rather than linearly. It is aware that everything is connected.

Masculine energy is strong and predictable. It moves in a linear fashion with structure and rules. It is focused and clear. Masculine energy is knowledge while feminine energy is knowing. One is decisive and concrete, while the other is changing and malleable. Masculine energy is protective, honest, and steadfast. It always wants to do the right thing.

Scientifically, our brains are also composed of both male and female. The right side of your brain is female and the left is male. We cannot have one without the other. As with anything in life, the quest is finding the right balance. Give some thought to which attributes you gravitate towards and practice introducing the other energy to bring balance to your life.

JUNE 16

WHAT IS ENLIGHTENMENT?

"Enlightenment is when a wave realizes it is the ocean."
- *Thích Nhất Hanh*

I believe enlightenment is an awareness that everything is the same. You see that everything is just as it should be. We perceive things as so, but they are just the way they should be.

Enlightenment is when you see clearly without meaning. You see that everything exists as one. Your happiness and your sadness, your birth and your death, your strength and your weakness.

Enlightenment is when you let go of seeking outside of yourself. You let go of identifying with the events in your life and the things in your life. You awaken to this moment and you meet it with complete acceptance and joy.

You let go of attachment to the fallacy that some*thing* will bring you happiness. You know that it all comes from within. There is nothing that can *make* you happy. There is nothing that can *give* you joy. Enlightenment is the understanding that you are your own creator of happiness and joy, of sadness and despair.

Accept this moment as it is. Let go of swimming upstream and float with ease to the natural current of your life. Enlightenment is when you let your life just be.

JUNE 17

EMPTY TO BE FILLED

"The flexible are preserved unbroken. The bent become straight.
The empty are filled. The exhausted become renewed.
The poor are enriched. The rich are confounded."

- Lao-Tzu

T he above passage from the 22nd verse of the *Tao Te Ching* illustrates that the more we are filled by attachments, the emptier we are in our lives. The only way to be fulfilled in your life and truly free is to let go of identifying yourself by your ego's attachments.

Once you release all that you hold on to, you can be filled with all that life has to offer you in this moment. You are able to become what you are capable of.

You must become empty in order to be filled. Clear away what is holding you back. Empty out the fear of the future and drink up the beauty of today. Be filled by the lesson. Be lengthened by the growth. Be nourished by the acceptance of the present moment.

We are always grasping. Always trying to be filled with something outside of ourselves. We overflow our cup and then become overwhelmed.

Notice when you are hoping that life will give you what you want. Life only gives you who you are. When you need life to always fill you up, life will only take from you. Live to give and your cup will always be filled with love and gratitude.

JUNE 18

WU WEI

"Just how do you do it, Pooh?" "Do What?" asked Pooh.
"Become so Effortless." "I don't do much of anything," he said.
"But all those things of yours get done."
"They just sort of happen," he said.

- an excerpt from The Tao of Pooh

*W*u *Wei* is a Taoist principle that believes there is action through inaction. This principle can be applied to everything in your life if you are present. Wu Wei is a way of being. It can be translated as "effortless action" or "actionless activity". This does not mean that you are sitting alone without participating in life. Rather it means living your life by not resisting and by being intensely alert.

Wu Wei is a way of not forcing. You approach life from a place of least resistance and as a result, you create more strength. Wu Wei does not go against the nature of things. It flows with life, instead of struggling against it. Watch how the natural world works this way: with little effort and in beautiful harmony.

There is a method-less method to Wu Wei. It leads in a way that never commands and results in understanding, acceptance, and voluntary obedience. Lao-Tzu said, "When the true Sage rules, good things are accomplished, and the people all say, 'We did it ourselves.'"

Notice when you try too hard to accomplish a task and it goes poorly. Let something soften and try again. Whether it is a tense mind or a tense body, mistakes will happen. Just be. Do without doing, and effortlessly all gets done.

JUNE 19

CLARITY

"A podium and a prison is each a place,
one high and the other low, but in either place
your freedom of choice can be maintained if you so wish."

- Epictetus

In all circumstances in your life you have a choice. Your life is advanced or defeated by every choice you make. You choose how you are going to react and then how you are going to respond to every event in your life. The more conscious you are, the more aware you are of the power you have.

When you are conscious and not attached to the belief that you or others have labeled a situation, you are able to pause and see what is in your control and what is not. You get to choose to let it go if it is outside of your control or choose the right action if it is within your control.

You are 100% responsible for what you do, don't do, and how you respond to what's done to you. Awareness that you have freedom of choice brings clarity. You get to choose how you think about a circumstance. You choose how you will respond to the circumstance. Whether it is a podium or a prison Victor Frankl explained in *Man's Search for Meaning,* "Everything can be taken from a man but one thing: the last of the human freedoms - to choose one's attitude in any given set of circumstances, to choose one's own way."

JUNE 20

CLOUDED VISION

"There is an optical illusion about every person we meet."
- Ralph Waldo Emerson

U nhappiness results when you are guided by your illusions. Your perception is directly correlated with your illusions. An illusion is a distortion of our senses which then distorts our perception of reality.

How you look at things affects the world you create. This is illustrated in a writing from Chuang-Tse: "An archer competing for a clay vessel shoots effortlessly, his skill and concentration unimpeded. If the prize is changed to a brass ornament, his hands begin to shake. If it is changed to gold, he squints as if he were going blind. His abilities do not deteriorate, but his belief in them does, as he allows the supposed value of an external reward to cloud his vision."

In yogic philosophy, illusion is referred to as *Maya*. It is a veil that sits between perception and reality. When we look through this veil, we see things as we are, not as they really are. So much of our fear is created by illusions. We misinterpret, add meaning and emotion, and then get swallowed up in the illusion.

Stay grounded. Remember that you are not separate from the natural world. Take your illusion glasses off and see what is right in front of you.

JUNE 21

BE CURIOUS

"I think at a child's birth, if a mother could ask a fairy godmother
to endow it with the most useful gift, that gift would be curiosity."
- Eleanor Roosevelt

L ife becomes a magical exploration when you are curious. Be curious
about nature. Be curious about how your mind works. Be curious
about learning. Be curious in every interaction and wonder what you
can learn.

Watch what is around you with new curiosity. Try to let go of prior
conceptions. Look at things as if you were seeing them for the first time:
the sun rising, water running from a faucet, the peeling of an orange.
Be curious and as Lao-Tzu said, "See simplicity in complexity."

Let your intuition open you to curiosity. Learn to be curious in a
nonjudgmental way. Look for the connections between things. Notice how
something makes you feel and do your best to not interfere with what you
are curious about. Just observe, then gather information, then let what you
have learned guide you.

What may open up for you is a deeper understanding of how life flows
exactly as it is. Because of your curiosity, you witness how things exist as they
are. Being curious awakens your senses, it brings you into the moment, and
opens your heart to the beauty that surrounds you.

JUNE 22

TRACELESS MOVEMENT

"So throw away your baggage and go forward. There are quicksands
all about you, sucking at your feet, trying to suck you down into fear
and self-pity and despair. That's why you must walk so lightly.
Lightly my darling, on tiptoes and no luggage,
not even a sponge bag, completely unencumbered."

- Aldous Huxley

Life is much easier when you can't trace your movements. Your every action, reaction, and response comes from a place of grace and acceptance. Walk lightly and your every move is like you are floating.

When you are faced with a difficult time, remember that it can't last forever—nothing does. Open yourself up to adversity. A shift will happen. A door will open. A path will become clear.

When you walk with a heaviness, you only see the mud but when you walk without a trace, you will see the light. You leave behind no messiness or consequence. What appears is the lesson that turns into wisdom.

Learn to soften when you feel your body tighten. When we try too hard our movements become heavy and dark. Let your footprint be like sunlight; casting warmth and light without a trace of movement.

JUNE 23

LET IT BE

"And when the night is cloudy there is still a light that shines on me.
Shine on until tomorrow, let it be. I wake up to the sound of music,
Mother Mary comes to me speaking words of wisdom, let it be."
- The Beatles

L et it be is a powerful phrase that you can use in your life in two different ways. Let it be can be used as a surrender to what is. A way of softening, letting go, trusting life. The second way this phrase can be used is to manifest your deepest wishes.

Every thought you have can be wrapped up in this phrase. You can either soften and let it be or you can be called to action by letting it be. Bring to mind something you desire. Maybe it is a new job, better health, world peace and then imagine it coming true. Say, "Let it be." How does this make you feel? Feel the impact it has on you and others. Create this in your mind, release the intention to the world, and then take action to let it be - let it become.

Now bring something to mind that is not serving you. A negative thought, something out of your control, the past. Take a deep breath in and then breathe out "let it be". Can you let it be by letting it go?

Begin to notice your thoughts. Ask what's here, right now and then let it be. Let it be and let go or let it be and let it be so.

JUNE 24

JOY

"Joy is a net of love by which you can catch souls."
- *Mother Teresa*

J oy is peace dancing. Joy is different than happiness. It is not a choice nor is it a response. It is energy; a feeling of being who you were intended to be. Joy is cultivated from within.

You don't seek joy. Joy finds you. It is found within you when you awaken to the joy of your authentic being. Eckhart Tolle wrote in *The Power of Now*, "Things and conditions can give you pleasure, but they cannot give you joy. Nothing can give you joy. Joy is uncaused and arises from within as the joy of Being."

Joy is felt because you have known pain. Both are in your heart and in your soul. They share you. Let joy fill you up. It doesn't require anything more than your own true self. It dances its way into your day when you are loving what you are doing unconditionally.

To witness more joy in your life, invite more stillness in. When you can hear your soul, you experience joy. Your mind creates a barrier to joy. Invite in more compassion, generosity, awareness, and courage and you will experience more joy.

JUNE 25

IMPOSTER SYNDROME

*"Such as are your habitual thoughts, such also will be
the character of your mind; for the soul is dyed by the thoughts."*
- Marcus Aurelius

I mposter syndrome occurs when someone doubts their abilities and feels they are not worthy. It is an internal experience of believing others perceive you as more competent than you feel you are. Those with imposter syndrome live in fear because they feel like a fraud. They feel like they don't deserve to be where they are. As a result, they work harder to appear the part and it becomes a vicious cycle that can lead to mental health issues.

We are all a work in progress. We all have something to offer, and we can all learn from others. Remember that you do belong. Wherever you are is right where you are supposed to be at that moment. If you believe it should be something different, then you are missing the magic of your life.

If you feel like you don't belong, try looking at your situation from a place of gratitude. Be grateful and notice what you have accomplished. Look around and know that others believe in you. In addition, notice your inner dialogue and rescript it to provide a pathway to calm, inner confidence.

If you feel like you don't know something, let it be an opportunity to learn. There is a difference in doubting yourself or doubting your skills. Life is about learning. Embrace it—don't hide from it.

Always remember, you are right where you are supposed to be.

JUNE 26

A.W.E.

"There are two ways to live:
you can live as if nothing is a miracle;
you can live as if everything is a miracle."
- Albert Einstein

I like acronyms. (Hence, the Daily JAM). I like the way they help you remember something. I like the mystery, simplicity, and cleverness to them. I am on a quest to help us awaken to our lives. To not get lost in thought. To learn and grow. To pause and soak in the beauty of the life we have been given. So, of course, I had to come up with an acronym.

A.W.E. Awareness, Wonder, Experience.

A is for Awareness. I believe the first piece to anything in life is awareness. It is an amazing ability to have the power to stand back and look at things. You cannot change what you're not aware of. Awareness allows you the opportunity to pause and choose your action and response. Awareness is being able to question your own thoughts. Awareness is being awake to your life because you are conscious.

W is for Wonder. We are always becoming and that takes wonder. Be curious about who you are becoming and why. Stand in the wonder of how nature works so effortlessly. Become dazzled by what lights you up. Be enchanted in stillness and wonder what your soul is saying.

E is for Experience. After becoming aware and embracing the wonder, you are ready for the experience. You have become grounded in your truth and, as a result, you are able to welcome the experience no matter the circumstance. In every moment, let there be A.W.E.

JUNE 27

PERSISTENCE

"Nobody achieves greatness
except through intense practice over a long period of time."
- *Kyle Eschenroeder*

W hatever goal or aspiration you have, be patient. To achieve, you will advance only with repetition and dedication. It will often be the mundane, the unnoticed, over and over again. To become skilled at something you master the first step before you move to the next step. It is a patient, persistent process.

Witnessing my daughter's evolution into a competitive CrossFit athlete taught me a great deal about persistence. Every aspect of her journey is a repetitive, patient, persistent action. She has practiced over and over again—for years.

Epictetus said, "No great thing is created suddenly, any more than a bunch of grapes or a fig. If you tell me that you desire a fig, I answer you that there must be time. Let it first blossom, then bear fruit, then ripen."

Success comes to those who stick with it. Those who have the courage to be persistent. It's not glamorous. It's often not fun, but when you believe in yourself, and you know that you can make your dreams come true... then persistence is your greatest ally.

JUNE 28

YOU ARE THE TASK

"When you have quieted your mind enough and transcended your ego
enough you can hear how it really is. SO: when you are with a
candleflame you ARE the candleflame and when you are with
another being's mind you ARE the other being's mind.
When there is a task to do you ARE the task."

- Ram Dass

E xplore what it feels like to become one with every interaction today. When you have a conversation with someone, can you visualize looking into a mirror? When you work on a project, can you feel yourself as the project? When you take a shower, imagine that you are the water flowing over you.

Become totally involved in everything you do by experiencing a union. There is a mindless quality that surfaces when you live this way. You will witness your ego becoming quiet and a freeing of attachment. What awakens is deep compassion and tremendous power.

You don't have a life, you are life. We are life. Come from a place of being, not doing. Be the candle flame. Be your friend's mind. Be the task in front of you. C.S. Lewis said, "You don't have a soul. You are a Soul."

JUNE 29

THINK IN MOMENTS

"See simplicity in the complicated. Achieve greatness in little things.
Take on difficulties while they are still small. The sage does not
attempt anything very big, and thus achieves greatness."

- Lao-Tzu

L ao-tzu's passage above communicates the ease in life when we think
in moments instead of days, weeks, months, years or more. All that
is truly important, all that matters is *this* moment. Life is so simple when you
stay right here in the now.

Catch yourself living in the past or worrying about the future. This is it.
Right here, right now, and you don't want to miss it. You will live without
difficulties when you live in the moment and welcome the next.

When you live in the present moment, there is no struggle.
Marcus Aurelius wrote, "Don't let your imagination be crushed by life as
a whole. Don't try to picture everything bad that could possibly happen.
Stick with the situation at hand, and ask, 'Why is this so unbearable?
Why can't I endure it?' You'll be embarrassed to answer."

Look at everything you do as small and simple. Look for the
simplicity and you will see that it is not complicated. Greatness is
achieved by staying small.

JUNE 30

COURSE CORRECTION

"If you don't like something change it;
if you can't change it, change the way you think about it."
- *Mary Engelbreit*

Y ou control how you process the world around you. Train your brain
to find the opportunity in everything. Believe that there is a hidden
blessing inside every situation. There's a great story about a little boy
throwing a ball up in the air to hit it with a bat. He kept missing it and after
a bit he said, "What a great pitcher I am."

Do a course correction every day and be grateful for it. It is teaching you
something. It's important to not focus on the outcome but to live your legacy
now. Let go of expectations and become filled with appreciation for the
wisdom you have gained.

Every situation is different and every situation calls for a unique response.
You are in control of your ship and only you can adjust the helm to current
conditions.

Sometimes we can't change our circumstances, but we can change
ourselves. We can change our relationship to our experience and that can
change everything.

You are capable of rising above any condition. You become the person
you want to be through your decisions, not your circumstances.

JULY

JULY 1

WHAT IS YOUR DHARMA?

*"It is better to live your own dharma imperfectly,
than to live an imitation of somebody else's life with perfection."*
- Bhagavad Gita

D harma weaves your passion with compassion to create your purpose. I believe every being on earth has a purpose. It may change and evolve over time but it is your reason for giving your best effort every day.

According to Deepak Chopra, there are three components to the "Law of Dharma." The first is to understand that we are spiritual beings having a human experience. Your true self is your spiritual energy. The second is discovering our unique talent or talents and offering them to the world. The third component is the feeling of joy that comes when your talent serves others. When you offer your talent to serve humanity there is a union of abundance.

You were placed on this earth with a special gift to help others. Your dharma is your calling. It's the energy underneath your feet. It's your path. In Sanskrit, dharma means "to uphold". When you live out your dharma, the entire universe holds you up.

You are here to serve in a way that brings you joy. What is your offering to this world? What fills you up and makes you lose track of time? What contribution can you make to answer the question, "How can I help?" Invest in that contribution. Learn as much as you can and keep on learning so that you can share your knowledge and skills to help others. This is your dharma.

JULY 2

REWIRE THE BRAIN

"Excellence is never an accident.
It is always the result of high intention, sincere effort,
and intelligent execution; it represents the wise choice of many
alternatives—choice, not chance, determines your destiny."
- Aristotle

Isn't it incredible that you can rewire your brain? The scientific name for this is *neuroplasticity*. It is the capacity of your brain to change connections and behavior in response to new information. Your brain is flexible and pliable.

You can strengthen your mental resilience. You have the ability to change your life by working to create new pathways in your brain. You can become a new version of yourself by forming new neural connections in your brain through consistent action.

When my son, Will, was born ten weeks prematurely we worked with him for years to create connections and pathways in his brain. Before my eyes, I witnessed neuroplasticity. It was repetitive work over and over again but his premature brain developed, connected, and became remarkable.

Your brain is reshaping and molding every second. Ultimately, everything you do or don't do shapes your brain. Use this incredible muscle to your benefit. Aristotle said, "We are what we repeatedly do. Excellence, then is not an act, but a habit."

JULY 3

WANDERING MIND

"The human condition: lost in thought."
- Eckhart Tolle

I believe we have a "wandering mind" and an "intentional mind". Today we will explore our wandering mind and tomorrow our intentional mind. How often do you find yourself doing one thing but thinking about another? Your wandering mind can be expressed this way: Although you might hear the rain, your thoughts are elsewhere.

The wandering mind cheats us out of the opportunities life is offering us in this moment. It is saturated with worries, doubts, and demands. Think of the wandering mind as a sports radio commentator with opinions, projections, judgments, and sarcasm.

The wandering mind asks questions like: Who's to blame? What's wrong here? What could be different? How could this be better? It is obsessed with the past and is comforted by distraction. The wandering mind seeks a cause for everything.

We tend to live most of our day in our wandering mind. This makes our life a story that hasn't happened. The more you want and desire, the more the wandering mind takes over. It is never happy with what it has. When the world feels heavy, it's the wandering mind holding onto things that aren't serving you.

Focus today on becoming aware of your wandering mind. Realize that it is not who you are. When you become the witness of the wandering mind, it creates space for the intentional mind.

JULY 4

INTENTIONAL MIND

"Wherever you are, be all there."

- Jim Elliot

When your attention moves from the wandering mind to the intentional mind, there is an alertness. It is like you are waking up from a dream; the dream of thought, the dream of past and future. The intentional mind is the present space in which your life happens.

Through your intentional mind, you find contentment, a sense of stillness, and of enough. Your best work comes from here. If you are always wanting more, you cannot live in the intentional mind. The intentional mind gives up the interpretation that there is something wrong.

Your intentional mind is present and highly attuned to your ever-changing circumstances. You must practice staying in your intentional mind because we tend to default to our wandering mind.

The intentional mind lets you meet your life with courage and action. It gets excited about the possibilities for your own life. You must train this part of your brain because we tend to default to our wandering mind. The intentional mind doesn't need to congratulate itself but rather focuses on how to improve. It doesn't focus on what other people think. It sets its own standards.

Notice which mindset you are in throughout your day. You are either retreating or moving forward. You are either lost or you are found. Choose to live in your intentional mind. It will carry you with grace, poise, and a sense of direction.

JULY 5

PROGRESS

"I learned this, at least, by my experiment:
that if one advances confidently in the direction of his dreams, and
endeavors to live the life which he has imagined,
he will meet with a success unexpected in common hours...
If you have built castles in the air; your work need not be lost; that is
where they should be. Now put the foundation under them."
- Henry David Thoreau

We all need a compelling tomorrow. In other words, we need the belief that our future will bring us joy and purpose. The way to achieve this is to always make progress because progress equals happiness.

We were designed for progress. Your self-esteem is earned through your own progress. It is not what you get that fulfills, but who you become. Make a shift in your identity and ask, "Who do I need to be to have what I want?"

All progress comes from breaking patterns. Become clear about exactly what you want. Visualize your outcome and know your reasons why. Progress towards that end will begin when you have clarity and observe your progress.

Crave your future. Every day make progress in the direction of your highest offering to this world. Stoic philosopher Epictetus said, "Progress is not achieved by luck or accident, but by working on yourself daily."

JULY 6

BE VIRTUE

"If you need rules to be kind and just, if you <u>act</u> virtuous, this is a sure sign that virtue is absent. Thus we see the great hypocrisy."
- *Lao-Tzu*

D oesn't it seem a bit odd that we have rules and laws in order to be kind to others? Imagine a world where we didn't need regulations because we knew it was our true nature to care for others like they were our brothers and sisters. You would do the right thing because it is authentically who you are.

Wayne Dyer expresses in his book, *Change Your Thoughts—Change Your Life*, "You can choose to see yourself in harmony with the regulations and laws of your business, government, family, and religion rather than *because* of them." If you live from a place of goodness because it is who you are, you will live with ease.

Rules are irrelevant because you *are* virtue. It is ingrained in you that it is your responsibility and desire to live without governing. We have rules to penalize and control people. What if we rewarded those that lived with virtue?

Stoic philosopher Cicero said, "The man who has virtue is in need of nothing whatever for the purpose of living well." Laws and punishment are non-essential parts of our human existence if we were to follow the rules of our hearts.

JULY 7

THE BUTTERFLY EFFECT

*"You could not remove a single grain of sand
from its place without thereby...changing something
throughout all parts of the immeasurable whole."*
- Fichte, The Vocation of Man (1800)

T he butterfly effect is the idea that a small change can allow other changes to occur. This concept is a beautiful, yet profound, way to understand how everything is connected. The theory is when a butterfly flaps its wings in one part of the world it causes a typhoon in another part.

It's the tiny things that change the world. Everything in the universe is caused by something before it. Often it is a natural progression and life is just as it should be, but unfortunately, humans often intervene to create alternate outcomes. Marcus Aurelius wrote, "Everything that happens as it should and if you observe carefully, you will find this to be so."

The butterfly effect is a symbolic representation demonstrating how the choices we make can have life-changing results. Our actions, even the small ones, can have a ripple effect that causes much larger outcomes.

Our world is fragile. We cannot control or predict the future, but we can walk gently and be a catalyst for positive change. Flap your wings and watch the beauty of the butterfly effect all around you.

JULY 8

VALUES AND BELIEFS

"Values are the emotional states that we believe are most important to either experience or avoid."
- Tony Robbins

What makes humans do what they do? The two things that control every thought, emotion, and every reaction while you are alive are your beliefs and your values.

Your values are your guiding compass. Your values determine the person you will become. Everything you do in your life is either moving towards your values or away from them. Examples of values that move you towards a life of fulfillment are love, joy, peace, adventure, security, passion, freedom, and many more. In contrast, experiences and states of being that might pull you away could be failure, rejection, frustration, anger, boredom, and depression.

Our beliefs have become part of who we are as we go through our life. According to well-known author and public speaker Tony Robbins, we have two types of beliefs: global beliefs and rules. Global beliefs affect your whole life. You have a feeling of absolute certainty of what something means. An example would be, life is… or I am… or people are… If you change your belief, you can change everything.

Rules are an if/then type of belief. If I were to become wealthy, then I would be happy. If I lost 20 pounds, then I could find someone to love me. As Tony says, "Beliefs have the power to create and the power to destroy. Human beings have that awesome ability to take any experience of their lives and create a meaning that disempowers them or one that can literally save their lives."

JULY 9

WHO YOU ARE IS WHAT YOU'RE NOT

"Thirty spokes converge upon a single hub;
it is on the hole in the center that the use of the cart hinges.
Shape clay into a vessel; it is the space within that makes it useful.
Carve fine doors and windows, but the room is useful in its
emptiness. The usefulness of what is depends on what is not."
- 11th verse, Tao Te Ching

I t's important to understand the part of you that can't be seen. This is your true self, your very essence. It is the non-being part of you that makes you who you are.

I know it is a hard concept to understand because we all use external measures to bring meaning into our lives. I invite you to feel more from your heart and soul and less from your mind and outer being. Take time to pause, breathe, and feel the non-being part of you. Just allow the awareness of your sacred self to surface. When thoughts come in, acknowledge them and then let them go.

Our mind and our outer being are like an interstate highway: Moving quickly, reacting, and lost in thought but within that frenzy is a peaceful, white noise that moves with grace, responds with love, and finds joy in the moment.

We have put on so many layers. Think how good it will feel to peel that armor off. You will discover that who you are is what you are not.

JULY 10

FOUR STOIC HABITS

"Our rational nature moves freely forward in its impressions when it: 1) accepts nothing false or uncertain; 2) directs its impulses only to acts for the common good; 3) limits its desires and aversions only to what's in its own power; 4) embraces everything nature assigns it."

- Marcus Aurelius

The above entry from Marcus Aurelius's *Meditations*, presents four habits that can enable us to make our lives simpler, fuller, and more compassionate.

Habit number one: Accept nothing false or uncertain. What is true is this moment; not the narrative in your head or what you think someone else may be thinking or feeling. Follow your own truth.

Habit number two: Direct impulses only to act for the common good. Every action you take and every thought you think should revolve around what is best for others. You are a piece of the whole. What is best for you should be best for all.

Habit number three: Limit your desires and aversions only to what's in your own power. Simplify your life by making it a habit to align your needs and wants with only what is in your control.

Habit number four: Embrace everything nature assigns it. Live your life with acceptance to what is. Embrace the moment and stop trying to make it mean something different.

JULY 11

MATTER OF MOTIVATION

"You are fettered," said Scrooge, trembling. "Tell me why?"
"I wear the chain I forged in life," replied the Ghost. "I made it link by link, and yard by yard; I girded it on my own free will, and of my own free will I wore it."
-Charles Dickens

We are driven by what motivates us. If I were to tell you there was a hundred-dollar bill waiting for you in a burning building would you go in and get it? If I told you your child was inside a burning building would you go in and get her/him? Action or change is never a matter of ability, it is a matter of motivation and drive.

There is a great illustration of this in Charles Dickens, *A Christmas Carol* and Tony Robbins has coined the process the "Dickens Pattern". If you remember from the story, Ebenezer Scrooge was happily miserable. He thought money brought him happiness and his success came from being mean. He had no desire to change.

Everything changed in one night when he was visited by three ghosts: past, present and future. During this dream, Scrooge sees and feels with massive pain the consequences of his actions. He realizes when he wakes up, his future has not yet happened. He can stop all the future pain now. He wakes up with a new association that giving means pleasure. He had linked enough pain to his bad habits that he was able to make lasting change.

We can all apply the Dickens Pattern to our life. What is a habit or belief that you want to change? What will happen if you continue this for the next five years? The next ten years? How could this hurt the people you love in the future? Really wake yourself up to this. Visualize it, feel it, and then change it.

JULY 12

MAKE MESSY PROGRESS

*"Courage is not something that you already have
that makes you brave when the tough times start.
Courage is what you earn when you've been through
the tough times and you discover they aren't so tough after all."*
- Malcolm Gladwell from David and Goliath

We spend so much time thinking about what we want to do. The only way to make it happen is to do it. When you are wrapped up in something that you once feared, you would notice that there is no room for anything else but your involvement. Think about learning to ride a bike. At first, you're afraid to even get on. Then you are afraid of falling, but once you achieve momentum, there is only glee in the present moment.

So, what if you make mistakes? So, what if it's messy? Just act and distract yourself from what scares you. Then, when you achieve your goal, you will see that all the falls off your bike taught you the joy of the wind in your hair and you will have earned courage through your struggle.

Have a courageous heart. Let your heart be unafraid to open to the world. Brené Brown said, "Courage starts with showing up and letting ourselves be seen." Stop trying to get the courage. Make messy progress towards what you want in life, and see the clarity unfold.

JULY 13

UNSELFISH JOY

"Here, O Monks, a disciple lets his mind
pervade one quarter of the world with thoughts of unselfish joy,
and so the second, and so the third, and so the fourth. And thus the
whole wide world, above, below, around, everywhere and equally,
he continues to pervade with a heart of unselfish joy,
abundant, grown great, measureless, without hostility or ill-will."
- *Buddha*

Rejoicing in someone else's happiness is a wonderful place to be. We don't have a word for it but Buddhists do—*mudita*. We only have words for the opposite like jealousy and envy. Our world would be a better place if we added the virtue of mudita. Finding joy in the happiness and success of others creates deeper connections. There is a bond created by compassion, joy, and love.

You must get out of your own head to cultivate mudita. Begin by truly listening to someone, feel their words in your heart, and then express how happy you are for them. It comes back, as always, to awareness that we are all one. Therefore, someone else's joy is your joy.

Choose to soak up the joy of others. When you are in a state of sympathetic joy, you are connected and present. Maybe we can create a new word for the English language that means mudita. How might you express and share this sentiment with others?

JULY 14

SOURCE OF HAPPINESS

"A compassionate concern for others' well-being is the source of happiness."
- Dalai Lama

I truly believe the key to a fulfilled, happy life is compassion. We all have pain and suffering: It is a part of life. For the majority of us, we sit in that pain by ourselves. Basically, you are watering your own pain so it will continue to grow. What if, instead, you thought of the pain and suffering the whole world was experiencing right now? What happens? There is a shift to compassion and, as a result, your pain is lessened.

Compassion arises when we see another's suffering and feel motivated to help relieve that suffering. Simultaneously, your own suffering is reduced. When you are compassionate, you want what is best for the other person. The Dalai Lama described it as, if we see a person who is being crushed by a rock, the goal is not to get under the rock and feel what they are feeling; it is to help remove the rock.

Our basic human nature is to be compassionate but we have become so competitive that we are losing this ability. We fear suffering so greatly that we shy away from compassion because we don't want to feel the pain of others. The paradox is the more we retreat, the more suffering we will experience. Conversely, the more we care for others, the more our suffering will subside and true happiness will be achieved.

Psychologist Paul Gilbert said, "Compassion can flow naturally when we understand and work to remove our fears, our blocks, and our resistances to it. Compassion is one of the most difficult and courageous of all motivations, but is also the most healing and elevating."

JULY 15

BE LIKE THE SEA

"Why is the sea king of a hundred streams?
Because it lies below them. Humility gives it its power."

- Lao-Tzu

W ater is nature's most beautiful symbol. We observe how it naturally flows without resistance, how it nourishes, and how it is required for survival. Water is also an incredible symbol of humility and leadership.

The ocean teaches us that by staying low and humble, you become a leader that all want to flow into. Wayne Dyer writes about the above quote in *Change Your Thoughts, Change Your Life*: "The ocean is king of all because it knows to stay low. All streams must ultimately flow to the sea, and in the process, it becomes a servant to all."

Your life will be like water if you make a conscious effort to never put yourself above others. Ask yourself the question, "Who am I to not?" Maybe you own multiple successful companies or you are highly educated, but that does not mean you still can't mop the floor.

Be like the sea; open, yielding, never demanding and watch how people gravitate toward you. Encourage and empower others. The ocean doesn't take credit for its magnificence. The more humble you are, the more you can serve and benefit others just like the sea.

JULY 16

YOU ARE A STORY-TELLER OF FEAR

"You must realize, that fear is not real. It is a product
of thoughts you create. Do not misunderstand me,
danger is very real, but fear is a choice."

- Will Smith

Fear is created in the imagination. Think of your fears as storytelling. You are both the author and the reader of your fear. You create the character (which is you), you write the plot and then you ask the question, what will happen next? This mental time travel is like a murder-mystery novel or a tale of dark romance.

Our imagined suffering is far more dangerous than suffering itself. Seneca said, "He who indulges in empty fears earns himself real fears." We create our own worst-case scenario. Fear envelopes us so we refuse to hear or see the facts.

Your sense of self creates your fears. The more anchored you are in your life, the less fear you will imagine. Fear is a choice. It is not concrete; it is transient and you can let it pass by.

TRUTH

"There are three levels of truth:
Experience, reasoning, and knowing.
All other assertions should be rejected."
- Deng Ming-Dao

We gain truth through experience, reasoning, and knowing. When you have experienced something in your life, like the birth of your child or the loss of a loved one, you know your emotions and your experience to be true. Even when someone tells you their experience was different, you cannot be persuaded otherwise.

You also gain truth through reasoning. You are not able to actually experience the truth, but you can analyze, reason, and conclude the truth. In yoga philosophy, the word *Satya* means truthfulness. This is a way to gain truth through unconditional reasoning. Satya is seeing and communicating things as they actually are, not as you wish them to be.

The third type of truth is a spiritual knowing. This truth does not come from external circumstances or measures. It is a quiet knowing deep in your soul. A truth that there is a higher energy that orchestrates your life and all lives. A knowing that you are right where you are supposed to be. Spiritual truth doesn't need words. It is not rationalized or questioned. It is just the truth.

JULY 18

CURVE BALL

*"Everything can be taken from a man but one thing:
the last of the human freedoms - to choose
one's attitude in any given set of circumstances."*

- Victor Frankl

Life is a series of curve balls—how well we handle them determines our outlook on life. There's an old saying, "We plan and God laughs." We never know what the future holds, but we can prepare and be open to different possibilities.

Hardships will happen in life and you have a choice on letting the curve ball lead you down the path of despair or down the path of hope and action. You choose the interpretation. You choose the meaning.

The one constant that you can count on is change. No matter what is going on in your life, it will not stay this way forever. Even a forest fire will always burn itself out. Life balances itself out by seeking its opposite.

Think of the curve balls in your life as a way to bring balance. You have to get unsteady to become steady. You have to suffer, to heal. Be open to the possibility that joy and sorrow are interwoven. You will experience both in your life, so instead of getting hit by the curve ball or dodging out of the way, embrace it and you may be surprised when you hit a home run.

JULY 19

LIFE'S GREATEST PARADOX

"If you want others to be happy, practice compassion.
If you want to be happy, practice compassion."
- Dalai Lama

The more we think about ourselves, the less happy we are. The more we think about others, the happier we are. This, I think, is life's greatest paradox. We seek joy and happiness to fulfill us, but the search is always unfulfilling. We must go beyond our own self-absorption.

When your focus is on "me", your life becomes very small but when your focus is on "we", your life becomes meaningful and abundant. There is a delicate balance because you do have to care about yourself, but when you step over the line to self-absorption you get swallowed up by the ego.

When our focus is on others, there is a jubilant energy that is received both internally and externally. Close your eyes and remember a time when you helped someone achieve something. Can you feel that? Can you remember the look in their eyes? It is the best kind of give and take. There is actually a chemical release in the brain that leads to this euphoric state. It is called "helper's high".

Practice turning to others and watch the magic unfold. This is why we are here. The way to happiness is having an open heart and caring about others.

JULY 20

In Control of Opinion

*"Some things are in our control, while others are not.
We control our opinion, choice, desire, aversion, and, in a word,
everything of our own doing. We don't control our body, property,
reputation, position, and, in a word, everything not of our own doing."*

- Epictetus

Life becomes so simple when you realize what you are in control of and what you are not. And the empowering part is even when something is outside of your control, you still have control over your opinion about the event. You may not control your circumstances, but you can control how you think about them.

Notice your opinion about events that happen today. What do you make them mean? Can you redirect your thoughts? Be curious about how you typically respond and see if your response is serving you. If it is not, take control of your opinion and make it mean something that uplifts you and those around you.

My daughter broke her ankle preparing for a CrossFit competition. Of course she was frustrated and disappointed, but she knew that how she responded to something outside of her control would change everything. Instead of wallowing in the fact that she would not be competing the following weekend, she said how excited she was to watch and cheer on the other athletes at the gym.

JULY 21

WHAT IS GOOD AND WHAT IS BAD

*"If you are pained by an external thing, it is not this thing
that disturbs you, but your own judgement about it.
And it is in your power to wipe out this judgement now."*
- Marcus Aurelius

T here is a famous Chinese story about a farmer whose horse runs away. I think it is a wonderful example of how we define life events and how making up a story about what something means does not always serve you.

The story goes that when a farmer's horse ran away the neighbors quickly commented on his bad luck. The farmer replied that no one knows what is good or what is bad. The horse returned with a wild stallion and the neighbors reversed their verdict and offered him congratulations on his good luck. The farmer replied with the same response: No one knows what is good and what is bad. Days later the farmer's son broke his leg riding the stallion and the neighbors told the farmer how sorry they were for his bad luck. Again, the farmer had the same response: No one knows. Shortly after, war breaks out and all able men are enlisted into battle except the farmer's son, who was pardoned because of his broken leg.

It is often because of our adversity that we find peace and happiness. When you are faced with a challenge, try not to define it as good or bad... it just is. Perhaps what seems so wrong to you today, is exactly what is right for you in the future.

JULY 22

UBUNTU

"I could not walk as a human being. I could not think as a human
being, except through learning it from other human beings.
I learned to be a human being from other human beings.
We belong in this delicate network."

- Archbishop Desmond Tutu

U buntu is a South African concept that we are who we are because of others. It is a universal bond that connects us all through humanity. We see this concept come alive when there is a great disaster. We care for other countries in times of crisis, but why can we not spread Ubuntu as part of our daily character?

We think about what we want and how it affects our own personal happiness. What is missing is the awareness that we achieve our goals and dreams by supporting the goals and dreams of others. We cannot survive without each other. When we are threatened by others, we lose Ubuntu. When you put yourself in the shoes of others, there is a compassionate connection. You see that we are the same. We may have differences like color, race, religion, and nationality, but we are one as human beings.

Ubuntu teaches us to look past the superficial and see the beautiful connection of humanity. Nelson Mandela said that Ubuntu was "the profound sense that we are human only through the humanity of others; that if we are to accomplish anything in this world, it will in equal measure be due to the work and achievements of others."

JULY 23

GREATEST NEED

"I prefer to go to hell than to heaven.
I can solve more problems in hell. I can help more people there."
- Dalai Lama

Wherever there is the greatest necessity, there is the greatest opportunity to serve. Our world needs you and your greatest joy will come from helping others. When you see a problem, see the opportunity to make a difference.

Be an instrument of grace. Any progress you make towards making a difference is an act of grace. Your soul will be satisfied if you become the best you can be. Your soul will soar, if you help others be the best they can be.

Suffering is always about ourselves. When you do for others, your suffering subsides. You see, the secret to living is giving. Do for others and your life will be a blessing. The beautiful paradox: The more you give, the more you receive.

Ask yourself: "How have I changed the lives of others? Are their lives better because of me?" Start valuing people and then see how you can contribute to adding value to someone else. Focus on being useful, not successful. You will find certainty in uncertainty when you lead a life of service.

JULY 24

THE BUDDHIST KOAN

"The koan serves as a surgical tool used to cut into and then
breakthrough the mind of the practitioner... Koans aren't just puzzles
that your mind figures out suddenly and proclaims,
"Aha! The answer is three!" They wait for you to open enough
to allow the space necessary for them to enter
into your depths—the inner regions beyond knowing."
- Don Dianda

A *koan* is a paradoxical statement that Zen Buddhists meditate on. It does not have a logical solution and its purpose is to confuse the mind so one can go deeper. The purpose of a koan is to show how our ultimate reality cannot be solved logically. It is intended to exhaust the analytic intellect.

A famous koan is the idea that you become enlightened by going through a gateless gate. What one must realize is that if you think there is a gate to go through you will never enter the awakened state. You enter enlightenment by realizing there is no gate to go through because you are already there. You do not need to *become* awakened. Everything you need to know is already present within you.

Another example of a koan is: Two hands clap and there is a sound. What is the sound of one hand? A koan teaches us to not just depend on reason, but to follow our intuition. It is often a riddle or puzzle that unlocks greater truths about the world.

JULY 25

HUMILITY

"To keep on filling is not as good as stopping. Overfilled, the cupped hands drip, better to stop pouring. Sharpen a blade too much and its edge will soon be lost. Fill your house with jade and gold and it brings insecurity. Puff yourself with honor and pride and no one can save you from a fall. Retire when the work is done; this is the way to heaven."

- Lao-Tzu

Humility is surrendering to a force greater than your ego. It is a way of being grounded, patient, still, and attentive all at the same time. Humility is our teacher of contentment. Instead of adding more to our life, humility opens the door to gratitude and simplicity.

Humility comes from the Latin *humus* which means earth. Humility literally grounds us. Nature knows when enough is enough. It doesn't ask for more or less. Have gentle humility to be like nature. Know when you have accumulated enough and stop to enjoy and be grateful.

Before you add to your life, practice humility. Less truly is more. Question everything you do today:

Do I need one more thing on my "To Do" list?

Do I need one more bite of food?

Do I need to order that shirt?

Do I need to post on social media again?

Notice how it feels to not overflow your cup. You will feel lighter, your heart will be more open, and you will be more grounded to the earth.

JULY 26

MIRROR NEURONS

"We are social beings. Our survival depends on our understanding
the actions, intentions, and emotions of others. Mirror neurons allow
us to understand other people's mind, not only through conceptual
reasoning but through imitation. Feeling, not thinking."

- Giacomo Rizzolatti

W e have the capacity to feel what others are feeling. How often do
we tear up when we see someone cry? How natural is it to smile
when someone smiles at you? It is the mirror neurons in your brain that
allow this to happen. Mirror neurons play an important role in empathy and
compassion because we are able to imitate others and experience how they
must be feeling internally.

Mirror neurons are an essential part of the learning process. I remember
when my son was born prematurely, one of the many therapies we did
worked on referencing. We taught him to look at us to learn. Referencing
would then enable the mirror neurons inside his brain to become engaged.
We learn not only how to do things but what our emotional state should be
by watching others.

One of the best ways to communicate with others is to mirror their body
language. When you match the posture, tone of voice, breathing, and
gestures of someone you want to connect with, the energy will automatically
draw you toward each other in a positive way.

JULY 27

LAUGH AT YOURSELF

*"If you can laugh at yourself, you are going to be fine.
If you allow others to laugh with you, you will be great."*
- Martin Niemöller

It is so important to not take yourself too seriously. Laughing at yourself shows humility and brings us closer together. It relaxes us, it grounds us, and it connects us. Humor shows that we are imperfect and attempts at perfection are futile. When you can laugh at yourself, you invite others to laugh with you in a compassionate way.

Self-denigrating humor that is shared among those that you care for and trust is uplifting. Archbishop Desmond Tutu believes this kind of humor says, "Come stand next to me and let's laugh at me together, then we can laugh at you together." He continues by saying, "It does not belittle either of us but uplifts us, allows us to recognize and laugh about our shared humanity, about our shared vulnerabilities, our shared frailties. Life is hard, you know, and laughter is how we come to terms with all the ironies and cruelties and uncertainties that we face."

Humor deflates a situation in a good way. When you can laugh at yourself it displays a softened ego. It shows that you do not think you are better than others. Learn to laugh at yourself. Look for the opportunity to be less serious. Accept the situation as it is and then laugh at what you made it mean.

JULY 28

STACKING

"If you look at what you have in life, you'll always have more."
- Oprah Winfrey

S tacking is a way of adding on top of a belief. It can have negative or positive consequences. Anything that you stack mentally or verbally will influence how you feel. For example, if you make a list of all the things you love about your partner, you will greatly deepen the relationship. On the other hand, if you list all the things you don't like about a person, you will lose connection with that person even if you once cared deeply for them.

If you let negative thoughts pile on top of each other, you will eventually tumble. Positive stacking will have the opposite effect. It will create gratitude, confidence, love, and more. In any situation, a negative and a positive can be found. Practice stacking positive interpretations.

Emotional stacking can have an adverse effect. If you keep adding emotion on top of emotion, there will be a breaking point. That's why, sometimes, the smallest thing can set you off. When you have kept so many emotions inside, one on top of the other, it's likely that the straw will break the camel's back.

Pay attention to how you feel when something irritates you. Then when it happens again, and you are even more irritated—you are stacking. Stack as high as you would like the positive but be mindful of stacking the negative.

JULY 29

DIFFERENCE IN RELIGION AND SPIRITUALITY

"Religion is belief in someone else's experience.
Spirituality is having your own experience."
- Deepak Chopra

I am a big believer in doing what is right for you. I also believe what is right for you at one point in your life may be different at another. I have been asking a lot of questions recently: Is there a God? Who is Jesus? What happens after you die? What role does religion play?

I don't have the answers because I'm not sure they can be contextualized. I do think there is a difference between religion and spirituality. Religion can bring people together but it can also divide. It is often based on people's opinions which in turn may become their absolute truths.

Spirituality is quiet. It is an understanding that life beautifully flows just as it should. Spirituality is acceptance of what is. It can be felt by looking up at the stars. It can be seen in the face of a newborn. It can be heard in the sound of the ocean. It can be smelt in a flower's center and it can be tasted in the first snowfall.

Religion is an external practice, while spirituality is internal. Some religions can be exclusive while spirituality is always inclusive. They can both have a wonderful place in your mind, heart, and soul.

JULY 30

ART OF MAKING MISTAKES

"The greatest mistake you can make in life
is to be continually fearing you will make one."
- Elbert Hubbard

Life is like learning to play an instrument. You know that you will pluck some wrong strings as you practice. You also know that there is a correct order to play the strings to get the result you want. It is part of the process to play the wrong chord in order to play the right one. This is the music of your life.

If you were fearful every time you practiced, how would you learn? How would you ever hear and feel the beauty of the music? Don't fear your life. Don't fear failing and learning.

Learn to turn your negative thoughts into productive thoughts. Our minds think but we have control over those thoughts. Let your thoughts serve you; let them be productive. Ask, "What step do I need to take to move closer to my goal? How can I learn from my mistake? How can I turn this into an opportunity for growth?"

There is an art to making mistakes. Buddhist teacher and American author Jack Kornfield said, "To undertake a genuine spiritual path is not to avoid difficulties but to learn the art of making mistakes wakefully, to bring them to the transformative power of our heart."

JULY 31

BE PREPARED

"Being unexpected adds to the weight of a disaster,
and being a surprise has never failed to increase a person's pain.
For that reason, nothing should ever be unexpected by us.
Our minds should be sent out in advance to all things and we
shouldn't just consider the normal course of things,
but what could actually happen. For is there anything in life that
Fortune won't knock off its high horse if it pleases her?"

- Seneca

I t's not if, but when. We go through life thinking, "That won't happen to me." Make preparation part of your character. This is not done through doomsday scenarios. It is through gratitude and being completely at peace with yourself.

If you are grateful when you are healthy, you will be calm when you are not. If you are grateful for your life now, you will be patient when it changes. You become prepared by having setbacks. Let your hardships soften you. Every time you have a setback, think about others who have experienced the same suffering.

When you are at peace with yourself, life's challenges become wisdom. Be prepared to become wiser. The painful experiences are going to happen and when they do, remember that you know pain because you know love.

AUGUST

AUGUST 1

SMILING IS GOOD FOR YOUR HEALTH

"Sometimes your joy is the source of your smile,
but sometimes your smile can be the source of your joy."
- *Thích Nhất Hanh*

Your smile makes everything better. Did you know that smiling is good for your health? Smiling helps you to live longer. Research suggests that happiness increases your lifespan by years. Smiling can reduce stress and it elevates your mood.

The physical act of smiling, even if you don't feel like smiling, activates pathways in your brain that influence your emotional state. You can trick your brain to enter a state of happiness by smiling.

Smiling is contagious. Your smile can help elevate the mood of those around you. Your smile makes others smile. When you smile at someone their brain coaxes them to return the favor. In addition, when you see someone smile it activates your orbitofrontal cortex which processes sensory rewards. You feel rewarded when someone smiles at you.

Smiling is a natural drug because endorphins, dopamine, and serotonin are released when you smile. You feel good all over. Smiling helps you to stay positive and improves your immune function because you are more relaxed.

So what are you waiting for? Turn the corners of your mouth up and go out there and spread good health with your beautiful smile!

AUGUST 2

WHAT IS THE TAO?

"The Tao is constantly moving, the path that all life and the whole
universe takes. There is nothing that is not part of it—harmonious
living is to know and to move with the Tao—it is a way of life,
the natural order of things, a force that flows through all life."
- Deng Ming-Dao

The *Tao* is the Source of everything yet it is not a thing. It does not begin and does not end. The Tao is something that is felt and experienced. It is not intended to be defined but experiencing its essence can change your life.

The Tao is often referred to as "the Way". It is a state of inner serenity while being completely and gratefully aware. The Tao teaches us to look beyond the word, beyond the definition, even beyond the meaning. The Tao is the silent voice of your soul, it's the equanimity of the universe, and it's the knowing in the unknowing.

Taoism is not about searching for something you do not have, but enjoying who you are. You do because you want to, not because you have to.

The most beloved representation of the Tao is the *Tao Te Ching* by Lao-Tzu. This collection of 81 verses was dictated 500 years before the birth of Jesus. A verse reads: "The great Tao flows everywhere, to the left and to the right. All things depend upon it to exist, and it does not abandon them. To its accomplishments it lays no claim. It loves and nourishes all things, but does not lord it over them."

AUGUST 3

THREE TREASURES IN YOUR BODY

"Take care of your body. It's the only place you have to live."
- Jim Rohn

According to the *Tao*, there are three treasures in your body: your essence, your breath, and your spirit. Your essence is like the fuel in a car. It is the biochemistry of your body that is nurtured by the food you eat. To stay in harmony with your true self, or as scientists call it "homeostasis," eat food that is packed and glowing with energy. Make sure to eat food as close to its source as possible. Be grateful for who helped bring it to your plate and how it nourishes you.

The second treasure is your breath. Your inhale provides you new energy, while your exhale releases old, stale energy. Inhale through your nose, fill up your belly, and then exhale through your nose. Build your breath through meditation, exercise, and work.

The third treasure in your body is your spirit. While the first two help to nourish your existence now, your spirit nourishes you for eternity. Let your spirit be a part of your life now. Remember that underneath all your many layers, lies your soul where your spirit is dancing.

Nourish your essence, expand your breath, and awaken your spirit to allow your three treasures to harmonize and prosper.

AUGUST 4

WHAT IS TRULY YOURS

"Anything that can be prevented, taken away, or coerced is not a person's own—but those things that can't be blocked are their own."
- Epictetus

We often spend a great deal of energy, time, and money on making things "ours." How can something truly belong to us if it can be taken away by fate, circumstance, or death? This doesn't mean that you don't enjoy what you have, but it's important to not become identified by it.

There is a difference between being detached and practicing non-attachment. When you are detached, you see yourself as separate from others. As a result, you identify with titles and roles and cling to "other" things like people and relationships.

When you live with non-attachment, everything is interdependent—nothing stands alone. You do not cling to any one thing. Everything is met with fresh eyes, an open mind, and a compassionate heart. Non-attachment leads to joy, while attachment leads to suffering. In the words of the Dalai Lama, "Attachment is the origin, the root of suffering; hence it is the cause of suffering."

Start by practicing non-attachment to your ideas. This will soften your grip on the labels and concepts you have identified with. You will see that your attachments do not own you, you own them and as a result, you can let them go if they are not serving you.

AUGUST 5

REFRAMING

"The quality of your life is the quality
of your communication, with yourself as well as with others."
- *Tony Robbins*

E very minute of every day you have the opportunity to reframe what you choose something to mean. Cognitive reframing is a psychological technique that helps you to change your perspective.

Reframing is about seeing opportunities in the chaos. It is staying in your intentional mind and seeing reality but knowing you have the capability to look for the good and act upon it. It's not "What should I think about this?" It's "What am I going to do about this?"

Reframing is substituting an original belief with a replacement belief. For example: Original belief—junk food tastes great and is easily available. Replacement belief—nothing tastes as good as healthy feels.

Reframing is about discovery. It's seeking the positive in what you may have made a negative in the past. Your mind receives and responds to your interpretation and makes it your reality.

Reframing redefines your existence. Instead of a problem, see a challenge. Instead of using anger, use the opportunity to practice patience. Instead of sadness following loss, experience gratitude for the connection that was made. Instead of judgment, embody acceptance.

You have the power to reframe any situation in your life.

AUGUST 6

DRINK UP, FILL UP

"Our grand business is not to see what lies dimly at a distance,
but to do what lies clearly at hand."
- Thomas Carlyle

There is a great little book called the *Pocket Guide to Action* by Kyle Eschenroeder. It contains 116 meditations on the art of doing. There is one titled, "The Half-Way Glass," and it reads:

"There's been a lot of concern with a certain glass over the years. It's 50% filled with water. Some people think it is half full, others see it half empty.

There's a room full of people arguing about the fullness or emptiness of the thing. A kid walks in, drinks what's there, and then fills it up. The room goes quiet. That's the only person taking action."

Often, we become consumed in trying to figure something out. We debate perspectives. We analyze, question, and argue. We also applaud ourselves for looking at something differently. Great— but where is the action?

When we overcomplicate things, we miss the simplicity in just doing. Why does there need to be a debate on whether the glass is half full or half empty? Give yourself permission to just drink up what life offers you and then fill it back up for others.

AUGUST 7

STRESS

"Nothing great has ever been achieved without enthusiasm."
- Ralph Waldo Emerson

W hen you feel stressed it is because you are focused on the end goal. To lighten your load, shift your goal to what you are doing now. Then change the word stress to enthusiasm. Your body actually reacts the same to both feelings. This "fight or flight" response rooted in the sympathetic nervous system, might manifest itself in your body with a faster heartbeat, a dry mouth, a churning stomach, muscle tension, and sweaty palms or skin.

Both stress and excitement originate from the same place, but it's how you respond that informs the emotion you experience. So, if you tell yourself that you are excited instead of stressed, you transform the situation from a threat to a challenge or opportunity.

You may think that what is needed when you are stressed is to learn how to be calm. When you make yourself calm, the opposite occurs in your body. Your parasympathetic nervous system kicks in and slows your heart rate, returns your digestion to normal, and regulates your temperature. This "rest and digest" mode is not what you want when you are engaged in something intense. So, instead of calm, flip to excitement and enjoy the ride.

AUGUST 8

HOLDING SPACE

"Empathy is simply listening, holding space,
withholding judgement, emotionally connecting, and
communicating that incredibly healing message of you're not alone."
- Brené Brown

There is a beautiful way to comfort another by holding space for them. When someone you care for is going through a hard time, you would do anything to make their pain go away. As we are learning, suffering is part of life, and the journey makes you who you are today. So instead of wishing away their hardship, remember that it is their teacher and practice holding space for them.

When you hold space for someone, you put them in your heart. You wrap them with loving compassion, you send them healing energy, and you remember a joyful time with them. Close your eyes, breathe them in and then exhale the vision of them being better because of their struggle. Send the message that they are not alone.

I will often tell someone that I am holding space for them. I can't take away their pain, but I can hold their suffering in my heart and then release it. Holding space is more than, "I'm thinking of you." It's connecting one heart with another. You can also hold space for a group of people or for a country or the whole world. We need each other. We need to hold space for one another.

AUGUST 9

HEALTHY EGO

"Our soul wants to manifest our true self in the world. Our Wounded
Ego says, "You can't do that." The Healthy Ego says, "Watch me."
- Wendy De Rosa

When you ask yourself, "What did I get right today?"
and "What can I work on?" your healthy ego is speaking.
Your healthy ego allows you to explore yourself and believes in you.
Your healthy ego comes from your heart, while your unhealthy ego
comes from a voice in your mind.

Have an ego that is grounded to the earth. If you can see your
weaknesses, it makes you stronger. Your healthy ego allows you to explore
yourself. It changes your thoughts to comfort you, inspire you, and move you
to positive action. The healthy ego is confident and accomplished. It believes
that you can make a difference.

The healthy ego is comfortable in its own skin. It allows you to become a
master of your own emotions and a master of yourself. When you have a
healthy ego, you understand yourself. Time is not wasted on trying to make
others understand you.

The healthy ego lets you connect with others, learn from others, and have
empathy for others. It doesn't compare—it unites and sees all as the same.
The healthy ego is directed to the common good. It is responsible for its
actions and doesn't make someone else wrong.

Let your healthy ego shine today and see all the good
that can come from it.

AUGUST 10

BE WEALTHY

"If you realize that you have enough, you are truly rich."
- Lao-Tzu

When you are grateful for everything that you have, you are wealthy. True wealth comes from within. When you are living out your dharma—your purpose in life, you are prosperous. True wealth makes you feel alive.

You are wealthy if you are balanced in all areas of your life. These areas include your physical body, emotions, relationships, time, work, finances, spirituality, and contribution. Invest in building yourself. Become wealthy by constantly becoming the best version of yourself. Prosper from the inside out. You are wealthy if you are fulfilled. Be fulfilled by always growing, making progress, and sharing your contribution with others.

Let your wealth come from your soul. We all want to thrive and prosper, and you will if your wealth comes from the inside and you share it outwardly with others. As Marcus Aurelius said, "The only wealth which you will keep forever is the wealth you have given away."

Have your energy be bountiful. Be rich with empathy. Be abundant with love and compassion. True wealth is not about adding more things but adding more joy.

AUGUST 11

JUMP IN

"O I could sing such grandeurs and glories about you! You have not shown what you are, you have slumber'd upon yourself all your life, Your eyelids have been the same as closed most of the time...

Whoever you are! Claim your own hazard! These shows of the East and West are tame compared to you, These immense meadows, these interminable rivers, you are immense and interminable as they..."
- Walt Whitman

You are not who you appear to be. The reality of your world is a manifestation of the stories you have created in your mind. You have repeatedly replayed your created reality so many times that it is now your belief.

Together, we are practicing being the observer of these thoughts. Over and over again, we step outside of the story and just watch. This will become your new habit. As the observer, you now have awareness that life is occurring as it is with or without your commentary. There, the space is created for you to become you. You can move into action. You are in the arena instead of being a bystander.

Wake up to how important you are to this world. Stop judging and talking about it...jump in and be an integral part of life.

AUGUST 12

IT WEARS OFF

"Yes, getting your wish would have been so nice. But isn't that exactly why pleasure trips us up? Instead, see if these things might be even nicer—a great soul, freedom, honesty, kindness, saintliness. For there is nothing so pleasing as wisdom itself, when you consider how sure-footed and effortless the works of understanding and knowledge are."

- Marcus Aurelius

What you think will make you happy, usually wears off rather quickly. Think back to a time when you thought, "When I get *x,y,z*, then I will be happy." How long did you stay happy for? An hour? A day? A week? When we think something external will make us happy, we soon conclude it's not enough.

The things that bring us true happiness begin internally, are within our control, and do not wear off. Lasting happiness is found in your heart and in a clear mind. It is found in compassion, love, hard work, and freedom in your soul. These things cannot be taken away.

You may find temporary satisfaction in achieving an external goal, but if you base your happiness on it, you will quickly become disappointed. True happiness is found in your contribution to others. Increase your responsibility toward others and the world and you will have internal happiness that shines externally.

AUGUST 13

WORK

"Work is love made visible."

- Kahlil Gibran

To some, work can be a four-letter word and to others it is complete joy. It doesn't matter what you do but it does matter how you do it. It all comes from your heart. No matter the task, the joy comes from knowing you are contributing to the lives of others. Kahlil Gibran writes about work in *The Prophet*:

"And what is it to work with love?
It is to weave the cloth with threads drawn from the heart,
even as if your beloved were to wear that cloth.
It is to build a house with affection,
even as if your beloved were to dwell in that house."

Shift from thinking work is something that you have to do, to something you get to do. Open your heart to allowing your work to be an expression of love. Do your job like you were doing it for a loved one. If you are a builder, build the home thinking it is for your family. If you are a barista, serve the coffee like you would to your spouse. If you own a company, talk to your employees like they were your family.

Work with joy. Let your job be an extension of your heart. If you find yourself not able to shine your light, find a different job that allows you to be a contribution of goodness.

AUGUST 14

GAIN AND LOSS

"When the senses contact sense objects, a person experiences cold or heat, pleasure or pain. These experiences are fleeting; they come and go. Bear them patiently, Arjuria. Those who are not affected by these changes, who are the same in pleasure and pain, are truly wise and fit for immortality."

- The Bhagavad Gita

When you treat gain and loss the same, you are not intimidated by your life. You accept things as they come to you because you know that it is all part of the plan. You can stand to the side and watch the situation with detachment. You let your senses feel, but you don't need to act upon them.

Let's look at a few examples. Imagine you just got promoted at work. You feel your ego take over. You listen to your mind tell you how incredible you are. You look around the office and want everyone to congratulate you. Then, you remember that these emotions are not who you truly are. You are the one observing.

Now imagine losing your job. What do you make that mean? Can you become the witness of your emotions but not the participant? The ultimate goal is to treat gain and loss the same. This does not mean that you don't feel happiness or sadness because you most certainly do. The keyword and goal is to treat them the *same*. Be in equilibrium. Seek evenness of mind and remember, in every gain there is loss, and in every loss there is gain.

AUGUST 15

GRATITUDE FOR COMPLAINING

"A complaining tongue reveals an ungrateful heart."
- William Arthur Ward

Next time you hear yourself complaining about something, pause and be grateful for whatever it is. I know that sounds strange but when you look below the surface, you will see that whatever is bothering you in that moment is most likely because of a situation you are blessed to be in.

The other day I found myself complaining about a prescribed workout that I was choosing to do. Catching myself complaining and moaning, I stopped and thought, "How lucky am I that my body is able to do this. How blessed I am that I have a gym that supports me and helps me to become a better athlete."

We complain about the weather. Instead, have gratitude that you are able to go outside and feel the change in seasons. We complain about traffic. Be grateful that you have a car to drive and a destination to drive to. We complain about our job. Stop yourself and be grateful you have a job. When your children are driving you crazy, pause and think about all those who weren't able to have children or lost a child.

Look at what you are complaining about and see how lucky you are.

AUGUST 16

PRANA

"Prana is the driving power of the world,
and can be seen in every manifestation of life."
- *Swami Vivekananda*

P rana means "life force" or "vital energy". Everything is a manifestation of prana. It's the same energy that runs through your body as the energy that comes from the pen you write with.

Prana is the connecting link between the material world, consciousness, and the mind. This energy of life was first documented over 3,000 years ago. It plays a role in our health, our spirituality, and our psychological well-being.

The prana in your body must flow unencumbered to have optimal health. There are thousands of methods to help the flow of prana including yoga, acupuncture, eating spicy food, etc. The most beneficial way to keep prana flowing is breath work. When you focus on your breath, you expand your life force.

You will gain harmony and health in your body and mind by letting your prana flow. This energy flow gives you life and lights your way.

AUGUST 17

LEARN HOW TO BREATHE

"Each breath is like a little rebirth, a renaissance
that can only be celebrated if we recognize that it's happening."
- Cristen Rodgers

Learning to breathe properly is essential to your health and well-being. Breathing is something we take for granted and the majority of us do it incorrectly. The first step is awareness because how can you fix or improve something if you aren't even aware that there is a better way?

After simply becoming aware of your breath, notice if you breathe through your mouth. There is a proverb that says: The nose is for breathing, the mouth is for eating. Many people breathe through their mouth when they are sleeping which leads to many health risks including sleep apnea which causes your airway to close intermittently while asleep. Mouth breathing raises your blood pressure, stresses your body, and leads to disease.

The next step in learning to breathe properly is to practice breathing slowly in and out through your nose. You want to take an inhale to a count of five, and a slow exhale to a count of five. You can do this anywhere and at any time.

Another way to increase your ability to breathe purposefully is to chew your food. The bones in our face continue to grow so we can reshape our face and improve our ability to breathe by chewing our food.

There are countless breathing techniques that you can practice. I encourage some breath hold work to expand your lung capacity and to become comfortable with the uncomfortable.

AUGUST 18

I Said to Myself

"The mind is using you.
You are unconsciously identified with it,
so you don't even know that you are its slave."
- Eckhart Tolle

How often have you thought, "I said to myself…"? Isn't that kind of funny? There we are right in the middle of being lost and finding enlightenment. If you are the "I", who is the "myself"? You are the one that witnesses your thoughts.

In a world of constant noise, how do you become the witness? Constantly have the mantra: "I am awareness." This will help to quiet the mind so you can be conscious of yourself. You are not your mind. You are the experience of Being. Your being is your true self. The one that is present, open, and one with humanity.

When you identify with your mind, you become the other—the one that is talking to you in your head. And this other you, can change from moment to moment. Again, come back to your true self and practice awareness. Begin to break the habit of identifying with your thoughts.

Be the witness and your life will change. Maybe think of yourself as an eye, not an "I". You are the one that sees but does not judge. The eye does not evaluate but notes. Keep reminding yourself that you are the one that observes the voice in your head and this will lead you to your soul.

August 19

Your Brain and Your Mind

*"The brain is not the mind. It is probably impossible to look
at a map of brain activity and predict or even understand
the emotions, reactions, hopes and desires of the mind."*
- David Brooks

The debate on the difference between brain and mind has been going on since the time of Aristotle. Many scientists believe that they are the same thing, but I find them to be different yet valuable to each other.

Your brain is an essential organ in your body while your mind is the manifestation of thoughts, perception, emotion, memory, and imagination. While the brain is tangible, our mind is hypothetical. We identify with our mind as who we are.

We often think of the mind as being part of the brain. What if we let our mind come less from our head? Research has shown the possibility that we have three brains: a head brain, a gut brain, and a heart brain. Our mind will have peace and clarity if we allow our thoughts and emotions to be drawn from our heart and gut brain more than our head brain.

Your mind and your brain are like siblings. They can learn to love and appreciate each other and thrive by working together. You can use your mind to change your brain to change your mind for the better. Let your mind create new thought patterns, and you will actually rewire your brain.

AUGUST 20

BE GRATEFUL TO BE PRIVILEGED

*"To this day I believe we are here on earth
to love, grow, and do what we can to make this world
a better place for all people to enjoy freedom."*
- Rosa Parks

There are so many things we take for granted. Many of the gifts we have been given are privileges. These gifts should not invoke shame when others do not have them, but we need to recognize them as blessings to be grateful for.

You are privileged because you are able to read these words. So many people are not able to obtain an education. You are privileged because you are safe. When you feel safe you go out and explore the world. When you don't feel safe, you are not curious and only stay with what is familiar. The ability to feel safe and secure is a privilege because so many people in the world do not have that sense of security.

You are privileged because you have food and water. You are privileged if you have a job. If you have access to health care, information at your fingertips, the right to vote, a bed to sleep in…you are privileged.

Recognize your privileges and become aware of the opportunities that these gifts offer you. Then focus on how your privileges could help others. Today, when you remember the importance of saying "I get to…" try adding "…when so many people cannot."

AUGUST 21

EMOTION

"Feelings or emotions are the universal language and
are to be honored. They are the authentic expression
of who you are at your deepest place."
- *Judith Wright*

All emotions are important because they clear the way to joy. An emotion is your body's reaction to your mind. Since you have control over your mind, you have the power to let the emotion flow through you and to release it.

The key is to not let your emotions define you. You are not a lonely person; you feel lonely in this moment. You are not an angry person; you feel anger at a situation. You are responsible for your feelings. Peace is at the heart of all emotions. Maintaining equanimity is the answer.

Listen to your body. When you feel sadness, release the tears. When you feel anger, safely release it by punching a pillow or yelling when no one is around. Ralph Waldo Emerson said, "Sometimes a scream is better than a thesis."

Yoga is a gentle way to open your heart and to release pent up feelings. If you keep these emotions inside, you are only hurting yourself. Unexpressed emotions can cause long-term suffering. Expressing your emotions is not a sign of weakness—it is a sign of strength.

AUGUST 22

SOUL

"When you do things from your soul,
you feel a river moving in you, a joy."

- Rumi

I believe our true self is our soul and our soul is love. Therefore, when you look at others you should see their soul. Our soul is who we truly are. When all the outside layers are stripped away there is only love. Your soul, my soul, the souls of those in other countries, those that are suffering, those that have wronged others, those that serve, all beings…we are all one. Underneath it all, we are the same.

Of course, we are on different paths, put on different armor, have different thoughts and dreams, but we are the same. What makes us different is our ego, what makes us the same is our soul. When I pass people on the street or in a store, I try as often as I can to look at them and say in my heart, "We are the same."

When you see soul to soul only love and compassion can arise. To see your enemy as your friend, to feel the suffering of others is difficult, but it is the answer to true happiness.

Think of yourself as an archery target. Your body is the outside circle. Your mind is the inside circle and your soul is the bullseye. When you stay as close as possible to the bullseye, you will live your life from the inside out and that is magical.

AUGUST 23

LINGER IN THE GOOD MOMENTS

*"As we express our gratitude, we must never forget that
the highest appreciation is not to utter words, but to live by them."*
- John F. Kennedy

Times have changed since our ancestors walked the earth, but unfortunately our brain still defaults to the same fight or flight response. To help our ancestors survive in harsh conditions, the brain evolved a *negativity bias*. This means that it is easy for us to learn from bad experiences but hard to learn from good ones.

Our brains were trained for millions of years to always be in high alert—looking for what might hurt us, hunting for food, etc. In our modern world these threats are rare, but our brains have wired our alert system and the saber-tooth tiger danger might now appear as our boss or as the opinions of others. We ruminate and worry instead of running for our lives.

How do we change our brain to not be on constant high alert? You must linger in the good moments; pausing, appreciating, and letting positivity soak in. All those moments when you are feeling relaxed, joyful, successful, appreciated, loved, and more...let them marinate. Take time in the moment to let them make an imprint on your brain and in your heart.

AUGUST 24

EXCEL AT WHAT YOU WERE ASSIGNED

"Remember that you are an actor in a play, playing a character according to the will of the playwright—if a short play, then it's short; if long, long. If he wishes you to play the beggar, play even that role well, just as you would if it were a cripple, a honcho, or an everyday person. For this is your duty, to perform well the character assigned you. That selection belongs to another."

- Epictetus

A great deal of where you are in life is not chosen by you: the family you were born into, the color of your skin, the sickness that takes over your body, the beautiful singing voice you were born with. A lot of where we are, who we are, and where we are going is determined by the cards we were dealt.

You have two choices. You could play the victim and decide that since life threw you a bad hand, you will just settle and possibly fold. Or, you could play the victor and excel at what you were assigned.

Choose to look at your life as a card game. You were given a hand of cards and you can thoughtfully navigate a way to make them work for you. You can trade one card for another so your hand works more in your favor, but how you truly win the game is to accept what you were dealt and make the very most of it.

AUGUST 25

A LOJONG PRACTICE

"I judge you unfortunate because you have never lived through
misfortune. You have passed through life without an opponent—
no one can ever know what you are capable of, not even you."
- *Seneca*

L *ojong* is a Tibetan mind training in which you turn your adversity
into growth and development. Instead of seeing what was lost, you
find what was gained. For example, if you were in a car accident and totaled
your car but came out uninjured, you would focus on your fortunate good
health and not the damage to your car.

It is often through our suffering that we can empathize and have
compassion for others who are going through something similar. You can
make the Lojong practice part of your life. Notice and become aware of
where you are experiencing suffering in your life. Step outside of your own
pain and think of all those who may feel the same way or worse. Send them
love and compassion. Then think about how you might learn and grow from
your hardship.

As hard as it may be, be grateful for your suffering. See the experience
as a step towards greater wisdom and more compassion. Be open to the
opportunity to help others through what you have learned. Find the good
in adversity. You become a better person by staring into the eyes of your
suffering and conquering it with growth.

AUGUST 26

BE SELFISH

"I can do nothing for you but work on myself...
you can do nothing for me but work on yourself!"
- Ram Dass

It's so important to know yourself. It may seem like a paradox but the most selfless thing you can do is to be selfish. Selfish in understanding who you really are. When you understand your true self, you will see the true self of others.

Self-mastery of your actions and self-realization of your being will guide you to enlightenment. Remember that your true self is your soul and we all are the same because of this. It is the same in every *thing* not just every being. That is why nature offers such peace and connection.

The work we have to do is on ourselves to strip away the layers to let our soul lead us for the greater good of all. It is an illusion to think you are separate from others. We are all woven into one tapestry. Your job is to be grounded to the earth and be a contribution.

When you identify with your soul your actions will come from this effortless, peaceful place. St. Catherine of Genoa said, "And the state of this soul is then a feeling of such utter peace and tranquility that it seems to her that her heart, and her bodily being, all both within and without, is immersed in an ocean of utmost peace."

AUGUST 27

STAY

"When you are sorrowful look again in your heart, and you shall see that in truth you are weeping for that which has been your delight."
- Kahlil Gibran

When times are difficult—stay. Do everything in your power to stay. Don't run away. Don't use something to mask the pain. Sit in it and feel it. It is important to embrace our emotions because they play a vital role in our lives.

Sharing your difficulty with others is part of the healing process. Archbishop Tutu said in *The Book of Joy*, "We don't really get close to others if our relationship is made up of unending hunky-dory-ness. It is the hard times, the painful times, the sadness and the grief that knit us more closely together."

By truly feeling your suffering, you are reminded of joy. Your grief is love on some level. Stay, because if you don't, your pain will manifest into greater pain. Stay because you will witness a transformation. Your difficulty will become your strength. Your pain will become your resiliency. Your struggle will become your gift. If you do not stay, this will not happen and you will incur more hardship.

AUGUST 28

FIELD OF FORCES

"All actions are performed by the gunas of prakriti. Deluded by identification with the ego, a person thinks, "I am the doer." But the illumined man or woman understands the domain of the gunas and is not attached. Such people know that the gunas interact with each other; they do not claim to be the doer."

- The Bhagavad Gita

The three *gunas* are from Hindu philosophy and are a beautiful way to be compassionate to yourself and to others. They are a type of energy found in every state of matter and mind. The gunas can roughly be translated to our three states of matter: solid, liquid, and gas. They are *tamas*, inertia; *rajas*, activity; and *sattva*, harmony or equilibrium.

Think of the gunas as different states of our mind—even different personalities. What is important is the awareness that we have all three within us. There are times when we are full of energy—the rajasic person, times when we are passive—the tamasic person, and times when we are compassionate, selfless, and calm—the satvic person.

Pay attention to the energy you are carrying. Remember that you are the one observing the guna. Be compassionate to yourself and others and focus on expanding your satvic energy to become closer to your true self.

AUGUST 29

EVERYONE SHOULD HAVE A DOG

"Once you have had a wonderful dog,
a life without one, is a life diminished."
- Dean Koontz

E veryone should have a dog. I know this is my opinion and perhaps there are legitimate reasons why you cannot, but if you can—get a dog. I waited 19 years for my husband to say "yes" to our No. 1 companion. She has brought so much joy, love, and laughter to our lives that I can't believe we ever lived without her.

Dogs truly bring unconditional love into your life. They love you no matter what. I think our family is closer because of our dog. Everything is better because of her.

If you need scientific research on the benefits of having a dog, studies show that: Dogs increase your mood dramatically. They reduce the risk of cardiovascular disease. Dogs protect children from skin conditions and allergies. They encourage a healthy lifestyle by dog-walking exercise. Humans with dogs recover more quickly from illnesses and children in households with dogs have higher self-esteem.

Having a dog makes you a better person. You learn about responsibility, companionship, patience, and more. You will never be so deeply loved. Oh, about my husband who didn't want a dog…he and our dog are now inseparable.

AUGUST 30

DIFFERENCE IN ACTION AND RIGHT ACTION

"Action wants to be busy, right action wants to be effective."
- Kyle Eschenroeder

A lways do the right next thing. Your life will be fulfilling if you do the right thing in every moment. Your life depends on making right choice after right choice. We don't know what the future holds, but there is certainly more certainty if your moments are a long string of right actions.

There's a difference in action and right action. Action is searching for a way to be productive while right action is getting to work. Eating is an action, but eating mindfully is right action. Listening is an action. Listening intently with compassion is right action. Reading is an action, but applying what you have learned is right action. Henry David Thoreau said, "To be a philosopher is not merely to have subtle thoughts, not even to found a school…it is to solve some of the problems of life, not only theoretically, but practically."

Right action is about transformation. It's about turning your fear into useful information, your mistakes into knowledge, and your pain into wisdom. Practice right action daily. From the words you use or don't use, to the thoughts you have, to the food you eat, to the quality of your time. What matters in life is what you do—make it right.

AUGUST 31

PRACTICE LISTENING

*"Acquire the habit of attending carefully
to what is being said by another, and of entering,
so far as possible into the mind of the speaker."*

- Marcus Aurelius

How often are you thinking of what you are going to say when someone is speaking to you? We must become better listeners if we want a more compassionate world. When you give your full attention to someone, you are giving them alert stillness. In your silence, you are saying, "I hear you." "I honor you." "I see you." Isn't that what we all want—validation?

Listen with curiosity. Be interested in people and leave each exchange having learned something. Use your words to learn from others. Epictetus said, "Be silent for the most part, or if you speak, say only what is necessary and in a few words. Talk, but rarely, if occasion calls you, but do not talk of ordinary things."

You can become a better listener (and person) by listening not just with your ears but with your heart and your eyes. Empathize and speak through your eyes. Use non-verbal communication to engage in the conversation and become comfortable with the stillness that is always there.

SEPTEMBER

SEPTEMBER 1

TRUE KINDNESS

"Kindness is the language
that the deaf can hear and the blind can see."
- Mark Twain

B ecome a seeker of those who need kindness in their life. To be kind to others you must see yourself as them. Look for the person that needs your smile. Offer a hand to someone that is struggling. Lend an ear and your heart to a friend in need.

Being kind to others is a sign of strength. You have taken the time to get out of your own way to express kindness to another. This can be your super power. Seneca said, "Wherever there is a human being there is an opportunity for a kindness." I would take out the word "human" because at every moment there are opportunities to be kinder to our earth, to animals, to our thoughts, and more.

Kindness can be exhilarating at times and exhausting at others. But no matter what the accompanying emotion is, kindness will always make you a better person. When you give, you will receive. Kindness opens a gateway to compassion. Even if you have difficulty with someone, express kindness. That expression of true kindness will transform you into a superhero.

SEPTEMBER 2

THREE KINDS OF GENEROSITY

"Before giving, the mind of the giver is happy.
While giving the mind of the giver is made peaceful.
After having given, the mind of the giver is uplifted."
- Buddha

In Buddhist teachings there are three kinds of generosity: 1) material giving, 2) giving freedom from fear, and 3) spiritual giving.

Perhaps material giving is the kind we are most familiar with. It involves sharing your resources to help others. It involves giving food to the hungry, shelter to the homeless, money to those in need, and more. This type of generosity is not limited to material things. You can also give of your time and share kindness with others.

Giving freedom from fear involves protection, counseling, or solace. The giving of fearlessness can come from first responders, from a parent consoling a child, or from a doctor or nurse comforting a worried patient. Mr.Rogers spoke of this type of giving when he said, "When I was a boy and I would see scary things in the news, my mother would say to me, 'Look for the helpers. You will always find people who are helping.'"

The third type of generosity is spiritual giving. It involves giving your wisdom, moral and ethical teachings, and helping others be more self-sufficient and happier. I believe this type of giving is so beautiful and accessible. It can happen when you read something and share what you learned with others. It can happen in companies by caring and mentoring.

Let your giving be joyous and without looking for anything in return.

SEPTEMBER 3

OUR THREE SELVES

"Tear off the mask. Your face is glorious."

- Rumi

I believe we have three selves: our thinking self, our watching self, and our true self. All three are part of who we are, but the one you spend the most time with creates your life.

Your thinking self resides in the realm of human definition. Here our reality is defined by our thoughts. Our self is created by "them". We care more about what others think of us than we do about how we feel. Our thoughts are plagued with always wanting what it doesn't have. Our thinking self—judges, creates false stories, separates us from others, is lost in thought, and is not at peace.

Your watching self is the one who is aware of your thinking self. You are able to pause the merry-go-round and become the observer. You see that your thinking self is making you unhappy and you realize the power you have to create the life you want. You begin to transform your life by taking action. Your watching self enjoys stillness, learning, possibility, creativity and begins to understand that true happiness is found in compassion, service, and self-love.

Your true self is who you truly are. It has been who you are since the minute you were born. Your true self is your soul and is found within a spiritual realm. It is you unburdened. Your true self is loving awareness. Aware that we are all the same—that everything is the same. That life is just as it should be. Your true self is perfect peace.

SEPTEMBER 4

CHANGE

"Loss is nothing else but change, and change is Nature's delight."
- *Marcus Aurelius*

C hange is hard because it involves loss, but it also involves creation. Change is the nature of the universe. Without change you cannot grow, learn, overcome challenge, love, and feel emotionally. Change is necessary for all things. When you resist change, you resist your life.

There will be times in your life you may not agree with the change, but you can accept it and learn to pivot. Loss is about what was, acceptance is about what is, and creation is about what can be. What are you willing to create from the change? What meaning will you put into it?

It's all about perspective. Do you look at change as the end of something or the beginning? It's the meanings that we attribute to change that determine how we feel and only you have control over where you live emotionally.

Let change be an opening, not a closing. Look for the opportunity to become better. Change invites you to be vulnerable. Choose courage over comfort. Choose living over suffering.

SEPTEMBER 5

YOUR JOB

"What is your vocation?
To be a good person."

- Marcus Aurelius

The Roman Emperor, Marcus Aurelius, journaled to himself and his private thoughts are published in the extraordinary book, *Meditations*. His philosophical thinking from almost 2,000 years ago is still relevant and helpful today.

The main value that flows through Stoicism and yogic philosophy is to be a good person. Above all else, be of good character. Always do the right thing. Always get better. Always tell the truth and always love everyone. In other words, do your job. Do what you were placed on this earth to do.

What if every day you woke up and said, "My job today is to be a good person." Imagine if every moment of your day you had this intention. Marcus writes, "You must build up your life action by action, and be content if each one achieves its goal as far as possible—and no one can keep you from this. But there will be some external obstacle! Perhaps, but no obstacle to acting with justice, self-control, and wisdom."

If every day your goal is to be a good person, any obstacle that comes your way will be a gift. Marcus continues, "Gladly accept the obstacle for what it is and shift your attention to what is given, and another action will immediately take its place, one that better fits the life you are building."

SEPTEMBER 6

BEING IS ESSENTIAL

"When we do not trouble ourselves about whether or not
something is a work of art, if we act in each moment
with composure and mindfulness,
each moment of our life is a work of art."

- Thích Nhất Hạnh

There is an art in just being. It is an art that is so simple but must be practiced over and over again. It is our life's practice. Keep coming back to this moment. The mind travels—bring it back. Feel the ground beneath your feet. Feel your heartbeat. Feel the energy you radiate out. The mind travels—bring it back. Be grateful for this moment. Find the joy in the task at hand. Practice the art of simply being.

We are so challenged by what is most important in life—being present. Everything you need is in this moment. Give up trying to get something from life. Just be fully present and you will receive. Instead of trying to find peace, be peace. Instead of seeking happiness, be happiness. Instead of searching for love, be love.

Everything you do, let it come from a place of being. Your true authentic self will be a work of art.

SEPTEMBER 7

THE SEASHORE MIND

*"The ocean stirs the heart, inspires the imagination
and brings eternal joy to the soul."*
- Robert Wyland

One of my favorite things to do is walk on the beach. I probably hear my soul speak the most around water. The union of sound, sight, smell, touch, and taste is alive with every step. One of the beautiful aspects of the ocean is the way the water purifies the sand. Any imprints are washed away and a clearing remains.

Imagine our lives if every day we allowed this to happen in our minds. What, if on a daily basis, we resolved conflict so we could always start without lingering impressions? What if we let go of regret and negative thoughts as soon as they appeared? When we hold onto these emotions, they make impressions in the sands of our minds.

To live your life without leaving consequences is difficult. If you are mindful and practice letting go of what is not serving you—you will succeed in living with peace and clarity. Let the past and worry about the future be washed away like footsteps on the seashore.

SEPTEMBER 8

LEADERSHIP

"Thus the master is content to serve as an example and not to impose his will. He is pointed but does not pierce; he straightens but does not disrupt; he illuminates but does not dazzle."
- *Tao Te Ching*

A great leader is one who creates an environment where others feel they did the work themselves. From the 17th verse of the *Tao Te Ching*: "The great leader speaks little. He never speaks carelessly. He works without self-interest and leaves no trace. When all is finished, the people say: we did it ourselves."

Great leaders don't actually lead; they guide, serve as an example, and allow others to explore possibilities. Their leadership is so subtle that the group doesn't even realize they are being led. They are seen in the actions of those in their group. Each member of the group will want to do the right thing and work hard because of the unseen force of their leader.

Great leaders are found in companies, religions, and government but they are also parents, teachers, and mentors. Great leaders empower others. They encourage others to make decisions and take pride in their work. These leaders are there to serve without asking for anything in return. They want others to achieve their own greatness. A great leader creates trust and respect which leads to responsibility and ownership.

SEPTEMBER 9

BRICK BY BRICK

"You must build up your life action by action,
and be content if each one achieves its goal as far as possible—
and no one can keep you from this."
- Marcus Aurelius

We often focus on the final product. Whether it be winning a game or completing a project, the end goal is always on our minds. We miss our lives and the joy of the process when we live this way.

Concentrate on what is most important to you now. Build your life brick by brick in an order that brings you joy. Everything in life is a process. Don't rush it. Work hard and be here now.

A young comedian once asked Jerry Seinfeld how he could become successful. Jerry told him to write one joke a day and put an X on the calendar each day he did this. You must work hard at your craft. Enjoying the daily work is what fulfills you. It is not the touchdown or the raise, but how present you are in each moment—this is true happiness.

I took Jerry Seinfeld's advice and wrote this book one JAM at a time. Almost every day, for 16 months, my motto was: Write with joy every day!

Build your life brick by brick, right action after right action, and you will always be right where you are supposed to be.

SEPTEMBER 10

OTHERING

"Our ability to reach unity in diversity
will be the beauty and the test of our civilization."
- Mahatma Gandhi

Othering has unfortunately been a part of our culture for a very long time. It is when one group of individuals makes another group feel not welcome and different. Othering is an *us vs. them* mentality. The thought is "they are not like me" or "they are not one of us."

Othering is often based on race, gender, social class, ethnicity, religion, sexual orientation, or political affiliation. Our world is hurting because of othering. There must be a transformation in the way we look at each other. If we were to see someone's soul when we stand next to them or when we talk behind their back or when we use violence to hurt them, we would see their soul as our own.

Othering is the opposite of belonging. Instead of including others, we exclude them. Why do we do this? It's because so many people enjoy the destruction of anything that is different from them. People are threatened if they feel they have to change. When you only see your perspective, you cannot be inclusive. Othering involves only seeing what someone is not.

Gandhi said, "Be the change you wish to see in the world." Walk united with everyone you encounter today. Make exterior differences a beautiful thing and always remember that deep in the heart we are one.

YOU ARE HOME

"Do not look for a sanctuary in anyone except your self."
- Buddha

Everything you need is inside of you. You are always home. When life pulls at you, keep coming back to your truth. Use your breath to center you, feel your feet grounded to the earth, and feel your heart beat. You've got this.

Discovering that you have it all is so beautiful. It's a magical awakening. You see beyond illusions and limiting beliefs. You see your home. You are home. You are right where you are supposed to be.

Home is your soul. It's the love and joy you were born with. You are aware that life has obstacles, but you are centered and peaceful because you are home.

Keep coming back home. When the tide pulls you out, gently swim back to shore. When the burden is heavy, lay it down at the front door. Breathe in, breathe out.

SEPTEMBER 12

DOWNWARD FACING DOG

"Yoga is not about touching your toes.
It is what you learn on the way down."

- Jigar Gor

Many yoga poses are influenced by animals and nature. By observing nature, you can see your own reflection. The yoga practice does a beautiful job of symbolizing and weaving the environment with our inner being.

Probably the most well-known yoga pose is downward facing dog. This pose reminds us how humans evolved from animals that walked on all-fours. Downward facing dog creates an opportunity for playfulness. Like our furry friends, we can be relaxed, silly, and fun.

Cobra pose in yoga symbolizes how a cobra sheds old skins for new ones. This demonstrates how we can let go of the old and begin again. In many cultures, snakes have come to represent the harmony of good and evil.

Did you know a pigeon can travel over 1,000 miles and find its way back home? Pigeon pose signifies how we can survive in challenging situations. Pigeons will often puff out their chest in pride. In yoga, this pose helps develop confidence and assurance.

Eagle pose cultivates concentration. Eagles can clearly see about eight times as far as humans can. They can spot and focus in on prey two miles away. Eagle pose helps us to live our life from our third eye center—the place of all knowing.

SEPTEMBER 13

AGING IS BEAUTIFUL

"The longer I live, the more beautiful life becomes."
- Frank Lloyd Wright

Doesn't it seem crazy to try to be something you are not? We spend so much time, effort, and money trying to be something different. As the clock turns, something beautiful happens: We become more comfortable in our own skin. We don't care as much (or at all) about what others are thinking about us. We are more thoughtful and caring because we are not as focused on the external.

As we age, we become wiser. We know that true beauty comes from within. We know who we are and who we are not. We want to be free from restriction. We enjoy stillness, laughter, friendship, food, comfort, and happiness more. We have a deeper gratitude for these things because we have endured without them in our life. We know what is important and what is not. We enjoy simplicity and marvel at nature.

Aging is beautiful. We let things soften—our hearts and our grasp on perfection. We see imperfection as our unique blueprint. The wrinkles on our faces are our tattoos of life: joy, sorrow, contemplation, and more. We find our voice. We don't try to change who we are to please someone else. We let life flow through us. We are our own expression and that is beautiful.

SEPTEMBER 14

BE ADAPTABLE

*"In this way you must understand how laughable it is to say,
'Tell me what to do!' What advice could I possibly give?
No, a far better request is, 'Train my mind to adapt to any
circumstance.'...In this way, if circumstances take you off script...
you won't be desperate for a new prompting."*
- Epictetus

T o learn to flow with life is an art that takes practice. We often turn to others for guidance and direction but your life comes from within you. Not from what others say or think. Being adaptable is a wonderful trait. You stand in your truth and like a boxer, you move side to side, up and down, backward and forward to adapt to the situation.

As you begin to let your life flow you will see that the circumstances that occur are on the outside. You are a being that cannot be shaken because you are centered. You maneuver through obstacles with grace and strength—like a boxer. You have trained your mind to be adaptable. Seneca said, "The whole future lies in uncertainty: live immediately."

Adapt to the circumstance you are faced with. Let it be natural. Don't look for someone else to tell you how to do something. Learn, create, cultivate, and adapt.

SEPTEMBER 15

GOING INTERNAL

"You know, you have to go internal if you want to go eternal."
- Robert Sargent Shriver Jr.

The above quote was said to Maria Shriver by her dad when he was suffering from Alzheimer's. Maria writes in her book, *I've Been Thinking...* "He didn't know my name or his own. He wasn't even talking much anymore. I was sitting with him at the table, trying to engage him about something that was clearly uninteresting to him, when he looked me dead in the eye and said, 'You know, you have to go internal if you want to go eternal.'"

The only way to truly live is to feel from the inside. Pause, breathe, gain perspective, find stillness and you will be One. You will be eternal—without an end or beginning.

If you find yourself lost, be with it. How often have you or someone you loved been at rock bottom only to come out the most incredible, new version of themselves? It's because they stepped off the path and took time to heal. They went internal—some for a very long time. When they stepped back into the external world, they had eternal love for themselves.

SEPTEMBER 16

TAKE ACTION

"First tell yourself what kind of person you want to be, then do what
you have to do. For in nearly every pursuit we see this to be the case.
Those in athletic pursuit first choose the sport they want,
and then do the work."

- Epictetus

What kind of person do you want to be? It's important to
know what your values are, what your goals are, and what
you want in life but after contemplation you must take action.

If you want to be more independent, you must take yourself out of your
comfort zone and venture out. If you want to start your own business, you
need to step away from all your notes and put yourself in situations where
you can practice what you want to create. If you want to be a more
compassionate person, be aware of everything happening around you and
then do something to share compassion.

It's one thing to write down who you want to be, but it won't happen
unless you practice who you want to become. Stoic philosopher Marcus
Aurelius said, "Waste no more time arguing what a good man should be.
Be one."

SEPTEMBER 17

MONK MINDSET

"The monk mindset lifts us out of confusion and distraction
and helps us find clarity, meaning, and direction."
- *Jay Shetty*

Former monk, Jay Shetty is the author of the book *Think Like a Monk*. He has taken his experience at the ashram and weaved what he learned into practical wisdom for us. The book is not about how to become like a monk but how to *think* like a monk.

In the yoga world, we often refer to the "monkey mind". This is the wandering mind that jumps from one thought to the next and then back again. Shetty compares the monkey mind vs. the monk mind. He says, "Our minds can either elevate us or pull us down."

The monkey mind is often overwhelmed while the monk mind is focused on the root of the issue. The monkey mind complains, compares, and criticizes while the monk mind is compassionate, caring, and collaborative. The monkey mind is distracted by small things while the monk mind is disciplined. The monkey mind seeks short-term gratification while the monk mind pursues long-term gain. The monkey mind looks for pleasure while the monk mind looks for meaning.

Notice today which mindset you are in. As often as you can—think like a monk.

SEPTEMBER 18

ASK WHAT IS NOT WRONG

"We should learn to ask, "What's not wrong?"
and be in touch with that. There are so many elements
in the world and within our bodies, feelings, perceptions,
and consciousness that are wholesome, refreshing, and healing."

- Thích Nhất Hanh

So much in life is about perspective—how turning things upside down can bring you greater joy. Instead of looking at what it is not, look at what it is. Instead of asking yourself or others what is wrong, ask what is right. When we focus on the negative, we create more negative. When we focus on the positive, guess what? We create more positive.

Look at what is right in your life. Focus on what you like about your body. Marinate in happiness. When you are healthy, notice being healthy and how you feel. We gravitate to suffering and get swallowed up like it's quicksand. If you become aware of all the goodness that surrounds you, you will be able to navigate through the hard things when they arise.

You see the secret to happiness is happiness itself. Ask not what is wrong but what is right. Fill yourself up with nature, with stillness, with gratitude, and love and you will become aware of all that is right.

SEPTEMBER 19

WHY ARE WE SO HARD ON OURSELVES?

*"You have been criticizing yourself for years and it hasn't worked.
Try approving of yourself and see what happens."*
- Louise Hay

W hy are we so concerned with how our body looks? It scares me that so many women (and men) spend their lives obsessing about the number on the scale or the size of their jeans. I know first hand how this obsession can turn into an illness. I battled anorexia for years during college and beyond, and while I definitely don't have all the answers, I did learn some things:

1. There is something deeper happening inside of you. When you are controlled by the way your body looks, it is because your heart and soul are hurting. It is usually something that happened in your childhood. Dig deep and heal.

2. You worry so much about what others are thinking about your body. Guess what? Nobody cares—they are thinking about their own body and what *you* may be thinking! Please, can we stop this madness?

3. When you focus on the way you look, you are wasting your life. When I had an eating disorder, every second of every day was about me. Looking back, that brings me the most sadness. I wasn't a good friend, I wasn't a giving person—I was selfish and not in a good way.

Be kind to yourself. You are not your body. You have a body that needs you to love it, care for it, nourish it but not make it an obsession.

SEPTEMBER 20

LEARN WHEN YOU SUFFER

"The truth is that relative income is not directly related to happiness.
Nonpartisan social-survey data clearly show that the
big driver of happiness is earned success: A person's belief that
he has created value in his life or the life of others."

- Arthur Brooks

People misunderstand the goal in seeking happiness. We think that happiness is not suffering but you cannot have happiness without suffering. The key is to make peace with your unhappiness. This happens when you sit with your unhappiness and become aware of the emotion you are experiencing. When you do this, your emotion moves from an unconscious reaction to a thoughtful, conscious response.

People want happiness without purpose. We worry that if our happiness has purpose, we could suffer. Here we are missing the goal. You learn when you suffer. Your negative emotions are important and can teach you so much. When your happiness has purpose, your life has value.

Learn to observe your emotions. Name them but don't let them become you. The next time you are unhappy make peace with your unhappiness and know that it creates space for happiness.

SEPTEMBER 21

WHICH ONE ARE YOU?

"The point of the *varnas* is to help you understand yourself
so you can focus on your strongest skills and inclinations."
- Jay Shetty

Acording to the *Bhagavad Gita* there are four personality types called the *varnas.* We are all still equal, but our personality demonstrates different talents and skills. Understanding our varna, helps us to become our true self.

The four varnas are the Guide, the Leader, the Creator, and the Maker:

Guides are those who enjoy serving others. You can find this personality in teachers, coaches, and mentors. Guides thrive on learning, sharing, and gaining wisdom.

The Leader is inspirational and driven. This personality does well engaging others and is often found in politics, law enforcement, military, and justice.

The third personality is the Creator. Creators are the salespeople, entertainers, producers, entrepreneurs, and CEOs. They love networking and brainstorming. They work hard and play hard.

The fourth personality is the Maker. Makers are driven by stability and security. This personality is supportive and inventive. Makers are social workers, therapists, doctors, nurses, engineers, cooks, and more.

Knowing your personality will help you to follow your dreams and create your best life.

PARADOXICAL UNITY

"Being and nonbeing produce each other.
The difficult is born in the easy. Long is defined by short,
the high by the low. Before and after go along with each other."

- Lao-Tzu

I t is our belief system that creates our reality. If you can change your belief system, you can change your life. We believe something to be true because we believe its opposite to be true.

To change your belief system it takes awareness, practice, and patience. Every time you identify something as one way, pause, become aware of what you have identified as its opposite, and then see them as the same.

In the *Tao Te Ching*, Lao-Tzu writes in the second verse, "So the sage lives openly with apparent duality and paradoxical unity. The sage can act without effort and teach without words. Nurturing things without possessing them, he works, but not for rewards; he competes, but not for results. When the work is done, it is forgotten. That is why it lasts forever."

Let go of defining something as so. Just be. When you let go, you find. When you eliminate opposites, you unify them.

SEPTEMBER 23

CHANGE YOUR DEFAULT HABITS

"Remember that your ruling reason becomes unconquerable when it rallies and relies on itself, so that it won't do anything contrary to its own will, even if its position is irrational. How much more unconquerable if its judgments are careful and made rationally? Therefore, the mind freed from passions is an impenetrable fortress —a person has no more secure place of refuge for all time."

- Marcus Aurelius

Train yourself to do the right thing without thinking. To do this you must first become aware of how you habitually react to a situation. Do you automatically react with anger in conflict? Do you judge before you get to know someone? Do you complain before you appreciate?

You can change your default habits. Observe how you react to a situation today. Use the insight to do something different. Stop yourself from your typical response if it is causing you and others pain and begin a new pattern of response. Smile instead of tensing up. Listen instead of talk. Be grateful for what is good.

Remember that you have the power to rewire your brain. It does take practice but you can do it. Turn your habitual reaction into a thoughtful response.

SEPTEMBER 24

THE WISE PERSON

"This is why we say that nothing happens
to the wise person contrary to their expectations."

- Seneca

What is it that makes someone wise? Is it age? Is it knowledge? The wise person is the one who can manage their expectations. The wise life is simple because it is curious, prepared, and resilient.

Wise people do not think anything is "unbelievable". They are prepared for both the best and worst case scenarios. There is no wishing or hoping for the wise, there is acceptance of whatever may come their way. Wise people have a reverse approach—they expect things to go wrong so they can learn and grow.

Instead of being surprised, marvel at what life brings you. Wisdom cannot be taught. It comes from your soul, while knowledge comes from your mind. The wise have a knowing that comes from something bigger than themselves.

The wise person not only accepts the present moment but learns from it and shares it. The wise person does not question what is outside of his/her control but self-inquiry is paramount. The wise know what they do not know. As Shakespeare put it, "The fool doth think he is wise, but the wise man knows himself to be a fool."

SEPTEMBER 25

TRUTH POWER

"Satyagraha is a weapon of the strong; it admits of no violence under any circumstance whatsoever; and it ever insist upon truth."
- Gandhi

Satyagraha is the Sanskrit word that Gandhi created to embody the idea that wars can be won by transforming your opponents. He believed and confirmed through his actions that you could overcome your opponents by changing them with respectful and patient persistence. This "truth power," as it is also referred to as, makes great change through love, truth, and non-violence.

Truth power brought the Indian Relief Bill in South Africa; it united long-separated political territories; it stopped civil war and more. The idea of truth power was conveyed centuries before Gandhi in Lao-Tzu's, *Tao Te Ching*: "Yield and prevail. Bend and be straightened. Empty and be filled... The great man embraces the One, and becomes its model to the empire. Not showing off, he shines. Not asserting himself, he becomes known. Not taking credit, he is acclaimed. Not boasting, he endures. He does not strive against others, so others do not contend with him."

Think of satyagraha, truth power, as eliminating antagonism without harming the antagonist. We can do this in our lives by transforming conflict to a higher level that brings peace.

SEPTEMBER 26

GET UP AND MOVE

"Emotion is energy in motion."

- Peter McWilliams

The best way to learn something and make it a part of you is through emotional movement. You must feel, move, and embody what you desire. Without this kind of energy nothing happens.

Just having intellectual understanding is not enough. You must then feel the information and link emotion with knowledge. Then, after taking the knowledge into your brain and into your heart, you must repeat and repeat so you embody it and it becomes your physical identity.

The best way to take knowledge and make it a part of you emotionally is to move. Bring energy to your desires. The higher your energy, the higher your performance. Bring action into your life. Train yourself to have energy. Make it a habit to get in a state of emotion. Maybe you sit up taller, put a smile on your face, pat yourself on the back. Choose something that trains your body and your mind that you are up to something that could change the world.

To keep this energy flowing it's important to take breaks. When you are working on a project, stand up often and shake out your body. Turn on some music and have a dance party. Jump on a mini trampoline for a few minutes. Go outside and do a yoga pose. When you move your body, information has time to rest and reset. Just a few minutes, recharges you mentally and physically.

SEPTEMBER 27

LET GO AS THEY HAPPEN

"That one is dear to me who runs not after pleasant
or away from painful, grieves not, lusts not,
but lets things come and go as they happen."
- The Bhagavad Gita

Let go as they happen. I will often say, "I don't *mind* what happens." They key word is "mind" because it is our minds that put meaning into everything. When you let go of naming, blaming, and putting meaning into the events that happen in your life, you will see you are right where you are supposed to be.

Life just is. We put the meaning into it. So, the question ,"What is the meaning of life?" cannot be answered. The question should be, "What do you make your life mean?" Instead of looking outside yourself for the answer, you have to look inward.

What do you make your life mean? Are you the victim in your life or are you a gift to this world? Do you choose suffering or joy? Is your life filled with learning or do you think you know it all? Are you grateful for what you have or do you always wish for more?

Let go of making things, especially things that are outside of your control, mean something. Just relax and be present to whatever life offers you. Soon enough you will see that you will not mind what happens. In the words of Marcus Aurelius, "External things are not the problem. It's your assessment of them. Which you can erase right now."

SEPTEMBER 28

TWO KINDS OF HAPPINESS

"If you want happiness for an hour, take a nap. If you want
happiness for a day, go fishing. If you want happiness for a year,
inherit a fortune. If you want happiness for a lifetime,
help someone else."

- Chinese Proverb

There are two ways to experience happiness. One way is the enjoyment of pleasure through our senses. I call this external happiness. This happiness initiates a response to a stimulus or behavior. External happiness is found in what heightens our senses: The taste of an ice cream cone. The smell of flowers. The sight of your child. The feeling from a wonderful hug. The sound of the ocean. These are the "simple pleasures" of life.

The second way to experience happiness is through our mind and our heart. I call this internal happiness. It is felt in your soul. This deeper level of happiness is found through love, compassion, generosity, and gratitude. This happiness is true joy.

Happiness found through our senses is fleeting and is experienced as a result of something outside of us. External happiness makes us feel good for a short time while internal happiness brings complete joy to us and to others for a lifetime.

SEPTEMBER 29

TEACH CHILDREN

"We take our kids to so many practices - sports, music, etc.
But do they practice being a good person?
We are good at practicing everything but humanity."
- *Dr. Michele Borba*

C hildren learn from us and from their environment. We need to make a conscious effort to teach our children that we are all one. Without even knowing it, we create our children's unconscious prejudices.

Our children find comfort in the familiar. When they see something that is "different" they become cautious and fearful. As a result, if they see a person of a different color or different to them in any way, children get anxious and retreat. We often don't even know it's happening.

Practice humanity with your children. Teach them the concept of "same-same". This means that trees, animals, the sky, humans, and even emotions are the same. We are all connected and dependent on each other. No one thing is better than another.

Teach them to look for the soul in every living thing. Souls are all the same—they are love and truth. We must bring more diversity into our children's lives. Do everything you can to change your child's perspective. Let them see themselves in others.

SEPTEMBER 30

DETACHMENT

*"The ego and the Self dwell in the same body.
The former eats the sweet and sour fruits of the tree of life,
while the latter looks on in detachment."*

- Mundaka Upanishad

The only way to truly acquire something in life is to let it go. When we are attached to the outcome, we will never truly have it. Look at your goals and aspirations in life as your reason for being—not the result of them.

You must believe in yourself to let go of your attachments. Deepak Chopra said, "The moment we combine one-pointed intention with detachment to the outcome, we will have that which we desire."

Detachment is simple when you love the *Now* with all you've got. Surrender to the outcome because you know that it will be just as it should be. When you are attached to something, you are doubting the universe— you are doubting yourself.

Your attachments are not you. When you detach from them, you find joy. Detach from outcomes. Detach from belongings. Detach from people. Detach from your thoughts. When you do this, your life will fill up magically. The outcome will be more than you dreamed. You will have abundance in all areas of your life.

OCTOBER

OCTOBER 1

YOU ARE LIMITLESS

"Don't you see the plants, the birds, the ants and spiders and bees
going about their individual tasks, putting the world in order, as best
they can? And you're not willing to do your job as a human being?
Why aren't you running to do what your nature demands?"
- Marcus Aurelius

Y ou are pure potentiality. You were given this life to be great and
anything is possible for you. Your potential comes from knowing
who you are—not who your ego or the world says you are.

You can create the life you want. If your dreams and goals come from
your true self, there is nothing stopping you. The cultivation of self is a daily
practice. Sit with yourself often. Listen and hear your knowing. Know that
you are an offering to this world and you are limitless.

When you are uncertain, observe nature. Watch, listen, and observe how
everything is possible and how it can be achieved effortlessly. Constantly
pursue what you love and every day become a little better at it. Have a
willingness to learn and a desire to grow. Your nature is to be great. Embrace
it and keep becoming better day after day.

OCTOBER 2

LET YOUR MIND BE YOUR ALLY

"The mind is everything. What you think you become."
- Buddha

I have probably said, "You are not your thoughts." This is true if you spend the majority of your time in your ruminating, made-up movie-making mind. You are not your thoughts if they are not serving you. If they are not helping you and the world, they are not you. But you are your thoughts if they are compassionate, curious, and open to learning more about yourself and others.

Be intentional with your thoughts. Train your mind to work for you, not against you. Let your mind be your ally. Work together to process life in a positive, evolving, and unconditional way. You and your mind are stuck with one another—why not become friends?

You can allow your mind to create the most incredible life for you or you can allow it to create suffering. You can allow your mind to look at all that you have instead of what you do not. Your mind can always be learning or it can atrophy.

Your mind can redirect your path. It is up to you. Marcus Aurelius wrote, "Indeed, no one can thwart the purposes of your mind—for they can't be touched by fire, steel, tyranny, slander, or anything."

OCTOBER 3

UNDERSTANDING

"When you plant lettuce, if it does not grow well, you don't blame the lettuce. You look into the reasons it is not doing well."
- *Thích Nhất Hanh*

What if we really tried to understand each other? Imagine someone you love and make it a priority to know them better. Even if this person has been in your life since you were born, there is still more to know.

Knowing leads to understanding which erases blame. When you blame someone, it is like closing a door in their face. While taking the time to understand someone, is an invitation to come in for a cup of tea.

Understanding is another word for love and for compassion. In *Peace is Every Step,* Thích Nhất Hanh said, "When you understand, you cannot help but love. You cannot get angry. To develop understanding, you have to practice looking at all living beings with the eyes of compassion."

Understanding takes patience. Instead of reacting by making the other person wrong, pause, and think about what they may be going through. Put yourself in their shoes and let understanding and compassion guide your response.

OCTOBER 4

LEAST EFFORT

*"An integral being knows without going,
sees without looking, and accomplishes without doing."*
- Lao-Tzu

There is a wonderful little book by Deepak Chopra called *The Seven Spiritual Laws of Success*. One of the seven is the "Law of Least Effort." We have talked about how life becomes effortless when you choose to let life happen for you, not to you. We've talked about how effort leads to effortlessness. If you practice what you love, in time it will feel effortless.

In Chopra's book, he says there are three things you can do to live a life of least effort. "The first thing is to accept people, situations, and events as they are, not as you wish they were, in this moment." This way of being is so important. There is nothing wrong with intending for things to be different in the future, but this moment is just as it should be.

The second way Chopra says to live a life of least effort is to take responsibility for your life and anything you believe to be a "problem". Turn your problems into opportunities for growth. When everything in your life becomes your teacher, your life is transformed.

The third way to put the "Law of Least Effort" into action is "to practice defenselessness. This means relinquishing the need to convince others of your point of view." Since you are open to all points of view, life flows with effortless ease.

OCTOBER 5

ACTION LOOKS BORING

"Nearly all the things that shake the world come out of nowhere.
A boring (looking) scientist or businessman hard at work changes
things far more than someone sitting around with a
mission statement and a proclamation to change the world."

- Kyle Eschenroeder

There are so many distractions in our life. From social media to keeping up with the Joneses, to all the apps where you compare yourself to others. Do you know the best way to succeed in life? Keep your head down and quietly do the work.

While everyone else is tooting their own horn, you are moving forward. Action by action, you get the job done. You don't look for praise or attention. You know that all of the outside noise will not bring you happiness, nor will it accomplish the task.

Keep your head down and you will reap the benefit. Kahlil Gibran wrote in *The Prophet*, "But I say to you that when you work you fulfill a part of earth's furthest dream, assigned to you when that dream was born, and in keeping yourself with labour you are in truth loving life, and to love life through labour is to be intimate with life's inmost secret."

OCTOBER 6

THE SMALL MOMENTS

"Life isn't a matter of milestones, but of moments."
- Rose Kennedy

It's the small moments that make up your life. The first sip of your morning coffee. The look from your partner as you head out the door. Your child's lingering embrace. The morning sun on your face. The smell of freshly baked bread. The quiet time in your home. The laughter with your friends. The feeling of fresh sheets. So much joy is communicated in these moments even while nothing is said.

When you look back on your life, yes you will remember the weddings, the baby being born, milestone birthday celebrations, but it is the trivial that truly becomes the most meaningful. It is because these moments are who you really are. When you feel gratitude for the small moments, your life becomes one offering of joy after another.

Take time to embrace the small moments today. Notice what makes you smile. Notice what makes you pause. Notice what fills you up. These are the small moments that make your life grand.

OCTOBER 7

PARTNERS

"Love one another, but make not a bond of love: Let it rather be a
moving sea between the shores of your souls. Fill each other's cup
but drink not from one cup. Give one another of your bread but eat
not from the same loaf. Sing and dance together and be joyous,
but let each one of you be alone."

- Kahlil Gibran

I believe that an intimate, lasting relationship with another human
being flourishes when each partner evolves independently. The union
of a couple is beautiful, but when each grows separately they have so much
more to offer each other and the world.

Love is a tricky word. Our culture has created love to be what we see in a
romantic movie—remember when Tom Cruise said, "You complete me" in
Jerry Macguire? A partner should not complete you. You are complete and
whole as you are. Love creates more love. When you love yourself first, that
love expands to be shared with others. It is not given to others. The love you
carry radiates out, but it always remains in you.

Make a life together, but make a life independently as well. Have your
own hobbies, different interests, your own thoughts, your own dreams, and
then together every day is a new adventure.

OCTOBER 8

WALKING

"Walk as if you are kissing the earth with your feet."
- *Thích Nhất Hanh*

There is something sacred about taking a walk. It nourishes you physically, mentally, and spiritually. It's beautiful and meaningful to take a walk just for the sake of walking—not to get your steps in or to talk on the phone, but to breathe, think, and soak up nature.

Walking can be a meditation. Breathing in and breathing out, you step as if to massage the earth with your feet. You walk gently with gratitude. Picture Times Square in New York City where everyone is rushing and there is a lot of noise. It is like the earth is being trampled. Wherever you are, walk mindfully.

Give yourself some time and space to walk with ease. Leave peaceful footprints on our earth. Thích Nhất Hanh visualizes it like this, "Every step makes a flower bloom under our feet. We can do it only if we do not think of the future or the past, if we know that life can only be found in the present moment."

As you walk, use your five senses. What do you see? What do you hear? What do you smell? What do you taste? And what do you feel? Breathe in— step, step, step, step. Breathe out—step, step, step, step.

OCTOBER 9

FINDING FULFILLMENT

*"Gain some internal control over your mind
and how you react to life's difficulties. Then, adopt an ethic of
compassion and altruism, the urge to help others.
Finally, act on that outlook in whatever ways your life offers."*

- Dalai Lama

Fulfillment comes from having something to do, someone to love, and gratitude for life's journey.

Seek out work that is a labor of love. You have unique talents that the world needs to know about. Create something that leaves a mark in a positive way. Be fulfilled by your work and share it with others. You are here to fulfill a purpose. Create your vision and then be that vision. Let your work come from a place of being, not doing.

Having someone to love fulfills our need for connection. Victor Frankl wrote in *Yes to Life*, "Do we know the feeling that overtakes us when we are in the presence of a particular person and, roughly translates as the fact that this person exists in the world at all, this alone makes this world, and a life in it, meaningful."

It is important to know that it is the obstacles in our lives that add meaning and fulfillment. Accepting, learning, and moving forward after suffering brings you closer to your true self. German poet and philosopher Hölderlin wrote, "If I step onto my misfortune, I stand higher."

OCTOBER 10

IDEOLOGY

"The world is always close to catastrophe.
But it seems to be closer now. Seeing this approaching catastrophe,
most of us take shelter in idea. We think that this catastrophe,
this crisis, can be solved by an ideology. Ideology is always
an impediment to direct relationship, which prevents action."
- Jiddu Krishnamurti

When you are faced with a crisis, come back to the current moment. Not what has happened in the past. Not what you think may happen. Take action in the Now. Pay attention to what is needed in the present situation and then act on it. Action will take you out of rumination and into the best choices to navigate the obstacle.

When you focus on how to solve the crisis at hand, you let go of your ideologies. How *you* think something should go is not the only answer. Be open to the endless possibilities. Life is constantly varied and this makes life interesting.

OCTOBER 11

NOTHINGNESS

"The essence of all things is emptiness."
- Eckhart Tolle

E verything comes from nothing and within nothing you can find everything. Look around you. The chair you are sitting on. The house that you are in. The family you have built. They all began as nothing.

Everything in life exists because it was once nothing. There is an emptiness that can be perceived as beautiful. Listen for the sound of birds… it exists because of silence. Just appreciate and be present. If you spend time trying to make the emptiness mean something, you will miss the song.

The *Heart Sutra* from ancient Buddhist texts states, "Form is emptiness, emptiness is form." Become aware of the space around you. Be less focused on the objects. Feel the spaciousness. Feel the emptiness that is wrapping its arms around you. This feeling is pure consciousness. In this stillness, you find your true self. Hence, you find everything.

If you need something more concrete - think of looking up at all the stars on a clear night. What allows for all the billions of stars to exist but space. Magnificence is nothingness and nothingness is magnificent. Remember: It is the space between your thoughts where true joy is found.

OCTOBER 12

GOING DOWN A RABBIT HOLE

"How satisfying it is to dismiss and block out any upsetting or foreign impression, and immediately to have peace in all things."
- Marcus Aurelius

Peace is found in the present moment. As living, thinking human beings, we repetitively turn our attention away from that peace. There is this expression about "going down a rabbit hole". We decide to check our social media and then an hour later we come back up for air. Or we start a conversation with a colleague about politics and thirty minutes later he storms out. Is the peace still there?

Know what your triggers are and avoid them. You have too much good to offer this world to go down rabbit holes. If the temptation is there, it is so difficult to turn the other way. If it is wasted time on social media, delete the apps from your phone or set a goal to only check for five minutes in the morning and five minutes at night. If talking about politics makes you angry, don't start the conversation or share your opinion.

Notice how you are feeling when you want to succumb to a negative habit. See if you can sit with the feeling for a few minutes before you begin. Visualize what is most important to you and ask yourself, "Will this action help me to achieve my goals?"

The more you practice self-control, the easier it will become. You will turn wasted energy into positive, productive energy.

OCTOBER 13

LIFE IS AN EXPERIMENT

"All life is an experiment.
The more experiments you make the better."
- *Ralph Waldo Emerson*

Isn't that a great way to look at life? Go out there and experiment! If you're not sure what you want to do for work...try lots of different things. Learn what you enjoy and what you do not enjoy. If you're not sure if you are ready to date after a long relationship ended...give it a try. If you're not sure what to do for a hobby...experiment with lots of them.

What holds us back from experimenting is fear. As Buddha said, "Fear does not prevent death. It prevents life." Fear of failure is life's greatest enemy. When you live your life as an experiment, then everything is an opportunity for growth. There is no such thing as failure when you live this way.

The more often you try new things and explore different possibilities, the further away fear travels. This will change your perception of fear. It will not hold you back but instead, the thrill of experimentation will drive you forward.

When life is an experiment, you are not attached to the outcome because you are enjoying the current experience. This life outlook will bring you profound happiness.

OCTOBER 14

MAKE THE ORDINARY A RITUAL

*"A daily ritual is a way of saying
I'm voting for myself, I'm taking care of myself."*
- Mariel Hemingway

Your life can be a spiritual experience. When you turn your ordinary activities into a ritual, your life will become sacred. This doesn't mean that you have to sit in meditation to reap the benefits. It could be your first cup of coffee in the morning. It could be your daily walk with your dog. It could be your lunch date with a friend. It could be your workout at your gym.

To experience deeper happiness, find rituals to organize your life. These moments will help you to pause, appreciate, and experience life more fully. It's a shift in the way you look at and perceive the activities in your life. Instead of just doing, you are being.

You will be surprised by how many things you are currently doing that you can turn into a ritual. The key is to be aware and present. If you decide to make your morning coffee a ritual, put your phone in the other room. Maybe light a candle and enjoy every sip as you gaze at the light.

Layer meaning into the ordinary. Find the gratitude, simplicity, and joy in your daily life. Instead of mundane—your life will be magical.

OCTOBER 15

OPTIMISM OF CHILDREN

*"A child's laugh could simply be
one of the most beautiful sounds in the world."*
- Unknown

Wherever you go in the world, the laughter of children is universally uplifting. Children help us pause and see that joy is found in the moment. They teach us about simplicity. They teach us about living in the present. They teach us about innocence.

The beautiful thing is that all of this is still inside of you. Look at life through the eyes of a child as often as you can. The wonder and excitement. The glee and curiosity. The possibility and the adventure. These are traits you were born with. The optimism of children can guide you to a better tomorrow.

It's important to let our children be children. When we rush them to the next stage, the laughter fades away. Let them play, sing, and dance. Let the world be filled with the sound of a child's laugh. It brings us hope. It lifts our spirits. It guides us to follow in their footsteps.

OCTOBER 16

SAY, "I DON'T KNOW."

"When they think that they know the answers,
people are difficult to guide.
When they know they do not know,
people can find their own way."

- Lao-Tzu

We think we are weak saying we don't know the answer to a question or how to accomplish a task. I believe the opposite to be true. It shows you are curious. You are eager to learn and open to being guided. You know yourself and part of that is becoming aware of what you do not know.

Trust the unknown. When you do not know, the door opens to a new perspective or way of being. You unlock a pathway to your true self. By saying, "I don't know" your ego softens and your soul moves forward. The more often you say it, the more fulfilled your life will be.

Allow others to say "I don't know" to you. Try not to force your ideas and opinions on them. Give them time to think and process. Then guide them to learn and benefit from your wisdom. Keep it simple, humble, and let the "student" feel they are learning on their own.

OCTOBER 17

CHOOSE PEACE

*"If peace mattered to you more than anything else
and if you knew yourself to be spirit rather than a little me,
you would remain nonreactive and absolutely alert
when confronted with challenging people or situations."*

- Eckhart Tolle

L et life act through you—not to you. As soon as something happens, become one with it. Use your breath to bring you peace in every situation. Then your response comes from a deeper place. It is not reactive but responsive.

As soon as you think something should have happened differently, then life is happening TO you and not FOR you. Peace floats away and discontent takes over. If you want the future to be different, take action now. But if you ruminate in what should have been, there is no peace.

Peace is in the present moment. Accept, respond consciously, and take action to learn, grow, and make change if you desire a better tomorrow. Eckhart Tolle says, "There are three words that convey the secret of the art of living, the secret of all success and happiness: One With Life. Being one with life is being one with the Now. You then realize that you don't live your life, but life lives you. Life is the dancer, and you are the dance."

OCTOBER 18

GRATEFUL EATING

*"And when you crush an apple with your teeth, say to it in your heart,
'Your seeds shall live in my body, and the buds of your tomorrow
shall blossom in my heart, and your fragrance shall be my breath,
and together we shall rejoice through all the seasons.'"*
- Kahlil Gibran

E ating is a necessity and a pleasure. How often do you give thanks
for your food? I invite you to begin a practice of grateful eating.
When you sit down for a meal, spend a few moments thinking about
and being grateful for the food you are about to enjoy. First give thanks to
the earth, the sun, and the rain that provided the environment for your food.
Think of the farmers that grew the vegetables. Then think about those that
packaged the food and those that transported the food to your hometown.
Acknowledge the store and the employees that work so you may have fresh
food. Bow in gratitude that you are able to have healthy food and that it will
nourish your body.

An important part of grateful eating is to send compassion to those that
go hungry. Think of the 957 million people in our world who do not have
enough to eat. Hold them close to your heart and with gratitude for what
you have, commit to helping those less fortunate.

Grateful eating brings a deeper connection to your food, to those that
you share it with, and to the greater good of our world.

OCTOBER 19

REMOVE BLOCKS

"Have you cleared the path you want to travel? Are you ready, willing, and able to do whatever it takes to have what you want?"
- Melody Beattie

M ake the road to what you want clear. As you set out on your journey, there will be obstacles. Become aware of what sets you back and plan to remove obstacles before you even start.

If your goal is to run a road race and you know that your nutrition needs improvement, get all the junk food out of your house and fill your refrigerator with healthy options. If your goal is to get a new job and you know procrastination is blocking you, clear out the distractions in your life. If your goal is to meet your life partner, but the past is like a boulder in the road, make the commitment to let go of the past and begin again.

What is it that is holding you back? Become aware of your obstacles and consciously remove them before you move forward. There will often be obstacles along the way that are unplanned, but they are there to teach us something.

When you know the obstacle before you begin, you have the power to remove it. Victor Frankl writes, "Man does not simply exist but always decides what his existence will be, what he will become the next moment. By the same token, every human being has the freedom to change at any instant."

OCTOBER 20

YOU ARE THE GURU

"Even if you haven't met your guru, your guru is there."
- Ram Dass

If you are searching for a *guru*, you can stop searching. Everything you need is inside of you. If you think finding a guru will help guide your way, you will become misdirected. Everybody has a guru. Your guru is your soul.

The word guru connotes "teacher" in Sanskrit. You will always be your greatest teacher. Searching for a guru will be fruitless because you are it! Look inside and you will find.

Slow down and listen to your guru. It is always speaking to you. That quiet voice, that nudge, the whisper of what is always right. You are your own guru. Follow your intuition and it will lead you to your inner guru. It has been said that intuition is knowing without knowing. This is because your guru knows what is best for you. Listen for the messages from your soul.

Be your own guru. Walk your own walk and allow your soul to guide you. Beautifully said by Natalie Brite, "One day you will have to make the choice to discover your own light and be your own guru instead of seeking it within other forces. On that day, you will take your power back, and see the game change."

OCTOBER 21

CONNECTION

*"Vulnerability is the essence of connection
and connection is the essence of existence."*
- Leo Christopher

I have this thing with paradoxes. I actually think life is a paradox. I often find that truth is found in the opposite. It's about looking at life from a different perspective. This is true when we look at vulnerability. When we become vulnerable, we back away because of fear and shame. What if we welcomed vulnerability? What if we dove in deep and opened ourselves up to what we were afraid of?

We all seek connection. It is why we are here. Often we are afraid to show our true selves because we think others will not like us. Here's the paradox: The more vulnerable you are, the more you are loved and connected with others. Being vulnerable is being true to yourself. If your vulnerability stops you from connecting with others, you will be disconnected. If you lean into your vulnerability, a whole new world will open up.

Embrace vulnerability. It makes you beautiful. It makes you authentic. It will profoundly connect you with others. Your choice: vulnerability as fear and shame or vulnerability as love and connection.

OCTOBER 22

BEST FRIEND OR WORST FRIEND

"You have power over your mind—not outside events.
Realize this and you will find strength."
- Marcus Aurelius

Your mind can be your best friend or your worst friend. You deserve kindness, compassion, and love. Is your mind being your friend or your enemy? Is your self-talk full of self-love or is your self-talk destructive and unkind?

Take time every day to observe your thoughts. Meditation is a great way to notice your thought patterns and distractions. As the negative thoughts come in, just observe as if you were watching clouds go by. See if you can practice non-judgment. As you become aware of your thoughts, then you can change them. Self-destruction becomes self-love.

Another great way to understand your mind and let it become an ally is by journaling. Writing brings clarity. By jotting down your thoughts, you will begin to see patterns and then you can weave a new way of thinking.

You do have power over your mind. From *The Bhagavad Gita*, Krishna says, "One who can control the mind and attain tranquility, to that man heat and cold, pleasure and pain, honor and dishonor are the same." Choose for your mind to be your best friend. What a beautiful existence that will be.

OCTOBER 23

SOLOMON'S PARADOX

*"The funny thing about advice is,
we always tell others the things we can't really do ourselves."*
- R.M. Drake

Isn't it interesting that we are able to help with other people's problems with more ease than our own? There is even a name for this: Solomon's Paradox. Solomon's Paradox is named after King Solomon who was the third leader of the Jewish Kingdom. He was known as a sage of great wisdom. Unfortunately, as wise as he was for others, he was the opposite in his own life. He made many, many bad decisions for himself throughout his life.

We tend to empathize better with others than with ourselves. When our friend has a problem, we are able to step back and look at the situation with a wider perspective. The paradox is that when you are removed from a situation, you can see it more clearly.

So, if we can help others with this perspective, can we distance ourselves from our own issues and zoom out to solve them? We can by thinking in the third person. Instead of saying, "Why do I feel this way?" Say, "Why does she feel this way?"

It comes back to being the observer of your thoughts. You can solve the Solomon Paradox by becoming the witness. Step outside of your mind and look at your personal problems as your best friend would.

OCTOBER 24

HIDDEN VIRTUE

"The Tao produces but does not possess;
the Tao gives without expecting;
the Tao fosters growth without ruling.
This is called hidden virtue."

- Lao-Tzu

Your life is an amazing gift to the world. You get to create, love, learn, and share all you have to offer. When you look at your life as an offering, it changes everything. In the 51st verse of the *Tao Te Ching*, Lao-Tzu refers to this way of being as "hidden virtue".

Hidden virtue is the awareness that you are responsible for your life. You get to choose who you want to become and how you will live your life. Many of us think we were born into a certain role or have to be a certain way to please others, but your hidden virtue welcomes you to be your true self. You are open to live without expectations. You can be like nature: natural, organic, just as it should be.

Think of this hidden virtue as your magic power. Instead of being part of a mold, you are part of eternity. Wayne Dwyer explains it like this, "... pay homage to the inner virtue that is your life. That power is in my hand as I write these words, and it's in your eyes as they read this page. Trust in it. Worship it. Feel safe in the force that remains hidden. This is all you need to feel complete."

OCTOBER 25

DO WHAT YOU CAN

*"I cannot do all the good that the world needs.
But the world needs all the good that I can do."*

- Jana Stanfield

There are so many things going on in our world today that have the potential to break our hearts. From climate change, to politics, to inequality, to hunger, to war…the list goes on and on. What can we do? How can we help? How do we bring light to a dark world?

It starts with you and the energy you release into the world. Complaining about these issues and being afraid of where we are going does not help. Make the commitment to only release love and compassion to our world. Do what you can every day to make change. Let your carbon footprint be gentle and nurturing.

Take action in ways you can make a difference. Maybe you become educated on where your food is coming from. Maybe you power your home with renewable energy. Perhaps you invest in education or volunteer for a non-profit that eases world hunger. The point is…the world needs you.

I believe our world runs on a vibration from the energy we release. You get to choose if you contribute to a low frequency or a high frequency. The energy you send out contributes greatly to the energy of the world. Do your part to lift us all up. Ram Dass said, "We're all just walking each other home." Let it be a walk of grace, hope, and action.

OCTOBER 26

TEACH HUMANITY

"We are the world. We are the children.
We are the ones who make a brighter tomorrow,
so let's start giving."
- Lionel Richie

We should teach humanity in school. Our children need to be taught how to be compassionate to themselves, to others, and to our world. Education is universal. We are missing the greatest opportunity to teach our children what is most important: kindness, compassion, self-love, and equanimity. They were born with it but life has buried it.

If I could create a class for the core curriculum beginning in kindergarten through senior year in high school, it would be called Humanity. It would teach children about their inner voice. How loving themselves comes first. It would teach children how to be compassionate toward others and themselves. It would teach empathy by understanding the needs of our world. Children would learn how to listen to their peers and listen to their own souls speak. Meditation and breathing techniques would become a daily ritual.

In Humanity class, children would learn that happiness comes from within and the greatest joy comes from being grateful for what you have and from helping others. Children would learn that we are all one. There is no doubt that this all starts in the home, but how life-changing it would be if it was part of our world's education plan.

OCTOBER 27

LINE OF SOULS

"Souls love. That's what souls do."

- Ram Dass

W hen you look at every being as a soul there is no separation. There is no one above you or below you. This is how we were intended to be. If you feel that you are better than someone else, try replacing that emotion with compassion. If you feel you are not good enough, try replacing that feeling with diligence.

We are here to help each other. We are here to learn from each other. We are here to become the best we can be. Everything else we do is superfluous.

Imagine a line of people waiting to go into a sporting event. Your eyes scan the people in front of you and behind you. You may make judgments. Your ego will most likely have something to offer your thought perspective. Your body language is influenced by those around you. Now, imagine a line of souls. All the layers stripped away and all that is left is love. You see that we are all the same.

One of my greatest mentors is Ram Dass and he beautifully says, "Souls love. That's what souls do. Egos don't, but souls do. Become a soul, look around, and you'll be amazed - all the beings around you are souls. Be one, see one. When many people have this heart connection, then we will know that we are all one, we human beings all over the planet. We will be one. One love."

OCTOBER 28

ULTIMATE EXPRESSION

"We are not human beings having a spiritual experience.
We are spiritual beings having a human experience."
- Pierre Teilhard de Chardin

I feel like we often give the mind a bad rap. We say, "You are not your thoughts." Or we compare our mind to a monkey. Without a doubt, we spend too much time unintentionally in the wandering mind. But, what if we gave ourselves the gift that spirituality is the ultimate expression of the mind.

Train your mind to think spiritually. As life happens, train your mind to look at the good. Spiritual thinking is an intimate and personal dialogue. Let the voice come up from your heart, not from your ego. Spiritual thinking is grateful. Spiritual thinking is open and compassionate. Spiritual thinking speaks through nature.

When everything becomes a spiritual experience to you, you become who you truly are—a spiritual being. The key to seeing the world through spiritual eyes is to appreciate the moment just as it is. To have a sense of wonder and delight. To have curiosity and forgiveness. To be so content with the beauty of the moment that you couldn't imagine it any other way.

OCTOBER 29

DIE WELL

"These bodies are perishable,
but the Dweller in these bodies is Eternal."
- *The Bhagavad Gita*

When you see yourself as a spiritual being, you become comfortable knowing your human experience is temporary. Death becomes not an end but a new beginning—a continuation on your path.

We fear death because of our attachments to this life. When we let go of our attachments, we let go of fear. Make peace with the evolution of your life. Death only brings the end to your ego but the awakening of your soul. Imagine your death as the grand finale of a firework show. It can be a celebration—a passage.

Yes, a full life is our goal. To be present. To love unconditionally. To become better every day. To make this world a better place. The fear of death does not allow space for your full potential. Imagine a baby bird who fears dying if she leaves the nest...the bird will never fly.

When the time has come, one's death should be peaceful and beautiful. I remember the last words my grandmother said to me, "It's a beautiful day." How you live your life can determine how you die. A joyful, productive, and peaceful life will offer you this as you pass. While a frantic, unhappy life will meet you at the end as well. To live well is to die well.

OCTOBER 30

WE ARE ALL WOVEN TOGETHER

"Meditate often on the interconnectedness and mutual interdependence of all things in the universe. For in a sense, all things are mutually woven together and therefore have an affinity for each other—for one thing follows after another according to their tension of movement, their sympathetic stirrings, and the unity of all substance."
- Marcus Aurelius

You are never alone. We are woven together like a spectacular tapestry. There is a connection amongst us all. If we were to take away thinking, there would be this palpable energy that unites us all. There would be an order to all things.

There is a hidden harmony to all of life. We must take the time to step back, breathe, and feel the interconnectedness. Next time you go for a walk in nature, leave your thinking mind at home. Fill your heart with the beauty of life around you. Notice how the trees are strong and rooted to the earth, yet graceful and serving at the same time. Notice the song of the birds. Notice how the sunlight touches the earth.

As you breathe in your surroundings, know that you are part of it. You are never alone. We are all on then same journey. Today, when you look into the eyes of another—see yourself.

OCTOBER 31

NOTHING EQUALS LOVE

"The most important thing that I know about living is love.
Nothing surpasses the benefits received by a human being who makes
compassion and love the objective of his or her life.
For it is only by compassion and love that anyone fulfills successfully
their life's journey. Nothing equals love."

- Sargent Shriver

Love truly is love. Love's only desire is to fulfill itself. Love has so many meanings but it truly is the vibration of everything on earth. Let love mean: Let Our Vibration Expand (L.O.V.E).

Be love. Send your loving energy out to the world and you will receive it back. The more love you send out, the more love you will receive. Expand your vibration by opening your heart. The reward far outweighs the risk. Love is your true essence and by closing off your heart you miss the love that you are and the love you have to give.

Keep your vibration high and connect with all those around you. Seneca wrote in his *Epistles*, "Nature bore us related to one another...She instilled in us a mutual love and made us compatible...Let us hold everything in common; we stem from a common source. Our fellowship is very similar to an arch of stones, which would fall apart if they did not reciprocally support each other."

NOVEMBER

NOVEMBER 1

UNCONDITIONAL HAPPINESS

"Things are going to happen. The real question is whether
you want to be happy regardless of what happens.
The purpose of your life is to enjoy
and learn from your experience."

- Michael Singer

You have two choices in life: Do you want to be happy or do you want to suffer? It is remarkably simple; the choice is yours. You can commit every moment, every day to choose happiness. The way to make this happen is to choose unconditional happiness. This means, no matter what happens, you choose happiness. Even in the darkest of times, you choose happiness.

When you take away conditions which bring you happiness, you open yourself up to internal sources of contentment. For example, if your happiness comes from another person, then everything stems from a source outside of yourself. If that person were to go away, then you believe your happiness has left you. If you lived your life unconditionally happy, then your source of joy comes from within.

Commit to unconditional happiness. Notice when you put conditions on your happiness. Let it be your teacher and redirect yourself. Notice when you choose to suffer. Let it be your teacher as well and practice finding gratitude in the suffering. This will lead you back to unconditional happiness.

NOVEMBER 2

LIVE LIKE YOU WERE DYING

*"Let each thing you would do, say, or intend,
be like that of a dying person."*
- Marcus Aurelius

What if you lived every day like it were your last? Songs have been sung about this, movies made, and we have all tried to grasp this concept. It's not a concept…it's real. It is true. We were all born and we will all die. It's the time in-between that matters.

We fear death because we want to live. Then, why are we not living? To live like you were dying is to appreciate and be joyful for every day you are alive. We do not know when our last day will be, but we do know we are alive today. To live is to experience life.

If you knew your dinner tonight was your last meal, wouldn't you savor it? Wouldn't you enjoy every bite? Wouldn't you take your time to smell, taste, and appreciate it? Every day should be like that.

Death is our teacher in life. Death teaches us the meaning of life. The Stoics and yogis believe in having mindfulness of death. Become mindful that life and death are one. Cherish your life. Hold people close. Be grateful for today and live like you were dying.

NOVEMBER 3

QUESTIONS ARE IMPORTANT

"It is not the answer that enlightens, but the question."
- Eugene Ionesco

I t is often the question that is more important than the answer.
Questions lead to an opening. They offer an opportunity to look more deeply at your life. Asking yourself questions can bring clarity and simplicity.

Discover more about yourself by asking questions like:

1) What are my values?
2) Can I love what is?
3) Can I be grateful for what I have?
4) Do I know what matters most?
5) Is this in my control?
6) Who am I?
7) Am I doing what is right?

It is the inquiry that is important. Those that ask questions are the wisest. Seneca wrote, "I examine my entire day and go back over what I've done and said - hiding nothing from myself, passing nothing by." Asking yourself questions creates a pause—a contemplation. The more you know about yourself, the more fulfilling your life can be.

NOVEMBER 4

SAVE ONE ANOTHER

"No man is an island, entire of itself;
every man is a piece of the continent, a part of the main..."
- John Donne

There is an old Hindu story about our purpose in life. A sage was seated beside the Ganges and noticed a scorpion that had fallen into the water. When he reached down to rescue it, he was stung. A few moments later he saw the scorpion struggling in the water again and he reached down to rescue it. A bystander claimed, "Holy one, why do you keep doing that? Don't you see that the wretched creature will only sting you in return?" "Of course," the sage replied. "It is the dharma of a scorpion to sting. But it is the dharma of a human being to save."

Our purpose is to save one another. What does that mean? What does that look like? I think it means believing in ourselves and the potentiality of every human being. It is the interconnectedness of us all on its deepest level.

We save one another by practicing compassion. It is our nature to be kind and helpful. It is the scorpion's nature to sting. When you see someone that may need to be rescued, follow your instinct. Reach out your hand and lift them up. When you need to be saved, allow others to bring you back to dry land. Our dharma is to save and is fulfilled by living a life of compassion and forgiveness.

NOVEMBER 5

UNSHAKEABLE EQUANIMITY

"But when you move amidst the world of sense,
free from attachment and aversion alike,
there comes the peace in which all sorrows end,
and you live in the wisdom of the Self."

- The Bhagavad Gita

U nshakeable equanimity. This truly is the key to life. To have unshakeable equanimity brings you the greatest peace and fulfillment. How do you achieve this? Let go of your attachment to the result. Let go of what you think it should be. Discipline your mind to be in the Now. Gently glide through your life. Have an open heart, calm mind, and vibrant spirit.

Make your goal in life to have profound peace of mind. Detach yourself from the dualities of pain and pleasure. Detach yourself from success and failure. You will be unstoppable. You will be happy.

Keep reminding yourself that life is happening for you. Find the grace in the moment and this will lead to a life of grace. A life that doesn't seek personal satisfaction but spiritual awakening.

NOVEMBER 6

ESPECIALLY THE ORDINARY

"Appreciate everything, even the ordinary. Especially the ordinary."
- Pema Chödrön

O ur lives are made up of ordinary moments: The drive to work, the conversations with our family, doing the dishes, walking the dog. It is how we perceive the ordinary and the gratitude that we feel that makes our lives extraordinary.

Sometimes we think our life should be one of accomplishment or one of adventure - one after the other. Your life is already that. Right here, right now. As you drive to work, be grateful you have a car and a job. Be present and compassionate when you talk with others. Find joy internally in the ordinary.

If we only appreciate the big moments, our life is always lacking. When we appreciate the ordinary moments, our life is a gift. As you go about your day, notice how you are feeling as you experience the ordinary. Can you bring joy and lightness to it? Can you smile? Can you be grateful? Can you share your experience with someone else?

One grateful, ordinary moment after another leads to a magical life.

NOVEMBER 7

YOUR IMPERFECTIONS ARE PERFECT

*"When you realize just how perfect everything is
you will tilt your head back and laugh at the sky."*
- Buddha

T he quote above brings me peace. We try to make everything perfect not realizing it already is. It is just as it should be— imperfections and all.

There's a great story about a monk who day after day carried water from a well in two buckets. One of the buckets had holes in it. One day a passerby asked him why he continued to carry the leaky bucket and the monk pointed to one side of the path that was barren and the other side which was lined with beautiful wildflowers. He said, "My imperfection has brought beauty to those around me."

Imperfection should be the goal. How boring it would be to be perfect. There would be no growth, no exploration, no compassion, no humility. When you make a mistake, applaud yourself for learning that there is a better way. When you think you are not good enough, remember that there is no one like you and that you are beautiful. When you are afraid of trying because you think you will fail, remember that perfection is not the goal. Epictetus reminds us, "We don't abandon our pursuits because we despair of ever perfecting them."

NOVEMBER 8

INTENTION AND ATTENTION

"We are all gardeners, planting seeds of intention
and watering them with attention in every moment of every day."
- Cristen Rodgers

B oth *intention* and *attention* are paramount to having the future
you desire. Intention comes first. It is the thought that you are
setting for yourself. It could be as simple as reaching for a plate in the
cabinet. Wayne Dyer said, "The word 'intention' is really important because
it doesn't leave any room for doubt or maneuvering: 'I intend to create
this in my life out of the circumstances that I'm now experiencing.'"

Your intention releases energy to start the ball rolling. Then attention
keeps it rolling. How much attention you put on your intention matters
a lot. Always remember to not become attached to the outcome.

Your future is created now. Set the intention. Focus your attention
on what you can do in the present moment to create your best tomorrow.

NOVEMBER 9

HIDDEN COST

"So, concerning the things we pursue, and for which we vigorously
exert ourselves, we owe this consideration—either there is nothing
useful in them, or most aren't useful. Some of them are superfluous,
while others aren't worth that much. But we don't discern this
and see them as free, when they cost us dearly."

- Seneca

D on't you love that feeling when you clean out your closet or purge
through years of clutter? For me, I find that I can breathe more
easily afterward. You create space not just on the outside but on the inside
as well.

Part of mindfulness is becoming aware of your excess. The obvious excess
is accumulating what you do not need but there is also a burden felt storing
all these possessions on your mind. Even if something did not cost you
money, it may be costing you emotionally.

Pay attention to what your attachments are costing you. When you walk
throughout your house, what do you feel when you look at your possessions?
Do they fill your heart up with love or do they weigh on you heavily?

It feels good to let go. Pass something on today that is not useful to you
anymore. Notice the ease it brings to your life.

NOVEMBER 10

THERE ARE NO PROBLEMS

"Problems are mind-made and need time to survive.
They cannot survive in the actuality of the Now."
- Eckhart Tolle

We do not have problems in our life—we have situations. If you planned an outdoor gathering and it rains, it's not a problem. It's a situation that needs your attention. Mother Nature definitely does not see the rain as a problem, she's just doing her job.

Catch yourself saying, "We have a problem." Instead, reframe to, "We have a situation and this is how we will work together to navigate through it." Problems are created in your ego because you think there is a better way to do something or that it should not have happened. When you linger in the "problem" you miss the opportunity to make the situation better.

Situations lead to action which leads to growth and results. Problems lead to suffering on some level. See if you can eliminate the word *problem* from your vocabulary. Everything in your life is an awakening to a situation that guides you on your path.

NOVEMBER 11

SHAME VS. GUILT

*"The difference between shame and guilt
is the difference between 'I am bad' and 'I did something bad.'"*
- Brené Brown

Shame is a universal human emotion that can be very destructive. You know that feeling of wanting to disappear? Shame doesn't want you to give it a voice so it hides inside of you. Shame comes from the fear of being disconnected. You feel you are flawed and as a result, you do not believe you are worthy of being connected with others.

Guilt is a different emotion than shame. Guilt is focused on your behavior while shame comes from within your being. Guilt can be helpful when you learn and change from it. Shame focuses on how you perceive yourself.

What kind of self-talk you lean towards plays an important role in how you show up to your life. Notice if your self-talk is focused on behavior or self. Do you say, "I am such an idiot." Or do you say, "I should not have done that." The former you are shaming yourself, while the latter is a manifestation of guilt.

We make mistakes—that is life. If you feel guilty, learn from it and become better. Shame has no place in your life. You may have done something wrong but you are not wrong.

NOVEMBER 12

You Belong to You

*"You are only free when you realize you belong no place—
you belong every place—no place at all.
The price is high. The reward is great."*

- Maya Angelou

We all want to belong. It is a natural human need. What is important to know is the more you seek belonging, the harder it is to find. Instead of seeking ways to belong, know that you are one with everything. You belong to everything and everything belongs to you.

The belonging comes from a place of being not doing. Be yourself. No matter what it takes—be authentic. Maya Angelou says, "The price is high. The reward is great." Stand in your truth and you belong. Take the difficult road and you belong. Listen to your soul speak and you belong.

Let go of the attachment to belonging and you will feel a lightness and connection with the universe. That feeling is you unconditionally belonging. Just being. You belong to you. When you know that on a cellular level, then you will know you belong to everything and nothing at the same time.

NOVEMBER 13

YOUR OWN PATH

"If you can see your path laid out in front of you step by step,
you know it's not your path. Your own path you make
with every step you take. That's why it's your path."
- *Joseph Campbell*

How often do we do something because it is what everyone else is doing? As we continue on our spiritual journey, there is a shift in doing, feeling, and being your true self. We understand that we are responsible for ourselves. That our path is unique to us—no one else has our journey. No one else can walk our path for us.

Find comfort in your uniqueness. It's boring to be like everyone else. I've always admired how my daughter walks to the beat of a different drummer. As a child, she dressed herself in whatever made her smile that day. As a middle schooler, it wasn't important to her to be the most popular. And now, a recent high school graduate, she has chosen to not go to college but to follow her dreams and become a professional CrossFit athlete.

It's your path. It's not your parent's. It's not your neighbor's or your best friend's. With every step you take, you are your own destiny. Be brave and vulnerable. Be silly and free. Be yourself.

NOVEMBER 14

THE OTHER SIDE

"Every event has two handles—one by which it can be carried,and
one by which it can't. If your brother does you wrong, don't grab it
by his wronging, because this is the handle incapable of lifting it.
Instead, use the other—that he is your brother, that you were raised
together, and then you will have hold of the handle that carries."
- Epictetus

Albert Einstein said the definition of insanity is doing the same
thing over and over again and expecting different results. We all
do that. We want something different, but we don't make the change that
is necessary to create a new outcome. We think that if we try the same
way again, we will get the result we are hoping for one day.

Think of something in your life that you have been trying to change.
Maybe it's related to your health, your relationships, or your environment.
What have you been doing to try to change the situation? Then change your
perspective on it. Look at what is going right and take action to create more
of that. When you focus on the negative and just keep repeating that
behavior there will not be change.

Epictetus wrote, "If you are defeated once and tell yourself you will
overcome, but carry on as before, know in the end you'll be so ill and
weakened that eventually you won't even notice your mistake and will
begin to rationalize your behavior."

NOVEMBER 15

WORDLESS TEACHER

"All profound things, and emotions of things
are preceded and attended by Silence...
Silence is the general consecration of the universe."
- Herman Melville

I love sitting and observing - simply watching a bird go about its day or watching the gentle ebb and flow of the water in the Cape Cod bay and noticing how the seagull just floats along with the tide. There are so many wordless teachers throughout our days.

Notice how watching a sunset teaches you about surrender. Notice how the sunrise is our reminder that we have a new day to begin again. Watch how your dog offers unconditional love through her eyes. Some of our best teachers are wordless teachers.

To hear these kinds of teachers, you must become quiet yourself. Here they are teaching you some of the most beautiful gifts on earth: To be still. To be in the moment. To become one with your surroundings.

Become aware of your wordless teachers. Nature is the most magnificent learning center. Then go inward. Listen for your soul to speak. Here you have found the greatest wordless teacher of all...your true self.

NOVEMBER 16

MY MOM IS MY HERO

*"To be yourself in a world that is constantly trying
to make you something else is the greatest accomplishment."*
- Ralph Waldo Emerson

My parents divorced when I was three. It wasn't because they fell out of love; it was because my mom is gay. It's taken me my entire life to realize that she is the strongest, bravest woman I know. In a time when being gay was almost forbidden, she stood in her truth. She knew that her love was for a woman. It has been almost 50 years and she and her partner are still together.

I have a lot of memories and emotions of growing up in the '70s with a gay mom. I was young and unclear of what it all meant. My mom tried to protect my brother and me. I remember that I was told to say that my mom's partner was my aunt. I remember not being able to have friends over. I remember over the phone telling my grandmother that lived in England that my dad was "at a meeting" so she would never know they divorced.

As a child this was confusing but as an adult, I understand that my mom was doing hard things to save us all from a world that did not understand. My mom is my hero because she could have stayed with my dad, but she chose to be true to herself. She has taught me that the greatest gift you can give yourself and the world is to be yourself.

NOVEMBER 17

AYURVEDA

"Ayurveda is simply the science of understanding
your own unique self and being who you are meant to be."
- Manyiri Nadkarni

*A*yurveda is a beautiful, holistic approach to understanding yourself more deeply. Your well-being depends on a delicate balance between the mind, body, and spirit. Ayurveda is personalized medicine that was created in India more than 5,000 years ago. It is often referred to as "the sister philosophy" of yoga.

Ayurveda involves the mental, physical, and emotional care of one's personal, evolving blueprint. Ayurveda means "knowledge of life". It is a way to gain wisdom of your special needs, imbalances, and unique offering.

There are two main goals of Ayurveda which are clearly stated in Deacon Carpenter's book, *A Little Bit of Ayurveda*: 1) To preserve the health of the healthy—keeping you balanced throughout the journey of your life. 2) To eradicate disease and imbalances in the sick—focusing on reversing the disease process and removing toxins and pathogens from the body to "cure" the physiology of disease.

Ayurveda addresses all aspects of your life. It can play an important role in preventative care for your body, mind, and spirit. You are unique and focusing on Ayurveda methods like managing your stress, eating seasonally, staying active, and practicing self-care will help you become the best you!

NOVEMBER 18

WHY POWER

*"If the fire in your heart is strong enough,
it will burn away any obstacles that come your way."*
- Suzy Kassem

You have probably seen throughout your life that willpower often does not work. When you focus on *not* doing something, it pushes you to do it more. Start having why power instead of willpower. It is your reasons why that will create lasting change.

While willpower is forced into your mind, why power comes from your heart. Ask yourself why you want to make a certain change in your life. Maybe you want to eat healthier or run your first marathon. Perhaps you decided to run a marathon to raise funds for your local hospital. Your why might be because they treated your child recently for a heart condition. Your why comes from a much deeper place than just crossing the finish line.

It's so much more authentic and meaningful when you know your why. Focusing on your why also fills you with gratitude. You become more grateful for the opportunity to make a positive change in your life. When you don't achieve your goals it's because your "why" isn't big enough.

Think of willpower as saying, "no" and why power as saying, "yes". Ask yourself often what your why is and you will achieve what you desire.

NOVEMBER 19

BE KIND TO MOTHER EARTH

"If all the insects were to disappear from the earth, within 50 years all life on earth would end. If all human beings disappeared from the earth, within 50 years all forms of life would flourish."
- Jonas Salk

We are visitors here on earth. Remember we are human spiritual beings living on this earth for a short amount of time. We think we rule the world but we don't. We trample the earth with our transportation. We constantly send out negative energy. We abuse and destroy our natural resources.

You can help by seeing yourself as one with your surroundings. You are the tree out your window. You are the breeze on your face. But, you are also the disappearing coral reefs and the extinction of animals.

Appreciate how magnificent Mother Earth is. Did you know that in California there are oak trees that are at least 13,000 years old? We think living to 100 years old is a major achievement but compared to nature, our lives are just a drop in the bucket.

We can all cohabit and flourish together. We need each other. Embrace nature and become one with it. Clearly said by Ram Dass, "When you are seeing the ocean, or the lake, or the river, you are seeing yourself."

NOVEMBER 20

CAUSE OF UNHAPPINESS

"Life isn't as serious as my mind makes it out to be."
- *Buddha*

It is our thoughts about a situation that brings us unhappiness. Each situation is as it is. Read that line again: Each situation is as it is. Unhappiness arises when you think it should be something different. Can you be present to this moment? Can you become aware of what you are making it mean?

Whatever is at this moment could not be otherwise. I love the answer from a 116-year-old man when asked the secret to his longevity—he replied, "When it rains, I let it."

When you get out of your head, you experience the joy of being. You get to choose whether you let the space in your head be filled up with stories, media messaging, fabricated fear, etc. or will that space be filled with experiencing the present moment, controlling what you can control, and letting go of the rest and experiencing life happening for you.

You are so much more than your thinking mind. Become aware of when it dictates your life. Step outside of your mind and look around at the beauty of the moment.

NOVEMBER 21

THE VOICE IN OUR CHILD'S HEAD

"If we are to teach real peace in this world, and if we are to carry on a real war against war, we shall have to begin with the children."
- Gandhi

Have you ever wondered what the voice in your child's mind is saying to them? Have you witnessed how they respond to negative emotions? It's important to help children understand the little voice in their head and the emotions that come from that.

I think a good approach is to share an experience you are having. I could say, "I'm really nervous about writing my first book. The voice in my head says it won't be good enough. But, then I realize that voice is not really me. That voice in my head is Fear. I'm going to feel that emotion but then send it on its way."

Help your children to understand that they have control over the voice in their heads. It's ok to let the voice speak, but don't allow this negative emotion to stay too long. As Buddha said, "The mind is by nature radiant. It's shining. It is because of visiting forces that we suffer."

These "visiting forces" that our children may feel include: fear, jealousy, inadequacy, and anger. Show them how you can invite them in for a short amount of time but then send them away. Maybe you have your child give the voice in their head a name to help them remember that it's not who they really are.

NOVEMBER 22

WHAT IS SERVICE?

"Service isn't something we do; it's a way of life.
Service is what our lives are when we're loving ourselves."
- Melody Beattie

W hen we think of service, we often think of serving others. Before you can be of service to others, you must continually bring joy to your own life. Everything you do to enrich your life is service. When you take care of yourself first, you can then take care of others.

Imagine a world where everyone loved themselves first. We filled our own cup before filling others. We lived our lives with passion and purpose. That is service. When something is presented to us and it doesn't bring us joy, we are able to say no and turn towards what is right for us at that moment in time.

Always be of service to yourself first. Open your heart and listen to your soul speak. Learn to love yourself unconditionally. This is true service. This will change the world.

NOVEMBER 23

TO BRING YOU PEACE

"As it was in the beginning, and now,
and always, and to the ages of ages."
- Gloria Patri

I t is peaceful to know that what has happened to you has happened to others since the beginning of time. It is true that you are beautifully unique and each moment brings its own grace, but your life consists of moments that have come before and will come again and again.

When you feel alone and that no one could possibly understand what you are going through—we do and we have. Reach out and ask for help; even if you just ask the universe. You will be blessed for the asking. Father Thomas Keating said, "Perhaps the shortest and most powerful prayer in human language is help."

Find comfort in knowing that what you are experiencing has been experienced before. Marcus Aurelius wrote in his journal, "If you've seen the present, you've seen all things, from time immemorial into all eternity. For everything that happens is related and the same."

NOVEMBER 24

BEST DAY

"He said, 'Write it on your heart that every day is the best day in the year. He is rich who owns the day, and no one owns the day who allows it to be invaded with fret and anxiety. Finish every day and be done with it. Some blunders and absurdities, no doubt crept in. Forget them as soon as you can, tomorrow is a new day; begin it well and serenely, with too high a spirit to be cumbered with your old nonsense. This new day is too dear, with its hopes and invitations, to waste a moment on the yesterdays.'"

- Ralph Waldo Emerson

There is something magical about beginning your day with gratitude. Before you even get out of bed, roll over on your belly and maybe put your hands in prayer and say how grateful you are that you were given another day to breathe, to learn, to love.

There is a shift in your consciousness when you begin with being filled instead of depleted. If our first thought in the morning is dread, how can the rest of our day bring joy? The more gratitude you have in your life, the easier it is to let life flow. You find gratitude in your mistakes. You let them go with ease so there is space to learn and grow. By beginning your day by saying, "thank you" you soften your attachment to yesterday.

NOVEMBER 25

JOY MATTERS

"When you do things from your soul,
you feel a river moving in you, a joy."

- Rumi

J oy is a beautiful word. It is a deeper word than happiness. Joy is felt in your heart and soul. Joy is the energy that runs through your body and through the universe.

Joy matters. Everything you do in your life should have an element of joy. Even in suffering, joy is underneath your pain. It is like the sun behind the clouds. The space between your thoughts. The ease of it all when you let go.

Let joy be your guide. Ask yourself constantly, "Does this bring me internal joy?" "Does my heart say yes?" The more you identify with your external world, the less joy you will have in your life. Your attachments bring a heaviness. Non-attachment brings a lightness—it brings joy. This joy is inside of you—it is you.

Choose joy day after day. Make it a priority in your life. Let it flow through you, let it be your shadow, let it be the song you sing to the world.

NOVEMBER 26

CORRAL YOUR LIFE

"Since the vast majority of our words and actions are unnecessary,
corralling them will create an abundance of leisure and tranquility.
As a result, we shouldn't forget at each moment to ask,
is this one of the unnecessary things? But we must corral not only
unnecessary actions but unnecessary thoughts, too,
so needless acts don't tag along after them."

- Marcus Aurelius

A re you going to do things today that are unnecessary? Can you corral your life to only do, feel, and think what is necessary? It takes practice. It takes committing to what is most important to you. It involves you taking control of your life.

Instead of becoming distracted, choose traction. Is what you are doing moving you forward or backward? This doesn't mean that you never relax. It's just a different way of being with your life. You choose to bring purpose to what you do. You design your life so every moment brings you closer to your highest self.

Visualize yourself as the billions of stars in the universe—scattered everywhere. Now visualize corralling all those stars into one—you would be the brightest light in the world.

NOVEMBER 27

BE AN EARLY BIRD

"The only time you're going to find more time is in the morning."
- *Jay Shetty*

There is something magical about mornings. I absolutely love the first hour of my day. I meditate, journal, read, and do a short yoga practice. That first hour makes me who I am.

I know getting up earlier is hard for many people. It does not need to be an hour earlier. Start with five minutes and then slowly increase it. Create a morning ritual that brings you joy. Watch the birds as you drink your coffee. Begin a meditation practice. Read a chapter from a book. Do something that is gentle and awakens your spirit.

You do have time—just wake up a little earlier. Starting your day with time for yourself will change your outlook on your life. Marcus Aurelius encourages us to find gratitude in the morning and remind ourselves "of what a precious privilege it is to be alive - to breathe, to think, to enjoy, to love."

These are all cliches but so true:
The early bird gets the worm, you snooze you lose, early to bed, early to rise makes a man healthy, wealthy, and wise.

Rise, my friends. Rise and enjoy the magic of the morning.

NOVEMBER 28

THE ANXIETY GAME

"When I see an anxious person, I ask myself, what do they want?
For if a person wasn't wanting something outside of their own
control, why would they be stricken by anxiety?"
- Epictetus

We are learning and practicing to let go of what we are not in control of. Stoicism has taught us that how we respond to what is outside of our control is the truth of our character. Yogic philosophy has taught us that the anxiety-ridden voice in our heads is not who we are.

It is a constant practice of awareness. When you become filled with anxiety for something that is outside of your control, like the future, for example, catch yourself. Each time you catch yourself drifting into the open sea of anxiety, you redirect your ship back home. The more often you redirect, the easier it will be to stay in the present moment.

Maybe turn your anxiety into a game. Every time you wander off into the sea of anxiety, make a tally mark in a daily notebook. Notice if you have fewer lines as the days pass. You could even write down next to the tally mark what you were anxious about and at the end of the week see if any of your worries materialized.

NOVEMBER 29

REALITY

"Don't demand or expect that events happen as
you would wish them to. Accept events as they actually happen.
That way, peace is possible."

- Epictetus

It comes down to what is real and what is not. Life is beautifully simple when you see that truth is the present moment. Truth, reality, your soul, God are ways to give a name to the only thing that truly matters... this moment.

Life becomes difficult when we go against this moment. We argue with reality when we think it should be otherwise. Put the word that resonates with you the most in the previous sentence: We argue with God when we think it should be otherwise. We argue with the truth when we think it should be otherwise. We argue with our soul when we think it should be otherwise.

Can you feel that? The simplicity of it. The surrender to what is. The awakening to living fully—here and now. Your thoughts of what is not real are why you suffer. Thoughts about the past. Thoughts about the future. Thoughts about wishing the present could be different. These thoughts are not reality. These thoughts are not the truth. These thoughts are not God. These thoughts are not your soul.

NOVEMBER 30

Is it Your Business?

"Your time is limited, so don't waste it living someone else's life."
- Steve Jobs

Notice how often your energy is focused on someone else's life. Thoughts of: "She should be doing this" or "I can't believe my husband said that" are examples of living someone else's life. Scrolling through social media you are living someone else's life. When you are filled with thoughts of someone else's life, you miss your own life.

Notice how much of your energy is focused on changing reality. Wishing the weather were different. Arguing with the television during a sporting event. These things are out of your control. You are trying to change reality.

American speaker and author Byron Katie has a clear and wonderful way of explaining this: "I can only find three kinds of business in the universe: mine, yours, and God's." She continues, "If you understand the three kinds of business enough to stay in your own business, it could free your life in a way that you can't imagine."

Wasted energy can fill much of our day. It separates us from ourselves. When our attention is on someone else's business or "God's business", we are disconnected from our own being. Every time you get wrapped up in someone else's business, come back to the present moment of your life. Be responsible for your life and shine your own light.

DECEMBER

DECEMBER 1

ACCEPT WHAT IS OFFERED

"Be content with what you have; rejoice in the way things are. When you realize there is nothing lacking, the whole world belongs to you."
- Lao-Tzu

Instead of looking for more, wanting more, accept what is offered now. Constant longing drains the life out of you. Sometimes it is helpful to remember how grateful you were for something in the past. Today, it may not seem enough for you, but at that moment, it fulfilled you.

I remember when my husband and I bought our first home together. I ran around the small home with elation! Maybe you remember your first car or your first suit. You were so grateful for where you were at that point in your life. What you were offered was better than you could have ever imagined. Epictetus said, "Do not spoil what you have by desiring what you have not: remember that what you now have was once among the things you only hoped for."

Hold onto the joy of where you are today. Accept what is offered in this moment as if it were created just for you—because it was. Be grateful for what you have. Know that you would be fine with less. Let go of longing for more.

DECEMBER 2

BE INSTEAD OF TRY

"The farther one goes, the less one knows. Therefore the sage does
not venture forth and yet knows, does not look and yet names,
does not strive and yet attains completion."

- Lao-Tzu

Τ here is a difference between *trying* and *being*. The more you try to achieve, the harder it is to reach your goals. Instead of trying, just be. Like the sun rises or our heart beats, they do not need to try because that is who they are. The sun doesn't try to be the moon and your heart doesn't try to be your lung. They work miraculously being themselves.

Being is a state of awareness that everything is complete as it is. Trying is a state of seeking more. Being is accepting this moment as it is. Trying is seeking to change the moment. Being is your soul speaking. Trying is your ego speaking.

If you surrender to just being, you will be guided. If you choose to try to make your own heart beat, you will be misguided. You will see your own path, without trying, by just being.

DECEMBER 3

PLEASE DON'T HATE

"Darkness cannot drive out darkness: only light can do that.
Hate cannot drive out hate: only love can do that."
- Martin Luther King Jr.

A nger can be a catalyst for change. We often think of anger as an emotion that we should not feel. If anger is coming from a place of wanting to make the world better, use it to fuel positive action. What does not help is hatred. Hatred is a feeling that only your ego can create. There is no space for love, forgiveness, or compassion alongside hatred. You can be angry at a loved one but you cannot hate and love at the same time.

When you cross the line into hatred, you are only hurting yourself. Anger can be transformed into goodness. Hate only creates more hate. Hatred stems from fear and pain. When you "hate" something or someone, they win. They win because you have given up on yourself.

Find the source of your pain. Dig into that. If anger bubbles up—feel it. You will probably feel it in your body while hatred resides within your mind. Move the energy of anger to something more productive and gentle: compassion, courage, change. Holding onto your anger is destructive. Buddha said, "Holding on to anger is like drinking poison expecting the other person to die."

DECEMBER 4

LIVE BY FAITH

"Faith is taking the first step,
even when you don't see the whole staircase."
- *Martin Luther King Jr.*

Years ago my sister gave me a sweatshirt that said, "Live by faith, not by sight." I didn't understand the message until recently. I believe it means: Let your heart and soul be your eyes. Living your life by sight is an illusion. Living by faith is opening your arms to each moment in your life.

Living by sight, your reality becomes a reflection of the illusion. Everything you see becomes a thought that you store in your mind. You identify with objects, names, and labels. What you make something mean becomes your reality. What you think, you become.

Be guided by the invisible—your energy, your soul, your faith. Living by faith is knowing you will be directed. Living by faith is leaving all your armor at the front door and stepping out into the world with abandon. Trust yourself—step out and you will find firm ground or you will learn to fly.

DECEMBER 5

DESTINY

"Let yourself live and be in each moment,
with each person, learning each lesson along the way.
Destiny isn't someplace we go. Destiny is where we are."
- Melody Beattie

How many times have you heard, "It's my destiny!"?
Someone is usually talking about their future. It's my destiny to become…What would you change if you realized your destiny were right now? Each new moment is your destiny and these present moments strung together create your life.

Destiny is not about waiting. It's about creating the life you want now. American bishop T.D Jakes said, "Destiny is the push of our instincts to the pull of our purpose."

Achieve your destiny now. Each choice, each action, each decision is your destiny. It is not a destination—it is now. Let each moment today be your destiny. Live this way and your life will be remarkable.

DECEMBER 6

FRIENDSHIP

> "We have to think of friends and community
> as investments, as our most important asset."
> - *Thích Nhất Hanh*

Building a community of friends is one of the most important things you can do in your life. Surrounding yourself with people that lift you up creates a source of security that money cannot buy. Investing in friendship will reward you for a lifetime.

It is true to have good friends, you need to be a good friend. Your friends are your family. Be there for each other. Listen well and laugh often. Friendship is a gift that nourishes you on a cellular level. Friendship can be felt without speaking a word.

From *The Prophet* by Kahlil Gibran: "And a youth said, Speak to us of Friendship. And he answered saying: Your friend is your needs answered. He is your field which you sow with love and reap thanksgiving. And he is your board and your fireside. For you come to him with your hunger, and you seek him for peace."

Cherish your friendships. Don't be afraid to start new ones and learn from each other. Open your heart and be grateful for the beautiful souls you have the privilege of calling "friends".

DECEMBER 7

ADORE SILENCE

"Seek silence. Gladden in silence. Adore silence."
- *Deng Ming-Dao*

As we walk deeper on our spiritual path, silence becomes the song of our hearts. It is in the silence, that we can hear our calling.

Close your eyes. Visualize yourself walking through the woods on a trail without a destination. Feel the ground support you. Feel the light above you guide you. Then just stand in mountain pose: feet gently pressing into the earth imagining an X on the bottom of each foot and each corner pressing, maybe massaging the earth. Arms are down by your side with palms facing forward in a gesture of receiving. The back of your head is in line with the base of your spine. Your face slowly lifts to the sky above you. Adore the silence in this moment. You are speaking the language of love without saying a word.

Often in silence, you hear the answer you have been seeking. Rumi said, "Listen to silence. It has so much to say." Silence is healing and joyful at the same time.

Silence is sacred but that doesn't mean you cannot enjoy its splendor many times throughout your day. Turn off distractions, close your eyes, breathe, feel the gladness in your heart, and hear the song in your soul. And when silence occurs naturally, embrace it. Drink it in with your whole being and be grateful for it.

DECEMBER 8

THINGS ARE NOT WHO YOU ARE

"If someone takes your shirt, let him have your coat as well."
- Jesus

T hings are not who you are. We all enjoy nice things but when we identify with them—that is when we lose ourselves. If you think you are important because you drive a fancy car and live in a big house, your self-worth comes from material possessions. Who are you if your self-worth comes from an object, title, or achievement?

There is nothing wrong with "having" as long as it does not become your "being". If something you have is taken away from you, does it change who you are? If the answer is yes, you have identified with wanting. If you can detach yourself from the possession and still feel complete without it, you are identified with your being.

When you let go mentally of your attachments, then you can truly enjoy them. It's kind of like getting that first scratch on a new car…you exhale because you're able to let go of perfectionism. Identifying with anything outside of yourself leads to an unfulfilled life.

Enjoy what you have and be grateful for it. But don't let it define you. Be so light as you connect with your possessions that if they were to float away you would smile and be even better without them.

DECEMBER 9

IDENTIFYING WITH THOUGHT

"The most vital thing in spiritual life
is to be able to watch your mind,
to be the observer of your mind,
so that the mind is not controlling you."
- Eckhart Tolle

I dentifying with your thoughts is similar to identifying with your material possessions. It's not wrong to have thoughts (that is what our incredible mind does), but when we become our thoughts, when we believe our thoughts, we are not our true selves. Remember, you are the one that is observing your thoughts. When you are the observer, you are in the present moment. When you are in your thoughts, you are in the past or future.

What happens to most people is thinking without awareness. Compulsive thinking is a pandemic that is causing us to miss our lives. We unconsciously let the voice in our head run our lives. We come to believe that we are this unconscious stream of thought. You become conscious when you notice your thoughts. You are the observer of your thoughts.

Your true self is the conscious observer and your false self is the unconscious mind. Practice becoming aware of your mind—of your thoughts. Pause often and separate yourself from the voice in your head. Shift from thinking to awareness as many times as you can today. You will soon fall in love with yourself and with life.

DECEMBER 10

THE WANTING GAME

*"No person has the power to have everything they want,
but it is in their power not to want what they don't have,
and to cheerfully put to good use what they do have."*
- Seneca

The wanting game is similar to being on a merry-go-round that doesn't stop. We want, we get, and then we want more. The wanting creates a desire that satisfies our ego. The ego loves the feeling of wanting. It's like a baby bird with its mouth wide open—hungry for more. Our ego keeps telling us to get more and this leaves us with the emptiness of not having or being enough.

By having more, you become less. Your ego turns you into an addict for more. It's never enough and it never will be until you realize: You *are* enough. You—just as you are—raw, beautiful, authentic you.

Practice walking in your own footsteps. Often the need for more comes from wanting what others have. When you let go of accumulating, you will find yourself.

We arrived on this earth with nothing and we will leave with nothing. Walk with less and you will be more. In the words of Lao-Tzu from *Tao Te Ching: A New translation by Sam Hamill*:

"The sage does not hoard,
And thereby bestows.
The more he lives for others, the greater his life.
The more he gives to others, the greater his abundance."

DECEMBER 11

THINK ABOUT WHAT IS HAPPENING NOW

"Discard your misperceptions.
Stop being jerked like a puppet. Limit yourself to the present."
- Marcus Aurelius

My greatest desire is to help us all live more fully in the moment. There are countless books, meditations, and techniques that teach methods of becoming more present. Unfortunately, we continue to fall back into our habitual way of thinking in the past and future because our minds do not know another way of operating.

I believe the answer is simple: Think about what is happening now. Retrain your brain to think in the Now. The answer may be simple but the training is difficult.

These are the five steps:

1.   Notice your thoughts. Become aware if they are in the past or the future. Then say, "Come back."
2.   Say, "Be here now."
3.   Put your attention on what you are doing at this moment. Let your mind think about what you are doing. Say, "Task at hand."
4.   Use your senses to become one with what you are doing. What do you feel? What do you see? What do you hear? What do you smell? What do you taste?
5.   Return to step 1.

Practice, practice, practice. Come back. Be here now. Task at hand. Repeat. You will change your brain to live fully in the present.

DECEMBER 12

FOCUSING ON FLAWS

"Don't be afraid to shine, the world needs your light."
- Gabby Bernstein

Yes, it's important to strive to be better, but it's also important to bathe in the fruit of our labor. We often get comfortable focusing on our flaws. So comfortable that we never reach beyond them. Our flaws hold us back from truly becoming.

Perhaps we focus on our flaws because we are fearful of shining our own lights. You can be everything that you ever imagined. Instead of focusing on the dark, focus on the light. Applaud yourself for how far you have come. Acknowledge all the gifts you share with the world. Be proud of what you have accomplished.

Ask, "What am I afraid of?" American author and spiritual leader Marianne Williamson writes, "Our deepest fear is not that we are inadequate. Our deepest fear is that we are powerful beyond measure. It is our light, not our darkness that most frightens us. We ask ourselves, 'Who am I to be brilliant, gorgeous, talented, fabulous?' Actually, who are you not to be?"

Focusing on your flaws releases negative energy while focusing on all the good you offer releases positive energy. Let go of your perceived imperfections and recognize your inner light.

DECEMBER 13

DON'T BITE BACK

"How much better to heal than seek revenge from injury.
Vengeance wastes a lot of time and exposes you to many more
injuries than the fist that sparked it. Anger always outlasts hurt.
Best to take the opposite course. Would anyone think it normal
to return a kick to a mule or a bite to a dog?"

- Seneca

Remember the key is equanimity: mental calmness. A way of being that does not try to be right or attached to a certain outcome. Watch yourself in situations. Do you become defensive, fearful, or aggressive? Do you retreat? Observe what you do, how you react, and how you respond. You are your own guru—what do you learn?

If you feel you have been wronged, revenge is not the answer. You can't fight fire with fire. Do the opposite: show love. Marcus Aurelius said, "The best way to avenge yourself is to not be like that." And Albert Einstein said, "Weak people revenge. Strong people forgive. Intelligent people ignore."

In Eastern thought, nonviolence is at its core. When we act in opposition to others, we are in opposition to ourselves. When we are at peace with ourselves, it is very difficult to be unkind toward others.

DECEMBER 14

COURAGE

"Life shrinks or expands in proportion to one's courage."
- Anais Nin

F inding courage can be difficult when our body had been designed to choose fear first. We don't have to do that anymore. You are physically safe but may not be mentally safe. Have the courage to stand in your truth before your mind takes over.

Courage is about staying and then moving forward. If you feel fearful, let your fear be your teacher. Courage is standing up for what you believe in. Courage is not attaching to an outcome. Courage is choosing the difficult path. Courage is doing the right thing.

The Stoics believed that courage was one of the four aspects of virtue. Thucydides said, "The secret of happiness is freedom and the secret of freedom is courage." Courage in yogic philosophy involves following your dharma—your life's purpose. We must have the courage to walk our own path and align with our reason for being.

Listen to your heart to find courage. The word courage derives from the Latin word *Cor* which means heart. Place your hands on your heart when you need courage. Open yourself up to being courageous.

DECEMBER 15

THE POLLUTED RIVER

"Once you know who you really are, being is enough. You feel neither superior to anyone nor inferior to anyone and you have no need for approval because you've awakened to your own infinite worth."
- Deepak Chopra

There's a story about a yogi taking his young son to the Mississippi River. Looking at the river, the son asked his dad if it was polluted. The yogi responded that no, the river was not polluted—it was only carrying the pollution. The river itself was pure.

This is what we do with our minds. They carry all these thoughts that cloud our judgment, our perception, our reality. We believe them to be true, and as a result, our life becomes polluted. You are pure. Underneath all those layers of pollution, your true self bears witness and patiently waits for you to discover who you really are.

Think of yourself as the river—carrying the thoughts, letting them float away, and don't identify with them. When you detach from your mind, you float with ease. Buddha said, "Life isn't as serious as my mind makes it out to be."

What are you carrying that you can let go of? Like the river, you are only carrying the pollution and underneath is pure. Let go so you are free to flow in the current of your life.

DECEMBER 16

TRUST IS A GIFT

"The best way to find out if you can trust somebody is to trust them."
- *Ernest Hemingway*

T rust is the way of the universe: A beautiful, light, synchronized way of being without judgment or expectations. The moon trusts the sun to rise as the moon shines its light somewhere else. The ocean trusts the tide to rise and fall. The sun, the moon, the ocean, and its tide trust the earth to rotate.

Sometimes we take trust for granted and sometimes we are fearful to trust. Look at trust as a gift. When you feel so comfortable with a person that you can trust them—it is a gift. If you are fearful to trust someone, let them have an opportunity to be trusted.

Trust creates stronger relationships. Believe in people doing the right thing. Trust each other and watch how trust leads to more trust. Learn to trust yourself and this will open the door to trusting others. Ralph Waldo Emerson wrote, "Self-trust is the essence of heroism." Trust your intuition. Trust the universe and notice how the gift of trust surrounds you.

DECEMBER 17

GOSSIP

"Strong minds discuss ideas,
average minds discuss events,
weak minds discuss people."

- Socrates

We gossip because it makes us feel better about ourselves. We feel better about ourselves because we think we know more than the other person. It is your ego that feels this way. Your ego thrives on more and is threatened when it feels less.

Gossip has become part of our everyday conversation. I recently heard that 80% of our conversations center around gossip. It has become a normal way to communicate. Talking about each other, giving opinions, judging… 80% of our communication?

Can you help to change the conversation? Can you bite your tongue before you speak about someone that is not there to defend themself?

When you gossip—you are only hurting yourself. It announces that you cannot be trusted. In addition, what you send out to the world, you will receive back.

Gossip creates conflict. Begin today to control your gossip. Let your conversations be about understanding, compassion, and learning. When gossiping occurs around you—practice redirecting the conversation.

DECEMBER 18

BYE, BYE BIRDIE

"Most people don't realize that the mind constantly chatters.
And yet, that chatter winds up being the force that drives us much
of the day in terms of what we do, what we react to,
and how we feel."

- Jon Kabat-Zinn

T ry this today: Imagine you have a little bird sitting on your shoulder. The little bird is the voice in your head. All day long… chirp, chirp, chirp, tweet, tweet, tweet. Every time you tune into the chirping, visualize the bird on your shoulder and say, "Bye, bye birdie."

So many people go through their lives thinking the little bird is who they are. There is this constant background chatter that has something to say about everything. Can you imagine your life without this little bird as a narrator?

Awaken to the truth in your own head. Just stop listening to that little bird. The endless chirping makes me want to shake my head and watch it fly away. We have made our little bird our reality. You are not that constant chirping.

Michael Singer explains it well in *the untethered soul,* "There are two distinct aspects of your inner being. The first is you, the awareness, the witness, the center of your willful intentions; and the other is that which you watch. The problem is the part that you watch never shuts up. If you could get rid of that part, even for a moment, the peace and serenity would be the nicest vacation you've ever had."

DECEMBER 19

THE GIFT OR CURSE OF THE WORD

*"It is through the word that you manifest everything.
Regardless of what language you speak, your intent manifests
through the word. What you dream, what you feel,
and what you really are, will all be manifested through the word."*
- Don Miguel Ruiz

We are the only species that has the gift of word. We get to choose to use the word as a gift or as a curse. The word is not just what is spoken and written, but what is thought and released.

How often have you been told something and it completely changes your day and possibly your life? The word is so powerful. I remember my boyfriend in college telling me I should lose some weight. Those words led to an eating disorder that lasted several years.

Make a commitment to use your power of word to strengthen yourself and others. Be responsible for yourself, but let go of judgment and blame. Remember that someone else's word is not your word. The more you love yourself, the purer your word will be. Be good to yourself. Practice self-love and your word will be a gift.

DECEMBER 20

YOUR PAST

"It is right it should be so;
Man was made for Joy and Woe;
And when this we rightly know, Thro the World we safely go.
Joy and Woe are woven fine, a Clothing for the soul divine."
- William Blake

I f you were asked, "What would you change about your past?" What would you say? What if your answer was, "I would change nothing." We have all made lots of mistakes. Events have happened that we wish had not. Life has brought us great pain and suffering. But, you are who you are because of what you have been through.

You see more clearly because of your past. You have deeper wisdom and greater love. We often hold onto our past because of regret or sadness or triumph and success. What's important is to take what you have learned to create your future and be grateful for the road you traveled. Living in your past is not why you are here.

Each moment in your life is exactly how it is supposed to be. Your past was your present at that moment. Your past is a beautiful lesson for today. It has created you: strong, beautiful, resilient. You have more compassion for others because of what you have been through. Your heart is more open and your spirit more alive. Your life: past, present, and future are exactly as they should be.

DECEMBER 21

WHERE IS WISDOM LOCATED?

*"We don't receive wisdom; we must discover it
for ourselves after a journey that no one can take for us or spare us."*
- Marcel Proust

Wisdom is a personality trait that centers around social behaviors including empathy, compassion, and altruism. According to Dr. Dilip Jeste in his book *Wiser*, wisdom also comes from emotional regulation, self-reflection, acceptance, decisiveness, and spirituality. Wisdom can be found in the brain through these traits. What is fascinating is they are found in the oldest and newest parts of our brain: the oldest is the emotional center—the amygdala and the newest is where we control our emotions—the pre-fontal cortex.

Wisdom comes from the balance of the two. To be wise one must have emotion but know how to control it. One should aim for a balance of self-compassion and compassion for others. The wise have a diversity of perspectives but can also be decisive.

Wisdom can be discovered at any stage in your life. Practice the art of balance. Rumi said, "The middle path is the way to wisdom."

DECEMBER 22

DO YOUR BEST

*"When the standards have been set, things are tested and weighed.
And the work of philosophy is just this, to examine
and uphold the standards, but the work of a truly good person
is in using those standards when they know them."*

- Epictetus

Set the standard of always doing your best. Hold fast to this standard no matter what. If you are working, exercising, parenting, doing chores…always do your best.

Your best will vary day to day depending on the situation. Perhaps you wake up with a cold, your workout may suffer but commit to doing your best with where you are. Theodore Roosevelt said, "Do what you can, with what you have, where you are."

It's important to not do more or less than your best. When you try too hard, you will weaken. If you do too little, you will judge yourself. When you do your best it quiets the ego. There is no space for judgment and regret.

It is through action that we feel alive. It validates us and offers contributions to others. Doing your best is a mindful action that brings happiness. Do your best in everything in life—not for an outcome but for the love of it. When you make mistakes doing your best, congratulate yourself. You've learned something and next time your best will be even better.

DECEMBER 23

TRANSFORMATION

"Transformation isn't a future event, it's a present day activity."
- Jillian Michaels

Y ou can transform anything in your life. We often think of
transformation as this big, radical, life-changing way of becoming
something different. Transformation can happen in the ordinary. It is
happening around you continuously in small ways and it can happen inside
of you in small ways too.

Think about your breath. It is a transformation turning air into the
breath that keeps you alive. It's when you turn an experience into a feeling.
Or when you look at all that you have, instead of what you think you
don't have.

Everything is an opportunity for transformation. Change your thoughts
from fear to excitement. Change your worry to gratitude. Transform your
way of being from external projection to internal love.

Walk this life with transformation. Be open to a new perspective.
Let your heart find the goodness in everything. Transform the mundane into
magic. Transform the ordinary into a beautiful ritual. Transform being lost
to being awake. Transform feeling not enough into more than enough.
You are a remarkable transformation.

DECEMBER 24

SIMPLY NOTICE

"Simply notice that you're aware."

- Yongey Mingyur Rinpoche

A simple and beautiful way to be more present in your life is to simply notice. How often do you take a moment to tap into your senses? What can you hear right now? You just brought awareness to your hearing and to the sounds around you. What is your mood right now? How is it making you feel? Light or heavy?

The act of noticing is a way to gently guide you out of your unconsciousness. You notice—you wake up. It's not hard to become aware, we just forget to notice. Everything can become something that you can develop awareness from.

Sit today, close your eyes, and notice sensations in your body. Can you feel the energy in your hands? Can you observe your thoughts? Can you breathe in a way that makes you feel lighter? When you are driving, can you notice the attitude in your mind? When you begin to go to sleep, can you feel the surrender?

Simply notice what brings you back to the present moment. Mark those moments and create more of them. Your mental habits determine the quality of your experience. Notice over and over again and you will wake up to your life.

DECEMBER 25

A CHRISTMAS STORY

"The most important things in life aren't things."
- Anthony J. D'Angelo

I was about ten or eleven and I was traveling cross country with my dad and my brother. We were driving from our home in Georgia to spend Christmas with my grandparents in Massachusetts. I loved being with them on Christmas. I still remember the smell of the house, decorating the tree, Christmas Eve candlelight service, and all of the holiday anticipation.

The long car ride was never a burden. It brings a smile to my face now thinking of going through the toll booths and saying, "Merry Christmas" as my dad paid the toll. It was a two-day trip and this particular year we stopped and spent the night at a motel. The next morning as we approached the car, we were shocked to see that the car had been broken into and all of our Christmas presents had been taken.

I remember feeling sad for how badly my dad felt. I don't remember missing gifts that Christmas. What I remember is all of the love from my grandparents and the traditions that could never be taken away.

Looking back at this event from my childhood, maybe the person that broke into our car had nothing and we gave them something. Maybe they had their first Christmas with wrapped presents.

Let the holidays fill you with gratitude for not what is under the tree but for those you love and for memories and traditions that can never be taken away.

DECEMBER 26

CLEAR YOUR MIND

"Too much knowledge can be a dangerous thing."
- Winston Churchill

There's an important story told by Leroy Little Bear about two scientists who traveled halfway around the world to ask a Hindu sage what he thought about their theories. When they arrived, he kindly brought them into his garden and poured them tea. Though the two small cups were full, the sage kept pouring. Tea kept overflowing and the scientists politely but awkwardly said, "Your holiness, the cups can hold no more." The sage stopped pouring and said, "Your minds are like the cups. You know too much. Empty your minds and come back. Then we'll talk."

We think the more we know, the better we will be. Knowledge can cloud the path to awakening. It's like the saying, "Clear your mind." Letting go of what is not serving you will create space for growth. Clear your mind, like your closet, of information that you are not using. Clear your mind of ruminating thoughts. Feel the freshness and clarity. When your thinking cup runneth over, pour it out and gently begin to fill it up again.

DECEMBER 27

LEAVE YOUR DOOR OPEN

"The most important thing in life is your inner energy."
- Michael Singer

Your energy may be the most valuable resource you have. Opening yourself to the abundant energy that flows through you leads to an unconditional life. The energy inside of you is limitless but it only flows when you are open. Without even knowing it, we have conditionally closed ourselves off to our greatest source of love.

Remember a time when you were depressed and unproductive. Were you open to new ideas and possibilities? Most likely you were not because you had closed yourself off from your own energy. Now think about a time when you were so absorbed in what you were doing that you forget to eat or check your phone. Here your heart is wide open and your internal energy is flowing with power and grace.

Be mindful of your energy. You control whether you are open or closed. You can be the teacher with the open-door policy or the one that always has their office door closed. Others feel your energy and it can become a contagious resource.

Keep coming back to being open. Make a commitment to not close your door even in the hardest of times.

DECEMBER 28

SAMSKARA

"The samskara can store a complete snapshot of the event. It is way beyond any computer storage system created by human beings. It can archive everything you were feeling, everything you were thinking, and everything that was happening surrounding the event."
- Michael Singer

S amskaras are impressions left on our hearts and mind from our past actions. In yogic philosophy, our Samskaras are the most important influences affecting our life. Samskaras alter our thinking process. Our mental world is deeply connected to them.

An example of a Samskara could be not forgiving your sibling for an argument you had ten years ago. You did not get complete with this past event and it created an impression that keeps showing up. Instead of releasing and letting go, it continues to move in a circle. You see this in your repetitive thoughts and you feel the ache in your heart. Your heavy heart is the result of the build-up of all your Samskaras.

You can hold onto positive and negative Samskaras. Both should be released as they happen. When you feel stuck, most likely your energy flow is blocked because of a Samskara. Letting go allows you and your life to flow.

DECEMBER 29

A LITTLE BIT LEFT

"We can't take away suffering,
we can't change what happened—but we can
choose to find the gift in our lives.
We can even learn to cherish the wound."
- *Edith Eva Eger*

Often there is a little bit that is left. It could be heartache, illness, or loss. We think that after time, the healing would be complete. But, there is still a little bit that is left. We can choose to linger in the suffering or we can awaken to the gift that is left.

The little bit that is left is your gentle reminder of all that is right. It is your gratitude, your compass, your center. There will always be a little bit of something, but you are strong and resilient. Allow the wound in your life to heal your outlook. You will be ok.

When that little bit saddens you, become your own best friend. Talk to yourself like your friends do. You choose if you want to dwell in the well or fly in the sky. Victor Frankl said, "Everything can be taken from a man but one thing: the last of the human freedoms—to choose one's attitude in any given set of circumstances, to choose one's own way."

DECEMBER 30

SIT WITH IT

"How do you free yourself?
In the deepest self, you free yourself by finding yourself."
- *Michael Singer*

D o you know how you move past what is holding you back? It is not stuffing it deeper inside you. It is not moving forward, thinking it will go away. It is sitting with it, letting the emotion boil up, understanding where it came from, and then letting it go.

The only way to heal and move past your pain is to sit with it. I know this is something you do not want to do. It seems too painful. It will be, but then it will be gone.

You can choose to keep hiding behind your emotional pain or you can choose to sit with it and then come out to the light. Practice feeling your suffering on a cellular level. This means noticing how your body feels when you sit with your pain. Where in your body do you feel the pain? Maybe in your heart or in your shoulders. Maybe your body tingles or your belly aches. Maybe your throat tightens or your legs shake.

Once you begin to feel the pain, then can you ask yourself where it originated. It's so important to be with that child or wounded self. It is here where you discover the story that you created and, as a result, you can let it go. Here you forgive. Here you rise up without the burden— without the pain.

DECEMBER 31

ONWARD

*"Remember the words you were told when this last
adventure began, the words whispered quietly to your heart:
Let the journey unfold. Let it be magical. The way has been prepared.
People will be expecting you. Yes, you are being led."*
- Melody Beattie

We come to the end of a year. What an exploration it has been! I am grateful for every turning page and every turning year. Thank you for learning with me. Thank you for exploring and meditating with me. It has been my hope that the past 364 days have: comforted you, awakened you, and helped you in some small way.

You've got this. Remember these important ideas:

1) You are in control of your response.
2) You are the observer of your thoughts.
3) All that truly matters is this moment.
4) Love yourself above all else.
5) Be grateful.
6) Learn from everything.
7) Soak up nature.
8) We are all the same.
9) Equanimity is the key.
10) I love you.

GLOSSARY

A SHORT GLOSSARY OF REOCCURRING NAMES:

Maya Angelou
An American poet, memoirist, and civil rights activist.

Marcus Aurelius
Probably the most well-known Stoic philosopher. Born in 121 AD, he was the Roman emperor from 161 to 180. His private journal is an extraordinary book titled, *Meditations*.

Melody Beattie
American author of self-help books.

Brené Brown
American professor, lecturer, and author.

Buddha (Siddhartha Gautama)
A Śramana who lived in ancient India. He is the founder of Buddhism. Buddhism is a religion and way of life or philosophy. The goal is enlightenment.

Deepak Chopra
An Indian-American author and alternative medicine advocate.

Winston Churchill
British statesman who served as Prime Minister of the United Kingdom from 1940 to 1945, during the Second World War, and again from 1951 to 1955.

Deng Ming-Dao
Chinese American author, artist, and philosopher.

Confucius
A Chinese philosopher and politician. His teachings (known as Confucianism) and philosophy formed the basis of East Asian culture. He coined principles such as: "Do not do unto others what you do not want done to yourself".

Dalai Lama
His Holiness the 14th Dalai Lama is the spiritual leader of the Tibetan people.

Wayne Dyer
Was an American self-help spiritual author and a motivational speaker.

Ralph Waldo Emerson
An American essayist, lecturer, philosopher, abolitionist, and poet. He led the transcendentalist movement of the mid-19th century.

Epictetus
A Greek Stoic philosopher who was born a slave in 55 AD. It was through his struggle, that he chose to live a life of philosophy. He taught Stoicism and instructed how to lead a life of responsibility, truth, and self-knowledge.

Victor Frankl
Born in 1905 in Vienna, Austria. He was a neurologist, psychiatrist, philosopher, author, and Holocaust survivor.

Mahatma Gandhi
Born in 1869 into a Gujarati Hindu
ModhBania family in India, he became
a lawyer, anti-colonial nationalist, and
political ethicist. He inspired civil rights
and freedom movements across the
world.

Kahlil Gibran
A Lebanese-American writer, poet,
and visual artist.

Thích Nhât Hanh
A Vietnamese Thiên Buddhist monk
who was a global spiritual leader.

Ryan Holiday
American author on Stoicism.

Martin Luther King Jr.
American Baptist minister and activist.
He became the most well-known civil
rights spokesman and leader. He led
the movement from 1955 until
his assassination in 1968.

Lao-Tzu
Born in 571 BC, he was an ancient
Chinese philosopher and writer. He is
the author of the *Tao Te Ching* and the
founder of Taoism.

Greg McKeown
Author and public speaker from
London, England.

Ram Dass
An American spiritual teacher, guru of
modern yoga, psychologist, and author.

He was born in Boston, MA in 1931
and died in Maui, HI in 2019.

Tony Robbins
American author, coach, speaker, and
philanthropist.

Rumi
A 13th-century Persian poet, Islamic
scholar, Maturidi theologian, and Sufi
mystic from Greater Iran.

Seneca
(Lucius Annaeus Seneca the Younger)
Born in 4 BC, Seneca was a Roman
Stoic philosopher who was exiled for
eight years. When he returned, he
became the tutor to Nero who became
emperor.

Jay Shetty
Former Hindu monk, current English
author, and life coach.

Michael Singer
American author, journalist, and
motivational speaker.

Socrates
Founder of Western philosophy from
Athens, Greece. Lived 470-399 BC.

Eckhart Tolle
A German-Canadian spiritual teacher
and self-help author.

Archbishop Desmond Tutu
A South African Anglican cleric and
theologian. He was a human rights
activist.

IMPORTANT
LITERARY WORKS:

Bhagavad Gita
A 700-verse Hindu scripture dated
to the second half of the first
millennium BCE. The story is a
dialogue between the warrior-prince
Arjuna and god Krishna. The message
is the person whose mind is always free
from attachment, who has subdued the
mind and senses, and who is free from
desires, attains freedom.

Meditations
A series of personal writings by Marcus
Aurelius, Roman Emperor from AD
161 to 180. He wrote deeply to himself
about Stoic philosophy.

Tao Te Ching
A Chinese classic text written by
Lao-Tzu. It is the most well known
literary work for both philosophical and
religious Taoism.

Yoga Sutras of Patanjali
A foundational text of classical yogic
philosophy. It is a collection of Sanskrit
sutras on the theory and practice
of yoga.